Task-Centered Practice

Task-Centered Practice

EDITED BY

WILLIAM J. REID

LAURA EPSTEIN

COLUMBIA UNIVERSITY PRESS   1977

NEW YORK

Library of Congress Cataloging in Publication Data
Main entry under title:

Task-centered practice.

Based on the papers of the Conference on Appli-
cations of Task-Centered Treatment, held at the
University of Chicago in 1975.
Includes bibliographies and index.
1. Social case work—Congresses. 2. Social
group work—Congresses. 3. Family social work
—Congresses. 4. Social service—Methodology
—Congresses. I. Reid, William James, 1928–
II. Epstein, Laura. III. Conference on Applica-
tions of Task-Centered Treatment, University of
Chicago, 1975.
HV43.T37   361.3   76-28177
ISBN 0-231-04072-5

Columbia University Press
New York—Guildford, Surrey
Copyright © 1977 Columbia University Press
All rights reserved
Printed in the United States of America

Contents

Preface

～.

Since its inauguration in the early seventies, the task-centered model of social work practice has been used by experienced and beginning social workers in a wide range of clinical situations. Reports on many of these applications were presented at the Conference on Applications of Task-Centered Treatment, held at the University of Chicago in 1975.

The present volume is an outgrowth of the Conference papers, whose original preparation was guided by a uniform topic outline. The papers were then revised in response to Conference criticism and discussion and, in some cases, in the light of subsequent developments in the work reported on.

The book is essentially a portrayal of the task-centered model in action: how it works when used by practitioners of varied orientations in varied settings with varied types of clients and problems. Although most papers address themselves to some theoretical concerns and most present research data, the central purpose of the book is not to extend in any systematic way the theoretical underpinnings of the model or to provide definitive data on its operations and outcomes, but rather to describe, in a graphic way, variations and developments in its application. The majority of the papers are based on the authors' own clinical experience in use of the model; the remaining papers have been authored by educators, supervisors, and researchers who have followed closely particular applications of the approach.

We thought that the book would be of interest to three groups of professional and student social workers. The first would comprise those interested in the task-centered model per se. In this group may be a portion of the several thousand students and practitioners who have participated in courses, seminars, and workshops on task-centered treatment given by the editors and others in this country and abroad. It may also include a portion of those who may not have had this exposure but who may read at least one of a half-dozen or so existing publications on the model. Members of this group may be interested in how the model has been applied to various types of clients and problems and, more generally, they may want to know about the various technical innovations described in the papers: for example, the use of mental tasks to deal with cognitive aspects of problems, the application of a particular sequence of activities to help clients implement highly specific tasks, the incorporation of behavioral techniques into the model, and the testing of a group treatment version. For this group the present volume may serve as a companion to, and extension of, our earlier book, *Task-Centered Casework*.

A potentially larger group would consist of those who may not be especially invested in the task-centered approach as such but are interested in one or more of the trends in social work practice which the model reflects. Clinical social workers are expressing growing interest in the following: brief, time-limited service; structured, goal-specific methods; use of treatment contracts; combining behavioral methods with more traditional approaches; and forms of practice that are closely tied to research and that lend themselves to systematic evaluation. All of these developments are very much a part of task-centered practice. Most of the papers provide demonstrations of them in actual cases and programs. The potential contributions of these trends to social work practice, as well as the issues they raise, can be viewed in a diversity of contexts.

A third group for which the book would have some appeal consists of readers who wish to gain a perspective on social work practice across a range of settings and client groups. While the book obviously does not offer a-cross-section of practice models, the practice it does describe takes place in most types of settings in which social work is practiced and with most types of clients, however classified, whom social workers treat. Thus we have samples of practice drawn from family, child guidance, medical, mental health, school, court, child welfare, public welfare, industrial, and private practice settings.

The clinical work reported on deals with families, children and adults whose problems include difficulties in family relations, emotional and behavioral disturbances, delinquency, inadequacies in academic and job performance, and lack of environmental resources. The volume as a whole provides exposure to issues arising from particular conditions of practice—issues that transcend any given model of treatment. One sees, for example, the technical complexities that arise when the unit of attention is a marital couple or family, or the dilemmas faced by practitioners when their clients' desires are at odds with the demands of authoritative agencies or the apparent interests of the community.

This book is the product of the efforts and assistance of many people and organizations. We were blessed with a group of diligent and competent authors who were able to relate their work and special interests to the requirements of the volume. Our work on the projects on which much of the book is based, as well as our work on the book itself, was greatly facilitated by the tangible and intangible support provided by our School's two chief administrative officers, Dean Harold A. Richman and Associate Dean John A. Schuerman. We also wish to express our appreciation to the Department of Health, Education, and Welfare (Grant No. SRS-98-P-005001-5-05) and to the CNA Foundation for funds that made possible much of the research effort underlying the book.

We gratefully acknowledge the able and versatile contributions of Esther Silverman, who assisted in the analysis of project data, handled correspondence with the authors, and prepared and typed the bulk of the manuscript. Thanks are due as well to Gerald Bostwick for his help in data analysis, and to Gloria Jones who typed portions of the manuscript and carried out numerous secretarial tasks essential to our efforts.

The authors will add their own acknowledgments to this list in the papers to follow. But we cannot close this expression of appreciation without recognizing the role of the many social welfare organizations cited in the papers that were willing to host innovative practice efforts and to contribute substantially to their cost.

WILLIAM J. REID
LAURA EPSTEIN
The School of Social Service Administration
The University of Chicago

Contributors

MICHAEL G. BASS
Probation Officer, Juvenile Division, *Circuit Court of Cook County, Chicago*

LESTER B. BROWN
Social Work Consultant, Department of Psychiatry, *Jackson Park Hospital Foundation, Chicago;* and Clinical Associate, School of Social Service Administration, *University of Chicago*

LAURA EPSTEIN
Professor, School of Social Service Administration, *University of Chicago*

PATRICIA L. EWALT
Assistant Chief Social Worker, *Youth Guidance Center of the Greater Framingham Mental Health Association;* and Clinical Assistant Professor, School of Social Work, *Boston University*

CHARLES GARVIN
Professor of Social Work, School of Social Work, *University of Michigan*

NAOMI GOLAN
Associate Professor, School of Social Work, *University of Haifa, Israel*

E. MATILDA GOLDBERG
Director of Research, *National Institute for Social Work Training, London*

VERONICA HARI
Director of Professional Services, *Family Service Society, Hartford, Connecticut*

MILTON O. HOFSTAD
Assistant Professor of Social Work, Graduate School of Social Work, *University of Nebraska*

WILLIAM J. REID
George Herbert Jones Professor, School of Social Service Administration, *University of Chicago*

JAMES ROBINSON
Research Officer, Social Services Department, *Buckinghamshire County Council, England*

RONALD H. ROONEY
Field Instructor and Research Assistant, School of Social Service Administration, *University of Chicago*

ROBERT B. ROSSI
Director of Social Services, *Colorado State Home and Training School, Trinidad*

WILMA H. SALMON
Chief, Community Based Care, *Louisiana Division of Family Services*

CARVEL U. TAYLOR
Director, Employee Counseling Center, *CNA Insurance Medical Center, Chicago*

ELEANOR REARDON TOLSON
Instructor, School of Social Service Administration, *University of Chicago*

ANDREW WEISSMAN
Director, South Works Counseling Center, *United States Steel, Chicago*

PHYLLIS WEXLER
Senior Social Worker, *Children's Memorial Hospital, Chicago;* and Instructor in Social Work, *Northwestern University Medical School*

FRANCES WISE
Caseworker, *Family Service of the Greater Cincinnati Area*

Task-Centered Practice

Chapter 1

~~~~~~

William J. Reid, D.S.W.

Task-Centered Treatment and Trends in Clinical Social Work

Task-centered treatment is a short-term model of social work practice designed to alleviate specific problems of individuals and families (Reid and Epstein, 1972). The model was an outgrowth of experimentation with methods of planned brief treatment (Reid and Shyne, 1969) and of work on intervention organized around helping clients define and carry out courses of action or tasks (Studt, 1968). It also drew upon Perlman's (1957, 1970) formulation of social treatment as a problem-solving process.

Work on the model has continued during the past several years. Part of this effort has taken place at the School of Social Service Administration, the University of Chicago, in conjunction with the School's task-centered program. This program, established in 1971, is built around a year-long, integrated sequence of classroom and field instruction for first-year students (Korbelik and Epstein, 1976). Each group of students, from 20 to 25 each year, learn task-centered methods in class and field as well as methods of clinical research. As part of the program, each student carries two research cases from which systematic data on task-centered treatment processes and outcomes are obtained. In addition, a number of second-year and doctoral students have carried out projects related to the model.

Another arm of the task-centered research and development effort has consisted of programs, projects, and clinical trials conducted by social work practitioners, administrators, and researchers at various sites in this country and abroad. These undertakings, generally designed and carried out in consultation with the editors of the present volume, have ranged from single case studies and small demonstration projects to a large scale implementation of the model in a state public welfare agency.

These in-house and extramural activities have resulted in applications of the model with children, adolescents, families, and adults in most settings in which social work is practiced. This book is a report of these applications.

An Overview of the Model

Before proceeding further, it may be well to present a brief summary of task-centered treatment as a system of practice. The summary is intended to provide necessary background for the papers to follow. It does not incorporate the many new developments described in the papers themselves.

The model is addressed to problems of living that the client can, with help, resolve through his own actions. The major kinds of problems dealt with in the approach (and referred to in the papers) may be described briefly as follows:

(1) *interpersonal conflict*, or problems dealing with interaction between persons—for example, husband and wife, parent and child, teacher and pupil;

(2) *dissatisfaction in social relations*, such as problems of loneliness, overdependence, and underassertiveness that define the client's distress over his relations with others;

(3) *problems with formal organizations*, or difficulties in the client's

relations with such organizations as social agencies, hospitals, residential institutions, and schools;

(4) *difficulty in role performance,* in which the client's main concern is his inability to carry out a social role (such as the role of parent, spouse, employee, or student) to his satisfaction;

(5) *problems of social transition,* which arise from actual or contemplated changes in a role or social situation, such as entering or leaving an institution or separating from one's family;

(6) *reactive emotional distress,* which consists primarily of problems of anxiety or depression precipitated by some particular event or situation;

(7) *inadequate resources,* such as the lack of money, housing, food, job, or medical care.

The clients' problems are elicited, explored, and clarified in the initial interview. This process proceeds in a give-and-take fashion in which the practitioner may point out problems the client has not acknowledged or the consequences of allowing such problems to go unattended. But at the end of this process, normally at the close of the first or second interview, the practitioner and client must come to an explicit agreement on the problems to be dealt with. These problems must be defined in terms of specific conditions to be changed. Also, an agreement is reached on the duration and amount of service, which generally consists of from 6 to 12 interviews (plus related environmental work) over a two- to four-month time span. These agreements form the nucleus of a service contract which may be added to or modified by additional agreements as service proceeds.

The practitioner and client then develop tasks the client can undertake to alleviate the problem(s) agreed upon. A task may be cast in relatively general terms, giving the client a direction for action but no specific program of behavior to follow. For example, Mrs. B is to develop a firmer, more consistent approach to handling her child's behavior; Mr. C or Mrs. C is to develop a plan for the care of their mentally retarded daughter. Or tasks may be very specific. Such "operational tasks" call for specific action the client is to undertake. Mr. A is to apply for a job at X employment agency within the next week, or Johnny is to volunteer to recite in class on Monday.

Ideally the client's task is based on the course of action he thinks would be most effective in alleviating his problem. The practitioner may then help the client modify the task, to make it more focused and manageable. If the client is unable to propose an appropriate course of action, the social worker helps the client develop a task through exploration and discussion of task possibilities which the worker may draw from the client or suggest himself. In this process we still try to focus on the client's own problem-solving actions—what he has tried to do, what has worked for him, if only for a short time or in a small way. The task is so structured that chances of its being accomplished, in whole or in part, are high. Consequently, the worker is able to convey realistic positive expectations that the client will be successful.

The practitioner's primary role in the model is to help the client formulate target problems and to carry out agreed-upon tasks. Two strategies to facilitate task implementation can be distinguished. One is to work directly with general tasks, which become, in effect, the client's own goals for change. The practitioner then makes use of techniques familiar to most clinical social workers but uses them in a concentrated way in helping the client achieve the task. Thus *exploration* is employed to elicit details of the problem and specific ways the client might proceed with the task. *Enhancing the client's awareness* of his own behavior, the behavior of others, or of social situations is used to help him understand and resolve obstacles to task performance. Considerable *encouragement* is given in response to constructive actions the client has undertaken, is carrying out, or is contemplating. The client may be given *direction* or specific suggestions about how to proceed with the task. Finally, a good deal of the practitioner's energy goes into *structuring communication* within the treatment session, in order to keep it focused on the tasks. Variations of these techniques are used when family members are interviewed together or in work with individuals on the client's behalf. This strategy, which is presented in full in Reid and Epstein (1972), does not represent a radical departure from focused "goal-oriented" models of short-term treatment now widely used in social agencies.

The second strategy has evolved from research and development work carried on in the task-centered program at the School of Social Service Administration. Since 1973 efforts have been made to break general tasks down into more specific, operational tasks that clients might undertake prior to the next treatment session, and to identify activities in the session that might be jointly undertaken by practitioners and clients to enable the clients to achieve such specific operational tasks. This work has been stimulated by a desire to place the model on firmer scientific ground by reducing our unit of attention—the task—to more measurable terms (Reid, 1976). It has also received impetus and direction from the apparently successful application of behavioral methods to the kinds of problems addressed by the model.

We eventually developed a sequence of joint practitioner-client activities to be used in the treatment session to help clients formulate and carry out operational tasks. Tasks were planned in detail with the client, incentives for task accomplishment were established, actions called for by the tasks were rehearsed or practiced, and obstacles to their achievement were analyzed. This set of activities, referred to as the Task-Implementation Sequence, was tested in a controlled experimental design (Reid, 1975). The results of the test suggested that the sequence was an effective means of helping clients carry out operational tasks, and it served as the springboard for a more extensive test, one still in progress (Reid and Epstein, 1974).

The techniques described under the first strategy (exploration, enhancing awareness, etc.) are used in the second, although they are concentrated at the level of helping clients plan and carry out more specific tasks. To illustrate the distinction between these two approaches, let us consider a client whose general task is to leave her parents' home and establish herself in her own apartment. In the first approach direction and encouragement might be used to help her take steps to leave and find her own place. Then a good deal of attention might be given to helping her understand her reluctance to separate from her parents, consequences for her if she remained or left, and so on. In the second approach, treatment would be organized, to a much greater extent, around specific things the client might do to facilitate her achieving an independent existence, such as locating living arrangements. An operational task might call for the client to tell her parents of her plans to leave and the treatment session might be devoted to working out the details of how this task might be carried out, establishing what she would gain from its execution and rehearsing with her exactly what she might say to her parents.

These strategies, of course, are not mutually exclusive and may be combined in various ways in a given case, although practitioners with psychodynamic orientations tend to follow the first, whereas the second is favored by workers who are more behaviorally oriented. Illustrations of each strategy are provided in the papers to follow. A full exposition of the second strategy will be given in a forthcoming publication (Reid, in press).

The model has been presented in the form used in one-to-one relationships. Adaptations employed in multiple interviews with family members and with groups have been developed and will be taken up in certain of the papers (Reid, Tolson, Wise, Rooney, Garvin, and Bass). The overview has also been limited to a presentation of the main operational features of the approach. Various characteristics of it that relate to broader trends in social work practice will be discussed in a subsequent section of the chapter.

Purpose of the Book

In its initial formulation the task-centered model was presented as a general approach to casework practice (Reid and Epstein, 1972). Although some suggestions were offered as to how the model might be applied to various client and problem groups in different settings, relatively little attention was given to specific adaptations of the model. Moreover, only a modest amount of field testing of any kind had been done, and this was limited largely to the work of students. Thus a main function of the present volume will be to reveal how the task-centered approach works in practice in a variety of contexts. At the same time, the papers report on recent developments in the model, such as the technology for the implementation of operational tasks and the application of the model to the treatment of clients in groups (Garvin, 1974; Garvin, Reid, and Epstein, 1976). Thus the book provides new dimensions to task-centered treatment as a general system of practice.

Any treatment model incorporates certain elements or addresses certain issues that are of interest in their own right, apart from whether or not one wishes to accept or utilize the model in its entirety. A second purpose of this book will be to examine selected elements of practice that are not only reflected in the task-centered approach but are having a significant impact on clinical social work as a whole. At least six such elements can be distinguished: planned brevity; specificity in treatment focus; use of contracts; a high degree of structure; emphasis on client action; and an empirical orientation. The remainder of this chapter will be devoted largely to an examination of these trends as they relate to the papers in this volume.

Planned Brevity

The task-centered model is one of a family of planned, short approaches to practice that includes psychodynamic forms of brief treatment and crisis intervention. We have in mind treatment that is short-term by plan, normally consisting of from 6 to 15 sessions occurring once or twice a week (Parad and Parad, 1968). There are many indications that this form of treatment is being used increasingly in social work practice. Beck and Jones (1973), for example, after noting an "increase in planned short-term service" in family agencies, report that in 1970, "35 percent of the cases accepted in the first interview were assigned to planned short-term service" (p. 62). Regardless of its theoretical orientation, any planned short-term modality raises certain questions: What is its range of application? What can it be expected to accomplish? Is it sufficient to meet the needs of most clients? How do clients view it? What problems might be encountered in trying to institute this form of practice among practitioners accustomed to using long-term or open-ended methods of treatment? What special advantages does this form of practice have that might override its problems and limitations?

All the papers in this volume are concerned with planned short-term treatment. In fact, the brevity of the services reported on was a more constant feature than their task-centeredness. All papers show how brief treatment can be applied in a range of settings and with a variety of client groups and provide evidence on kinds of achievements possible within short periods of time. Several of the papers deal explicitly with issues concerning planned brevity itself, including client and staff reactions to limits on the duration of service (Hari, Reid, Salmon).

Focus

A closely related trend in clinical social work has been toward use of a greater degree of focus and specificity in defining target problems and treatment goals. In part this trend is a reflection of increasing use of planned short-term treatment, since that form of practice must usually be confined to delimited problems and goals. But the shift toward more highly focused treatment has taken other forms: one sees it in the movement toward goal-oriented social services and, more strikingly, in behavior modification.

As Simon (1970) has noted, there seems to be a consensus among casework theorists that "treatment is focused or partialized" (p. 379). The main issue concerns the *degree* of focus or delimitation in defining the major problems and goals in a case—for example, whether a practitioner should strive to help a child improve his impulse control generally or to help him stay in his seat in a particular class at school. As the scope of treatment is narrowed, therapeutic efforts can become more concentrated and perhaps stand a better chance of achieving at least some demonstrable change. Moreover, it becomes easier to study and to comprehend the processes of change. At the same time, the gains achieved may be small in relation to the problems remaining, and there is often the concern that underlying disorders, untouched in the process, will produce new "symptoms." In addition, highly focused treatment raises a host of technical questions. How does one carve out a circumscribed piece from a large and vaguely defined problem area? How is the focus, once achieved, maintained? Is it usually possible to do so? Under what circumstances is it not? And so on.

In respect to degree of focus, task-centered treatment probably falls somewhere between traditional practice, on the one hand, and behavior modification, on the other, although a given task-centered case may be more or less delimited, depending on such factors as the nature of the problem and the style of the practitioner. The potentials, limitations, and methods of sharply focused practice are discernible in most papers, particularly in those by Tolson, Rossi, and Brown.

Contracts

The use of explicit agreements or contracts with the client to specify problems and goals to be worked on is another element of task-centered treatment that is being used increasingly in social work practice (Maluccio and Marlow, 1974). The major function of the contract is to ensure that the practitioner and client have a shared understanding of the purposes and content of treatment. The contract is formed at the beginning of service and, unless both parties agree to changing it, serves to guide the course of service. A contract may be oral or written; the understanding reached may be fairly general or quite detailed.

Use of contracts helps avoid certain perennial problems in social work practice: misunderstandings between worker and client as to the nature of the former's intentions and the latter's difficulty—well documented by Mayer and Timms (1970) and Silverman (1970); lack of clarity on the part of both as to what they are to do together; drift and scatter in the focus of treatment. Contracting, as do most things in social treatment, works best when the client has an active interest in getting help and some notion of what he wants to accomplish. Unfortunately, many if not most of the clients of social work do not fall into this category. Forming contracts becomes far more difficult when the client is reluctant to accept the services of a social worker or is uncertain about the nature of his problems or the kind of help he wants. Although contracts are hard to develop with such clients, we would argue that they are even more important with this group. A vast amount of time in clinical social work is unproductively spent in unclarified, ambiguous, and covertly conflicted relationships with recalcitrant clients. If a client is unsure of what he wants from the social worker, then perhaps the first order of business should be to assist him to achieve some sense of direction in using help. Most important, use of contracts with the unmotivated or uncertain client provides some assurance that he will not be treated "behind his back" for conditions that have not been made clear to him.

Papers by Ewalt, Salmon, and Bass, in particular, demonstrate the feasibility of using contracts with these kinds of clients, illustrate the kinds of contracts that can be formed, and present methods and procedures useful in contract formation. But as Goldberg and Robinson suggest, explicit agreements with an unwilling client on target problems may be quite difficult if the practitioner is acting primarily as an "agent of control or protection." Hofstad's paper suggests a rather different kind of issue: do clients mean what they say when they contract to work on problems in agencies such as a juvenile court, which hold considerable power over their lives? More generally, verbal agreements may not reflect felt commitments.

Structure

The elements discussed thus far—planned brevity, focus, and contract—may be thought of as elements of treatment structure or organization. A model is highly structured if it provides a substantial system of rules, methods, and procedures that serve to organize the treatment process. Highly structured approaches tend to proceed according to a sequence of steps or phases, with fairly detailed explication of the practitioner's operations at each stage of the process. Task-centered treatment provides one example; there are many others (Green and Morrow, 1972; Gambrill, Thomas, and Carter, 1971; Schwartz and Goldiamond, 1975).

In the past, highly structured forms of practice have been applied, for the most part, to the intake or diagnostic phase of a case. Of more recent origin have been attempts to develop a fairly high degree of organization for the "treatment" phases. Not surprisingly, such structuring is more likely to occur with brief, focused models, since they are less complex and easier to plan out than conventional approaches.

An assumption underlying highly structured forms of practice is that the guidelines they set forth will enable the practitioner to do his job more effectively than if he were to operate on the basis of very general principles, practice wisdom, intuition, and so forth. Ideally the structure should operate like a recipe for a complicated dish, by spelling out what one needs to do to achieve a desired result. If it is to work, it needs to set forth methods that are effective, and it needs to show how these can be applied in the range of situations the practitioner will be confronting. If these conditions can be met, then structured models offer powerful advantages since they would then provide a clear and efficient route to effective treatment. At best, however, these conditions are only partially met by structured models. There is always uncertainty about the efficacy of the prescribed methods and the guidelines seldom cover the welter of complexities that occur in practice. The recipe analogy quickly breaks down.

At the present state of the art, structured approaches are probably used to greatest advantage if the practitioner follows the structure when it makes sense to do so, or perhaps when in doubt, but is able to depart from it or add to it when circumstances warrant. At this point, perhaps, the greatest utility of structured models lies in training clinicians, especially beginners, in particular approaches to practice, in disseminating practice technologies, and in clinical research. Their role in experimental research on treatment effects is crucial. If maximum learning value is to be derived from an experiment, the investigator needs to explicate as thoroughly as possible the treatment modality he plans to test and to have it carried out according to plan.

A critical issue in the use of structured models is the extent to which they are, or can be, used by professional practitioners in their everyday work. The papers in this volume provide some insight on this issue. On the whole they suggest that the task-centered model was implemented in a partial and selective manner, often combined with other approaches or substantially modified according to the orientation or style of the practitioner. This proved so despite the conscious efforts of the practitioners to try out the model as designed, despite the training they received and despite the amount of instructional material available (a book supplemented by practice and recording guidelines). One might expect far less fidelity to a model disseminated and tried out under less favorable conditions. Perhaps the answer lies in the kind of long-term, intensive training program described by Golan in the concluding paper of the volume.

The uneven application of the model is not a cause for dismay. The model did not provide instructions for all circumstances of practice; innovations and adaptations were encouraged for the sake of model development. Nevertheless, one comes away with added skepticism about the possibility of achieving large-scale implementation of structured practice models in any pure form. Our experience is certainly in accord with various research findings which suggest that the model identifications practitioners may use (Rogerian, Gestalt, etc.) are poor indicators of their actual practice operations (Lieberman, 1972).

The papers do suggest, however, ways in which structured practice can be improved and better utilized. Adaptations or innovations not originally a part of the model can be incorporated into it, such as Ewalt's introduction of mental tasks, Rooney's technology for task-centered group treatment, and Rossi's and Brown's use of behavioral techniques. Applications of the model can provide information about types of clients or problems for which it may not be appropriate—a point amplified and illustrated by Goldberg and Robinson. Finally, a model of general scope, like task-centered treatment, can serve as the basis for the construction of specialized models for use in particular settings with particular client groups. Bass provides an excellent example of this kind of model construction.

Although adaptations and elaborations are necessary to model development, one can only add so much and still retain the essence of the approach—that which sets it apart from others. How far the model-builder can go is a sticky question, one that the volume raises but does not resolve.

Action Emphasis

During the past decade, growing attention has been given to forms of treatment that emphasize direct efforts to change behavior or stimulate and guide problem-solving action. Evidence of this trend may be seen in the interest in advice-giving as a treatment method (Reid and Shapiro, 1969; Davis, 1975), in the stress on client action in crisis intervention, in the increasing use of such directive, action-oriented modes of treatment as reality therapy (Glasser, 1965) and, of course, in the emergence of behavior modification and the behavior therapies.

Treatment with an action or behavioral emphasis can be distinguished from approaches that are directed at affecting internal processes—the client's feelings, attitude, level of awareness, psychodynamics, perceptions of self and others, and so forth. Modalities in the latter group, such as psychoanalytic-oriented therapy, Rogerian counseling, and encounter groups may be used by practitioners on the assumption that constructive changes in behavior or action will occur as a result of internal alterations but such changes are not the immediate targets of treatment.

While it is an action-oriented form of practice, task-centered practitioners make use of the client's cognitive capacities in problem specification and task planning and seek to affect internal processes when they become impediments to action. Since many practitioners who use the task-centered approach also make use of psychodynamic theory and ego psychology, the model, in practice, often gives even greater stress to intrapsychic factors, as papers by Ewalt and Wise illustrate. These characteristics of task-centered theory and practice seem to bring together the more traditional emphasis on the inner man and the newer focus on man as a doer.

A number of writers and practitioners in various fields are also searching for such common ground. Their efforts are reflected in attempts to find correspondences between psychodynamic and learning theory (Brady, 1967), to extend behavioral viewpoints to cognitive phenomena (Thoresen and Mahoney, 1974), and to combine insight-oriented and behavioral methods in practice (Sloan, 1969).

Thus the task-centered approach reflects two trends: increasing emphasis on action and behavior as treatment foci and, within that development, the push toward some synthesis between this newer emphasis and more accepted treatment foci on internal processes.

Stress on affecting what the client does emerges in all the papers. We see it as one of the strengths of the model and as a healthy trend in general. Papers by Rossi and Brown illustrate particularly well how this kind of focus can bring about rapid and decisive changes in the client's problem. Yet legitimate issues can be raised, not the least of which is the durability of change without the support of the client's awareness of the causes of the difficulty.

Papers by Ewalt and Wise illustrate different modes of combining foci on insight and action. Ewalt, in effect, eliminates the distinction through the intriguing idea of "mental tasks." Wise suggests how knowledge from psychodynamic theory can be related to a focus on tasks in treatment of marital problems. Each of these papers, as do others, produces an array of conceptual and technical questions on combinations of these kinds.

Empirical Orientation

The final trend we will consider is, in our judgment, the most significant of all: the movement toward empirically based modes of practice. Empirically based approaches have certain common characteristics: (1) target problems, treatment goals, practitioner operations, and outcomes tend to be cast in forms that lend themselves to objective measurement; (2) data obtained on these components are interpreted at a relatively low level of inference: speculative theorizing is avoided; (3) reliance is placed on such data to guide treatment of individual cases and the development of the approach as a whole; (4) research methods and procedures are used to collect data on problems, interventions, and outcomes as a part of normal practice operations, and research in some form tends to be built into ongoing programs rather than being limited to special projects.

This trend has been both stimulated and expressed by behavioral approaches, with their strong emphasis on research as a part of practice. Pressures on agencies and practitioners to produce systematic data for accountability purposes have also pushed practice into more empirical directions, as efforts have been made to define case goals and outcomes in more measurable terms and to collect systematic data on them (Reid, 1974).

These trends seem to be outcroppings of a long-term progression toward greater reliance on scientific knowledge and methods in clinical practice—one of the earliest and most persistent goals of the social work profession. The movement has gained momentum with the gradual improvement of clinical research designs and methodologies, advances in data collection and processing hardware (such as electronic recorders and computers), the growth in the number of social workers with doctoral degrees, and the introduction of scientific management methods into social welfare agencies.

Task-centered treatment was designed to be an empirical model of practice in accordance with the criteria previously given. Although these criteria are not always met in practice, the operations and outcomes of the model have been systematically studied in a variety of projects, many of which are reported in this volume. The model lends itself to research monitoring and evaluation, which may be carried out by individual practitioners, in special projects, or as a part of an agency information system. A number of research instruments have been developed for this purpose. A selection of instruments relating to projects reported in this volume is provided in the Appendix.

In keeping with the spirit of the model, most papers present research data. Papers that do not contain data still have connections to research. Wise and Hari discuss practice in a project the data for which are presented in another paper in the book (Reid). Salmon discusses use of the task-centered model as the service component in an agency information system designed to collect systematic case data.

The research presented in the papers does not provide decisive evidence on the effectiveness of the model. Experimental designs with control groups were not used and the data, often consisting of gross measurements, were either collected by the practitioners themselves or obtained from the clients' self-reports. More rigorous tests of the model are reported elsewhere (Reid, 1975; Reid, in press).

Nevertheless, the papers illustrate the kind of data that might be obtained in the course of everyday applications of a treatment model, that is, without the benefit of large research staffs or budgets. At present most social work agencies interested in building research into their ongoing programs seem to be limited to data of this kind; so are most agency information systems, despite their capacity to collect and manipulate data in much larger quantities. While we badly need to conduct more rigorous research, we also need to exploit the potentials of less sophisticated but more readily collected data.

The papers reflect another characteristic of task-centered treatment as an empirical model of practice: its stress upon events that can be assessed with a minimum of inference. In most papers, little use is made of highly abstract diagnostic and personality constructs, such as character disorder or ego strength, or of elaborate theoretical explanations of client problems and functioning. A positive consequence is that the practitioner can communicate more clearly to the client, to others, and perhaps to himself what he is about. One also avoids the wrong-headed conclusions that often result from over-reliance upon theories whose explanatory power is generally rather feeble. At the same time such theories, if used with restraint, can alert the practitioner to important considerations and provide hypotheses to be tested through the data on hand. We expect practitioners to use theory in this way but offer few specific guidelines as to how this is to be done. The papers then raise the issue of the use of untested but possibly helpful theories, in models that are rooted closely to readily discernible phenomena. They also raise such questions as: What is lost by not using diagnostic or personality theory more extensively and systematically? Can any of the case material presented be illuminated by the application to it of any particular theoretical system?

Plan of the Book

The papers are grouped in relation to the type of client or client system that constitutes the primary target of change in the application. Using this principle, the papers are divided into sections on families, children and adolescents, and adults. Admittedly these distinctions are arbitrary and certain papers could be logically placed in more than one category, but it is assumed that some differences in practice flow from these different foci. Thus if the family or family subsystem is the primary target, one is largely concerned with strategies for defining and affecting interpersonal problems. In the process, the interdependent interests of a set of clients must be dealt with. When the major target is a problem of a young person (child or adolescent), special knowledge of developmental processes and needs, and techniques related to that knowledge, are brought into play. At the same time, the dependent position of the young client on parents and social institutions must be taken into account. Although the treatment of most children and adolescents involves the family to some extent, the focus of attention may be on problems relating to school, to peers, or to other areas in which change in family relations may not be the central issue. Similarly, adults may have a wide range of problems apart from their functioning as family members. While family members may play a role in the creation and solution of many of these problems, the difficulties of the adult himself, and not his family, may be the main focus of attention. Work centered on individual problems of adults requires an understanding of the range of difficulties adults characteristically experience in their psychological functioning, interpersonal relations, and work situations. It also requires special knowledge of what individual adults may expect from treatment, how they may use it, and the helping methods best suited to their interests and needs.

Each section is introduced with a brief commentary on themes, viewpoints, and technical developments set forth in the chapters contained therein. The introductions also serve to relate the papers to work with the three types of client groups dealt with in the book.

References

Beck, Dorothy Fahs, and Jones, Mary Ann. 1973. *Progress on family problems: A nationwide study of clients' and counselors' views on family agency services*. New York: Family Service Agency of America.

Brady, John Paul. 1967. "Psychotherapy, learning, theory, and insight." *Archives of General Psychiatry* 16:304–11.

Davis, Inger. 1975. "Advice-giving in parent counseling." *Social Casework* 56(6):343–47.

Gambrill, Eileen D.; Thomas, Edwin J.; and Carter, Robert D. 1971. "Procedure for sociobehavioral practice in open settings." *Social Work* 16(1):51–62.

Garvin, Charles D. 1974. "Task-centered group work." *Social Service Review* 48:494–507.

Garvin, Charles D.; Reid, William J.; and Epstein, Laura. 1976. "Task-centered group work." In *Theoretical approaches to social work with small groups*. Edited by Helen Northen and Robert W. Roberts. New York: Columbia University Press.

Glasser, William. 1965. *Reality therapy: A new approach to psychiatry*. New York: Harper & Row.

Green, Judith Kopp, and Morrow, William R. 1972. "Precision social work: General model and illustrative student projects with clients." *Journal of Education for Social Work* 8(3):19–29.

Korbelik, John, and Epstein, Laura. 1976. "Evaluating time and achievement in a social work practicum." In *Teaching for Competence in the Delivery of Direct Services*. New York: Council on Social Work Education.

Lieberman, Morton A. 1972. "Behavior and impact of leaders." In *New perspectives on encounter groups*. Edited by Lawrence N. Solomon and Betty Berzon. San Francisco: Jossey-Bass, Inc.

Maluccio, Anthony N., and Marlow, Wilma D. 1974. "The case for the contract." *Social Work* 19(1):28–36.

Mayer, John E., and Timms, Noel. 1970. *The client speaks: Working class impressions of casework*. New York: Atherton Press.

Parad, Howard J., and Parad, Libbie G. 1968. "A study of crisis-oriented planned short-term treatment: Part I." *Social Casework* 49:346–55.

Perlman, Helen Harris. 1957. *Social casework: A problem-solving process*. Chicago: University of Chicago Press.

—— 1970. "The problem-solving model in social casework." In *Theories of social casework*. Edited by Robert W. Roberts and Robert H. Nee. Chicago: University of Chicago Press.

Reid, William J. 1974. "Development in the use of organized data." *Social Work* 19(5):585–93.

—— 1975. "A test of a task-centered approach." *Social Work* 20:3–9.

—— 1976. "Needed: A new science for clinical social work." In *The effectiveness of social casework*. Edited by Joel Fischer. Springfield, Ill.: Charles Thomas Press.

—— In press. *Helping clients act*. New York: Columbia University Press.

Reid, William J., and Epstein, Laura. 1972. *Task-centered casework*. New York: Columbia University Press.

—— 1974. *Task-centered methods for multi-problem families: A proposal for research and development*. Chicago: School of Social Service Administration, University of Chicago.

Reid, William J., and Shapiro, Barbara L. 1969. "Client reactions to advice." *Social Service Review* 43:165–73.

Reid, William J., and Shyne, Ann. 1969. *Brief and extended casework*. New York: Columbia University Press.

Schwartz, Arthur, and Goldiamond, Israel. 1975. *Social casework: A behavioral approach*. New York and London: Columbia University Press.

Silverman, Phyllis R. 1970. "A reexamination of the intake procedure." *Social Casework* 51:625–34.

Simon, Bernece K. 1970. "Social casework theory: An overview." In *Theories of social casework*. Edited by Robert W. Roberts and Robert H. Nee. Chicago: University of Chicago Press.

Sloan, R. Bruce. 1969. "The converging paths of behavior therapy and psychotherapy." *American Journal of Psychiatry* 125(7):49–57.

Studt, Elliot. 1968. "Social work theory and implications for the practice of methods." *Social Work Education Reporter* 16(2):22–46.

Thoresen, Carl E., and Mahoney, Michael J. 1974. *Behavioral self-control*. New York: Holt, Rinehart, and Winston, Inc.

Part I: Families

Introduction

The seven papers in this section deal with impediments to the welfare of families and family subgroups. They depict and analyze exploratory work on adapting the task-centered model to family treatment.

No particular "school" of family treatment dominates the work. In order to intervene in the functioning of a group as complex as a family, there must be a perspective to organize observations and guide conclusions. The authors of these papers tend to perceive families as networks of interpersonal relations. They attempt to give consideration both to the individual family members and to their combination as a family group or system. The concept of family members' role is used to imply the connections between individual and family group. Eclecticism is revealed in these papers by the selective reliance upon concepts from psychoanalytic theory and from the communication theories of the "Palo Alto" group (Watzlawick, Beavin, and Jackson, 1967; Sorrells and Ford, 1969; Satir, 1967).

The brevity, specificity, and structure of the task-centered approach precludes heavy or exclusive emphasis on either the psychoanalytic or the Palo Alto approaches. The psychoanalytic emphasis on the past and on intrapsychic matters is at odds with the concentration on the present time and on cognitive process in the task-centered approach. That aspect of the Palo Alto approach which concentrates on interactive process conflicts with the task-centered approach's emphasis on reduction of specific target problems. Nevertheless, the authors of the following papers have used ideas from both these sources to elaborate upon treatment strategies and techniques dominated by concentration on target problems, tasks, and time limits.

Ewalt's paper illustrates the combination of task-centered and psychoanalytically oriented approaches. She describes three programs conducted in a psychoanalytically oriented child guidance setting (The Framingham Youth Guidance Center): relief of stress due to loss of a family member; enhancement of social functioning of severely disturbed children and their families; and short-term treatment for diverse problems in living. Ewalt indicates that treatment was apparently successful in the great majority of cases and that drop-out was controlled. Differences in outcomes among the programs were found.

Experienced practitioners in this setting blended the structure of the task-centered model with their expressive psychodynamic practice styles. The attention normally given to subjective states in psychoanalytically oriented practice gave rise to a distinction between "mental" and "physical" tasks. The "mental task" designated in the reported cases refers to alteration of thoughts, feelings, and attitudes. The term "physical task" was used to refer to "external behavior." A combined "mental and physical" task designation was developed to depict tasks that involved both internal and external aspects of functioning.

The notion of a mental task may be useful in helping clients carry forward cognitive aspects of problem-solving. We would like to inject some notes of caution, however. First, we think that the concept of task should be limited to problem-solving actions the client can work on independent of the practitioner and the treatment session, although it is expected that the client's efforts will be assisted by the practitioner. This conception insures that the task will consist of some autonomous problem-solving effort that the client can engage in on his own. Such effort is central to the model as we conceive it. While mental tasks can certainly meet this requirement, practitioners sometimes use such notions to describe almost any variety of therapeutic stratagem. Thus, a client might be given a "task" in the treatment interview to recall and recount some painful childhood experience. It only confuses matters in our model to call such directives "tasks." Second, since cognitive activity is difficult to spell out and measure, there may be the danger of mental tasks fading into vague suggestions, such as "try to spend some time thinking about what this problem means to you."

Ewalt herself anticipates this concern and attempts to resolve it by suggesting that changes expected to result from mental tasks should be measurable. To this we would add that mental tasks should lead to an assessable product, such as a listing of the pros and cons of making a particular decision.

The staff of the Youth Guidance Center made flexible and ingenious use of contracts. In one program, written contracts were developed with older children who were given the chance to "edit" them. These contracts, which were brought to the interviews, served to remind the children of agreed-upon foci of treatment. In another, contracts with professionals from other agencies were used to formalize agreements— a device that appears to have considerable promise in coordinating agency services.

Wexler's case report, from the social service department of the Children's Memorial Hospital, clarifies two frequent technical problems in task-centered work with families: how to obtain participation from all members on task work, and how to get movement on tasks despite the existence of an intractable problem of personal relationships. Wexler depended upon reciprocal tasks. The family group consisted of a threesome: mother, father, and child. Wexler arranged for each member to take unique steps which were important to the individuals and which were feasible for them to do. Each action by an individual gave something to the others. A system of satisfying exchanges occurred. Their combined effort solved the problem.

Within the context of this set of marital and parent-child relationships, there were conflicting personality traits and marital disharmony. The clients showed no interest in work on these problems. Wexler capitalized on the family's motivation to address the target problem—their child's complex medical regime. Tasks were directed to that problem only. In this instance, observance of treatment structures enabled these clients to achieve necessary tasks without dealing with the intractable area.

Reid reports on a study of task-centered treatment in two family service agencies, located in Cincinnati and Hartford. The study observed the adaptation of the task-centered model to family caseloads, especially to marital conflict. In addition, Reid comments on issues involved in the dissemination of a new service model.

The practitioners in these agencies had evolved practice styles which emphasized expressive modes of interaction with clients. As the practitioners implemented the task-centered treatment design, their practice conformed to the model in some respects but not in others. The cases adhered to recommended time limitations and focused on specific problems and goals. However, concentration upon tasks was inconsistent. This pattern is not surprising. Formed practice styles do not change readily. Practitioners blended the task-centered model with preexisting technical repertoires. The model itself, however, has not developed procedures specific to the treatment of marital problems. Hence, clinical judgment must be exercised to construct techniques as the treatment occurs.

A technical problem which confronted these family service practitioners was that marital conflicts were connected to a host of dissatisfactions, emotional upsets, personality problems, and other difficulties. There was a tendency for intercurrent problems to take over the focus. Concentration on tasks proved hard to maintain.

Outcome measurements indicated that target problems, in this group of clients, were to some degree alleviated in a majority of cases, although there was no change or worsening in some. Task achievement corresponded closely to the degree of problem change. Numerous aspects of evaluating outcome are given in detail, such as predictors of task progress, clients' ratings of change, reactions to the service, and clients' perceptions of need for additional help.

Wise's paper is a colorful depiction of one practitioner's experience in the project discussed by Reid. As do many practitioners who use the model, Wise makes use of diagnostic concepts designed to increase understanding of the clients' personality dynamics. If this kind of perspective can elucidate the clients' problems as they perceive them and can help the worker guide task formulation and implementation, then in our judgment it is well used. Wise ably demonstrates how knowledge of character structure and functioning can be profitably employed in task-centered work. We question, however, if such theories have sufficient power to help the worker decide whether or not to use the task-centered approach in the first place. Here we disagree with Wise, who argues that the model should be "abandoned" and another approach substituted if early interviews indicate that "one or both partners have been too emotionally traumatized to be able to develop in relationship with one another." We quite agree that the model may be ineffective with partners who have little capacity to relate to one another but we think this incapacity (or other incapacities) to use the approach are better established through the clients' behavior in treatment than through the clinicians' prognostications. Wexler's techniques, mentioned earlier, suggest means of circumventing intractable problems of this type. Other papers in this volume are addressed to the same issue (Bass, chapter 13; Tolson, chapter 7; Weissman, chapter 17).

Hari's paper describes vividly the mixed reactions of a family agency staff to planned brief treatment. Anyone who has installed a brief treatment program can verify the aptness of Hari's observations and appreciate her commendable candor. Practitioner reluctance to use brief methods Hari attributes to misguided status perceptions (equating long-term practice with high status) and to fundamental human problems with separation (closing cases). While her arguments are convincing, an additional explanation of practitioner reluctance to use brief treatment needs to be considered. Many practitioners have become socialized into embracing long-term forms of treatment through professional education, selective reading, agency supervision, and other influences. They may be reluctant to use brief modes of intervention because to do so would be a departure from "established" principles. It is perhaps too simple to attribute such reluctance only to practitioner attitudes since many parts of the social work establishment have contributed to our long-term faith in long-term treatment.

Tolson's intriguing paper contains the flavor and immediacy of practice while observing the restraints and specificity of studious inquiry. Tolson's work addresses issues already explored by Reid, Wise, Hari, and to some extent Wexler, relating to treatment of marital conflict. These issues include: expressing problems in terms different from those used by the clients; effect of other problems on holding the focus steady; formulating tasks from the context of a complex problem; and, effectiveness of systematic treatment techniques on effecting behavioral change. Tolson's case analysis is of particular value because it points out a feasible technique for making concrete that pervasive, vaguely perceived but strongly felt marital problem called "difficulty in communication." It shows that the behaviors which contribute to communication difficulties are distinct, observable, and measurable. When thus specified, the communication problem lends itself to viable task formulations. Given such specificity in target problem and tasks, it becomes possible to control and maintain systematic treatment structure. Tolson's technical procedures suggest one way to circumvent the instability of problem definition and task formulation observed in marital conflict. Tolson's study indicates the importance of congruence between practitioner and client on target problem definition. There is need of a technology for managing the effects of other problems in addition to the specific target but that is beyond the scope of this particular study.

Salmon's paper ends this section with knotty issues. A range of influences, including federal accountability requirements and information-based management systems, are pushing public welfare agencies to develop goal-directed practice that can be explicitly described and readily monitored. There are substantial problems in three general areas: (1) the meaning, implications, and consequences of setting goals that become a part of contracts with clients; (2) the technologies to implement goal-directed services; and (3) alterations in administrative procedures to implement specified goals. An additional complexity is the strong tendency in child welfare for children to drift into open-ended placements. Lacking reliable criteria for placement and discharge, and losing momentum because of high caseloads and staff turnover, the objective of concrete goals, efficiency, and time-limited duration appears difficult to achieve. The task-centered approach applied to multiproblem families and to child welfare is potentially a mechanism for implementing some of the objectives of the 1974 Amendments to the Federal Social Security Act (Title XX). The model, more fully adapted to the population served in public welfare agencies, could provide a technology for implementing some types of goal-directed practice. Salmon clearly indicates directions for staff training. Some ideologies which pervade public welfare practice will need to be altered. Implicit commitments to alter lifestyles and control overt, and perhaps hazardous, deviance exceeds the capability of social treatment technology. There are vast misunderstandings in the public mind, shared also by some staff, which consider family conflict, adolescent bewilderment, and the overwhelmed condition of some parents to be "psychopathological," hence requiring magical incantations, sometimes referred to as "therapy." Salmon's uncluttered analysis of these problems provides a groundwork for careful analysis of means to develop new service approaches in public welfare. It cannot be emphasized too strongly that the probable contribution of the task-centered approach in public welfare will be enhanced by research. It is, obviously, essential to monitor practice according to rational standards and procedures. It is equally important to discover and install the key alterations in administrative practice which could develop goal-oriented public welfare practices effectively.

These seven papers, considered together, provide support for the feasibility of brief, structured treatment to reduce a variety of family problems. The contributors have identified numerous areas needing development in the task-centered approach. They have demonstrated orderly and clear processes, blending research and practice methods. When these papers were discussed by the participants in the Task-Centered Conference sessions there was general agreement that certain technical issues were common to all the adaptations of the model. The adaptations tended to reflect particular problems, regardless of settings. However, the social role of different settings created special boundaries and expectations.

Three general technical issues were seen to be common to all the work reported: diagnosis or assessment procedures, contract practices, and complexities of task formulation. Discussion about the role of assessment in task-centered practice revealed uncertainty about what use to make of concepts of personality development and pathology. Although it by no means settles the question, the tendency was to consider assessment to be a summing up of a limited number of key factors: characteristics and meaning of the target problem, and conditions in the environment which reinforce and maintain the problem. Most participants chose not to emphasize dysfunctional personality traits, viewing them as obstacles to problem-solving but not the major or sole hindrance. A good deal of task-centered practice concentrates upon altering the manifestations of the problem, rather than directly treating complex personality patterns.

The making of explicit contracts containing goals and time limits offered few difficulties, except in a minority of cases where clients appeared interested in securing a small number of additional interviews. Time limits, however, posed problems for agencies which assume some form of long-term care responsibilities, such as those dealing with corrections and those in the English social services system (discussed in a later section of this volume). There was an emerging consensus in support of extending individual client contracts to include symmetrical contracts with the agencies and authorities whose involvement sustains the continuing care patterns. In this way, dissonant and often unrealizable expectations are negotiated. The available supply of services is organized for a more efficient impact.

Problems of task formulation arose when clients did not spontaneously develop ideas for taking action, and when in marital cases tasks seemed ephemeral or peripheral. The aims developed by the Conference participants were, first, to encourage practitioners to take the initiative in recommending tasks, subject to client consent, and second, to increase the specificity of target problem formulations so that actions contained in tasks would refer to concrete situations. Expression of these aims will be evident in the papers that follow.

References

Bell, John E. 1971. *Family therapy*. New York: Jason Aronson Publishers.

Briar, Scott, and Miller, Henry. 1971. *Problems and issues in social casework*. New York: Columbia University Press.

Leader, Arthur. 1969. "Current and future issues in family therapy." *Social Service Review* 43:1–11.

Satir, Virginia. 1967. *Conjoint family therapy: A guide to theory and techniques*. Palo Alto, Cal.: Science and Behavior Books, Inc.

Sorrells, James M., and Ford, Frederick R. 1969. "Toward an integrated theory of families and family therapy." *Psychotherapy: Theory, Research, and Practice* 6:150–60.

Stein, Joan W., et al. 1973. *The family as a unit of study and treatment*. Seattle: School of Social Work, University of Washington, Regional Rehabilitation Research Institute.

Watzlawick, P.; Beavin, J.; and Jackson, D. D. 1967. *The pragmatics of human communication*. New York: Norton.

Williams, Frank S. 1968. "Family therapy." In *Modern psychoanalysis: New directions and perspectives*. Edited by Judd Marmor. New York: Basic Books.

Chapter 2

~~~~~~~~~~~~~~~~~~~~~~~~~~~~~~~~~~~

Patricia L. Ewalt, A.C.S.W.

A Psychoanalytically Oriented
Child Guidance Setting

Although task-centered and psychoanalytically oriented approaches have sometimes been considered incompatible, those methodologies were combined in three programs in an outpatient child guidance setting. All three programs served young children, adolescents, and adults: one was specifically intended for persons recently having undergone severe stress by loss of a family member; a second, for disturbed children and their families; and a third, for a more diverse group of people served in the clinic's short-term treatment program. The second program, that for severely disturbed children, included application of the task-centered approach to mental health consultation with school personnel.[1]

[1] The author wishes to express appreciation for the assistance of Janice Kutz, M.S., who analyzed data for the Limbo and MiniSchool Programs, and Andrea Levy, M.S., who similarly assisted with the Short-Term Treatment Program; also to Adele Sobel, M.S., Margrit Cohen, M.S., and Andrea Levy, M.S., administrators, respectively, of the three programs, and to all of the workers in these programs who implemented the Task-Centered Approach and provided the data.

In this presentation, emphasis will be placed on alterations in the model found useful in our setting, clients' reported progress through use of the model, and clients' and professional persons' opinions of the model itself.

The Setting

The Youth Guidance Center is a publicly supported child guidance clinic serving children and their families from a ten-town area west of Boston. The area population of 160,000 is predominantly white and about evenly divided among the social classes categorized by Hollingshead (1957). Clinic clientele, about 1,000 families annually, reflect the socioeconomic distribution of the area. The multidisciplinary personnel include 45 staff members and 25 graduate trainees. Except for a geographic limitation, admission to clinic services is nonselective. Hence, diagnostic distribution ranges from situational disturbances to severe, chronic, emotional disability. Any of these conditions may be accompanied by physical and intellectual handicaps of child or parents, as well as other seriously impairing reality situations.

The theoretical orientation of staff is psychoanalytic, and within that framework, strongly ego-oriented. Most workers, irrespective of the task-centered approach, tend to focus on problems identified by clients, to make such a focus explicit, and to draw upon clients' own abilities for problem-solving. The task-centered approach has, nonetheless, placed added emphasis on problems and tasks mutually agreed upon with clients, an approach consistent with the basic orientation of the clinic.

Assessment of Services

The empirical orientation of the task-centered model has also assisted our goal of assessing effectiveness, not selectively as in research projects, but as an inherent aspect of clinic services and within the clinic's relatively limited evaluative research budget. The model has been especially helpful in planning for externally funded short-term programs which often allow little time to develop an adequate evaluative methodology. One of the major advantages of the task-centered approach is its inherent capacity for the assessment of effectiveness. Because it requires at the outset mutual and explicit definition of problems to be alleviated and tasks to be achieved, a clear basis for assessment is provided for the client, the worker, and others at the conclusion of contact.

Although details of the evaluative system for the three programs to be discussed vary in some details, the general approach is as follows. An evaluation form is begun for each family at the beginning of contact. The general situation is recorded as each participating family member views it. During approximately the first two visits, the specific problem on which each member or combination of members wishes to work is identified. For example, a married couple may express difficulty in making demands they both agree on with respect to their child. Their child may feel he is having trouble letting his parents know that he wants more freedom from parental rules and feels that, if given more freedom, he can and will take more responsibility for his own actions.

Once problems of prime importance to each member have been selected, tasks (i.e., courses of action for each member to undertake during and between visits to alleviate the problem) are identified. Overall duration of treatment and the clients to be seen in interviews are specified. For example, adult or child family members may be seen individually or in specified combinations. Each of these contractual items, tasks related to each problem, the duration and frequency of treatment, and combinations of persons to be seen are all entered on the form. There is also space on the form to enter problems noted either by client or worker which are not to be focused on at this time. Additional problems and related tasks agreed upon during the course of treatment are also entered.

The major evaluative mechanism has been the clients' and workers' assessment of progress on tasks and problems. Very simple scales (similar to those in the Appendix) are utilized, asking clients and workers to assess whether problems have been alleviated and tasks achieved "greatly," "partially," or "not at all." Clients are requested to give verbal statements substantiating the extent to which they believe goals have or have not been achieved. For example, with respect to the problems cited above, an adolescent client may report: "I really think I have decided for myself my own rules for how to act with boys."

The evaluative aspects of treatment are emphasized throughout the final third of the contracted number of visits. This emphasis, which serves both clinical and research requirements, includes a summary of the clients' progress during treatment, identification of problems to be dealt with either by the client independently or with further professional help, and the meaning to the client of having had an alliance with a helping person who (perhaps like other significant persons in his life) has been available for a period of time and will be lost. While entries on the evaluation form are not made until conclusion of contact, evaluation of progress or its lack is a subject for discussion throughout the concluding phase. Based upon these discussions the client makes decisions as to whether further professional help is required and, if so, specifically for which problems and tasks.

While the benefit of an evaluative method capable of incorporation into general clinic practice stands on its own merit, a deficit from the investigative point of view should be pointed out. That is, once a system is applied in a primarily clinical as compared with a research program, workers tend to introduce idiosyncratic variations so that testing of the model in its prescribed form becomes difficult to ensure. Therefore, while we will provide outcome data for the sake of comparison with other settings, it must be kept in mind that, even with inservice training, the model has been imperfectly implemented. Reid arrived at a similar conclusion in his test of the model in family agencies (chapter 4).

Our Variation of the Model

By contrast with inadvertent variations in implementation, one purposeful variation has occurred in our clinical and evaluative approach. This variation will be presented at the outset since it pertains to each of the programs to be described. Others will be mentioned in connection with the specific programs.

Even though contractually agreed-upon, measurable, and mutually assessed problems and tasks are utilized, our workers' input may very well differ from that of more behaviorally oriented practitioners who use the model. Possibly our clients' contribution also differs from that reported in other task-centered studies. For example, if comparison is made between task examples given in such studies (Reid and Epstein, 1972; Reid, 1975) with tasks selected in our clinic's treatment contracts, it appears that our clients and workers more frequently select tasks having to do with alteration of mental, as contrasted with physical, activities. Accordingly, we have established an additional set of task categories: *mental tasks*, which involve change in patterns of thought, feeling, or attitude; *physical tasks*, which call for alteration in overt behavior, i.e., doing something differently; or *combined mental and physical tasks* in which there is an equal emphasis within a task on both aspects (for example, "understand why I daydream in class so I can stop that and get my work done"). These categorizations depend upon an *explicit emphasis* by both client and worker on the mental, physical, or combine result desired. Though it may be presumed that alteration in mental activity is likely to affect physical activity and vice versa, in establishing our categories such assumptions were *not* taken into account. Categorization required explicit agreement on a mental or physical change as a desired outcome.

A case example may serve to illustrate our concept of mental, as contrasted with physical, tasks:

Mrs. G, a 29-year-old, married, lower-middle-class mother of three, was preoccupied with the question of whether her mother and husband loved her. Recently, she felt, her major activities had centered around testing out their feelings or sitting and worrying about her questions. As a result she found it difficult to carry out child care, housework, or other activities for her own pleasure. Exploration indicated that while her inability to invest in home responsibilities led to greater disorganization than usual, it did not result in neglect. The major problem was the intrusion of worries, regardless of whatever else she was doing; this problem was therefore accepted by client and worker as the target problem. A contract for 12 sessions was agreed upon to deal with this problem.

In selection of tasks, consideration was first given to a gradually increasing schedule of specific activities, but the client seemed simply unable to invest herself in this focus. The first major task selected, therefore, was for the client to understand the reasons for her preoccupations.

Since the problem had had a specific time of onset, the first subtask was for the client to identify factors upsetting to her at the time. This task was readily accomplished: the client's mother had, in the client's view, paid a great deal more attention to her younger brother and his spouse, whose marriage had occurred two months previously, than she paid to Mrs. G. Moreover, Mrs. G's husband, during this same period, had been diagnosed as having early symptoms of a potentially disabling neurological disease. His longstanding pattern of dealing with anxiety was to ride around in his car. He had been doing this more lately, leaving Mrs. G alone many evenings. Mrs. G reacted to these behaviors by mother and husband by constantly asking for more attention and reassurance, which only seemed to result in driving them farther away. The second subtask was for the client to identify why her mother's seeming greater attention to her brother was so upsetting to her. This task also was readily achieved: Mrs. G, an adopted child, had long resented attention given to her brother, a natural child of her adoptive parents. Her parents' preference for the brother seemed to her a second rejection, the first having been abandonment by her natural parents. She had lifelong questions about why she had suffered these two rejections. She had been less concerned about them during adult life until the wedding of her brother, when the question of rejection again became predominant in her mind: did either her natural or adoptive mother love her?

Subtask three was for the client to identify why the extent of her mother's love for her was now of major importance. In interview five, the worker specifically asked: "What difference would it make if neither of your mothers loved you at all?" This question proved to be the turning point in the case. Mrs. G stated that she had always had the feeling that if her mothers hadn't loved her, she must be an unlovable person, would not be loved by anyone else, and would be incapable of doing anything worthwhile with her own children or in any other life activity. Once these fears were stated, it was possible to examine her actual relationships with adoptive mother, husband, children, and friends. Much of their behavior could be seen as demonstrating care for her, within the bounds of their own characterological patterns, rather than personal rejection. Her actual life achievements were also examined: for example, her abilities in child-rearing and maintaining a home, despite many reality problems. Her fear of not being able to do anything worthwhile was, as she could see, not substantiated in reality.

Up to this point what we have called mental tasks were emphasized: changes in patterns of thought and attitude about herself and others. The client was now ready for changes in her external behavior. With respect to her mother, she herself decided that she would now call her mother only when she had an activity in mind that she knew both would enjoy doing together, in contrast to her previous behavior, which consisted of calling and visiting with the intention of gaining attention or reassurance for herself. Regarding her husband, she decided to stop cross-examining him about his evening activites, which only seemed to cause him to stay out later. But at the same time she said she would no longer "make herself a slave to his every whim" about how she should manage the house and children, a role she had previously assumed resentfully in an attempt to gain more affection from him. With very little discussion during interviews, she reestablished a schedule for household management and social activities.

It may be noticed that once the initial problem was clarified in the client's mind, specific behaviorial changes with respect to mother, husband, and other obligations and activities were selected and carried out primarily on the client's own initiative. The worker merely helped the client to examine details of her own plans, and subsequently to sort out aspects which had and had not been effective and why. Perhaps most importantly, the worker listened to the client's report of her own achievements. In assessing her own progress, the client said, "I used to be about seven different selves trying to satisfy seven different people—now I'm myself, not perfect, but not such a hell of a bad person either."

Some professional persons may question whether the client's *understanding* of a problem, and of himself or herself in relation to the problem, is a worthwhile therapeutic goal in itself. In this connection, it may be of interest that, in a study conducted under the author's direction, clients reported that increasing their understanding of their problem was one of the two elements of greatest importance to them during brief service. Moreover, a statistically significant correlation was found between clients' reports of increased understanding and improvement in the problem at follow-up (Kutz, Lyon, and Stein, 1973). Moreover, Strupp (1971), well known for his studies of the therapeutic process, comments that:

> What the patient, in part, learns are new convictions or beliefs about himself and other people. . . . Patients after therapy talked much less about the symptoms that propelled them into therapy; that is, the place the symptoms played in their lives had changed or, stated otherwise, the experience of therapy had contributed to an emotional and cognitive restructuring of their view of themselves, others, and reality. (p. 327)

Such findings do not demonstrate, of course, that clients' altered views of themselves or others are the only changes they made or are necessarily the most important. Nonetheless, clients themselves did, in Strupp's studies, seem to place most emphasis and value on such changes.

Others may question whether inclusion of mental tasks transgresses the model on the basis that mental change is thought to be less measurable than alterations in physical activity. However, as long as care is taken to specify clearly the intellectual, affective, or attitudinal change desired, we have found no greater difficulty in assessing one type of change than another. Both clients and workers were able to provide statements illustrative of extent of change for both types of tasks. The evaluative problem, in my opinion, lies less in whether the task involves external or internal change than in whether therapist and client are willing to specify and assess desired outcomes.

Though some may prefer not to include mental change as an aspect of the task-centered approach, it is my impression that inclusion of this dimension may be important for those who practice in psychoanalytically oriented psychiatric settings. There has been a tendency by some in these settings to reject the model, stating that it is too "behaviorist." Apparently they feel that external behavioral measures alone do not fully reflect the goals toward which they and their clients desire to work. We feel that the option to include mental as well as physical tasks may assist such persons to find the model fitting for their actual practice situations. Indeed, our own experience in applying the model in this way has proved extremely useful as will be shown in the specific programs to be discussed below.

The Limbo Program

This program, in operation since 1973, is intended to help families to deal with problems resulting from divorce, death, serious illness, or other events causing separation from family members. The program has three components: (1) counseling with family members; (2) coordination and consultation with community agencies who might assist the families; and (3) short-term discussion groups for children of divorced or separated parents. The task-centered approach has been applied to the counseling aspect of this program.

By provisions of the grant, counseling for each family is limited to ten hours of in-person time, though flexibility in allocating this time is encouraged. Family members may be seen individually or in various combinations, with varying duration of contact. After an exploratory telephone call in which the purpose of the program is explained, interested clients are accepted directly into the program without an intervening diagnostic evaluation. The task-centered approach is then put into effect, first exploring whether mutually agreed-upon problems and tasks may be identified. If not, clients may be referred to other clinic programs or outside resources, or may choose to deal with their concerns independently.

The cases in this report include 23 families who began and completed contact with the program during the period January 1974–March 1975. One family, the single instance of termination without agreement during this period of time, is not included in this analysis.

By provisions of the program, each of the 23 families in the study had suffered a recent loss: 14 because of divorce or separation; 6, death of a parent; 2, severe illness of a parent; 1, loss of both parents owing to the child's leaving home. In each of the families, one adult and one to three children were seen, a total of 22 adults and 33 children. With all of these persons, contracts regarding problems and tasks were established within one to three visits, usually within the first two. Separated parents may also have been seen occasionally but contracts were not established with them. Nineteen contracts were made with individual children, 16 with individual adults, and 8 with combinations of persons—a total of 43 contracts among 23 cases. The children ranged in age from 3 to 17 years. Twenty-three were under age 12, 10 were age 12 or above. There were a nearly equal number of males and females. The number of appointments per family ranged from 4 to 13, with a mean of 8.5. Overall duration of contact varied from 5 to 21 weeks.

Within the 43 contracts, 78 target problems were agreed upon by individuals or combinations of clients. For the purpose of analysis, these problems were allocated to the seven problem categories established by the task-centered model. At least two persons, aside from the workers themselves, assisted with assignment of problems to categories in order to establish reliability. An eighth category, lack of problem clarity, was added to the problem classification scheme since the difficulty identified by clients in two cases was their inability to define their problems and therefore to decide what assistance, if any, might be needed. Contracts were therefore established for the specific purpose of clarification and planning. The following vignette illustrates such a contract:

Jane D, age 12, was referred to the Limbo Program for help in dealing with problems her mother felt she was experiencing as a result of her parents' recent separation and plan to divorce. Jane stated the problem as not being sure if she needed to talk about her situation, and agreed to focus on her uncertainty as an issue. She believed she was having some difficulty managing her sadness about loss of her father but was unsure whether she was dealing with these feelings on her own in a way that would turn out well for her. Tasks undertaken to resolve this issue were: (1) a discussion of the changes in her situation (enumerating and identifying them); (2) a discussion of her feelings about these changes; (3) an assessment of how she was actually dealing with each change; (4) reaching a decision about whether or not, in light of (1), (2), and (3), it was necessary to plan further use of therapeutic or other resources to assist her to deal with her new situation. After the first three tasks had been accomplished, the decision mutually agreed upon by Jane and the worker was that Jane could cope with her situation on her own. However, an important part of this plan to Jane was knowledge that the worker would be available if she decided she needed further discussion.

In other cases of this type, further services might have been planned and work done, if necessary, to enable the client to make use of those services.

A focus of the type described might be thought of as performing the first step only of the task-centered approach (problem search and specification), with termination after finding no problem requiring professional assistance. However, it seems to us that clarification of problems to be dealt with and of the client's own abilities to do so is indeed a specific, constructive service. Our concept emphasizes allying with client's *existing* abilities rather than, as is often necessary, mobilizing *potential* problem-solving abilities. Inclusion of such a focus as a definitive service rendered seems especially consistent with the ego-oriented, client-self-determining principles of task-centered casework. Indeed, it might be interesting to study instances in which only the problem-search aspect of the task-centered approach has been applied. It may be that some cases terminate at the end of the problem-search phase not because no problem was found but because, through discussion, the client had not only identified a problem but also had found his own ways (or "tasks") for dealing with it. In such cases, more may be achieved than workers believe.

The distribution of problems in accordance with Reid and Epstein's seven problem categories plus our added category is shown in Table 2.1. Also shown are the improvement ratings for each problem category. Improvement was assessed by clients and workers mutually with clients' opinions taking precedence if there was disagreement.

We had anticipated that since all clients in this program had suffered a recent stress, distribution among problem categories might be so disproportionate as to render the categories unhelpful. However, even though, as might be expected, a large number of problems fell into the category of reactive emotional distress, more than half of the problems were easily identifiable by the raters as belonging to four other categories.

It may be observed that nearly all problems of social transition showed *substantial* improvement as did a majority of difficulties in role performance. Substantial problem resolution less frequently occurred

Table 2.1

Target Problems and Problem Improvement, Limbo Program

| | | | IMPROVEMENT RATINGS (% OF CATEGORY) | | |
PROBLEM CATEGORY	NUMBER OF PROBLEMS	% OF ALL PROBLEMS	SUBSTANTIAL	PARTIAL	NONE
1. Interpersonal Conflict	7	9	29	57	14
2. Dissatisfaction in Social Relations	14	18	29	57	14
3. Relations with Formal Organizations	—	—	—	—	—
4. Social Transition	11	14	91	—	9
5. Role Performance	9	12	67	33	—
6. Reactive Emotional Distress	35	45	46	48	6
7. Inadequate Resources	—	—	—	—	—
8. Lack of Problem Clarity	2	2	—	100	—

in the categories of interpersonal conflict, social relations, and reactive emotional distress. Nearly all problems showing *no* progress occurred in these latter three categories. Overall, clients reported *some* improvement in 92 percent of all problems, substantial improvement in 49 percent of all problems.

Tasks were categorized both by the "unique" vs. "repetitive" dichotomy as suggested by Reid (1975) and by a typology distinguishing "mental," "physical," and "mixed" tasks. Within the 43 contracts, 179 tasks were agreed upon. Among these 179, clients and workers selected only 10 unique tasks, that is, tasks that would be considered achieved if done only once. An example of this would be to "get a book on divorce and read it with child." All 169 other tasks were categorized as repetitive, that is, behaviors which clients wanted to develop and repeat through time. Eight unique tasks were thought to have been largely achieved, two not at all. Forty-three percent of the repetitive tasks were thought to have been substantially achieved; 47 percent, partially achieved; and 10 percent, not accomplished at all.

Of the 179 tasks, 73 were considered mental, 99 physical, and 7 mixed. An example of a mental task would be: "get in the habit of giving myself credit for things I do well." A physical task would be: "tell mother when I am upset about something instead of shutting myself in my room." A mixed task would be: "figure out why I am mad and tell mother what the trouble is." Distributions of progress ratings for mental versus physical tasks were nearly identical: substantial achievement, 52 percent mental and 55 percent physical; partial achievement, 33 percent mental and 32 percent physical; no achievement, 15 percent mental and 12 percent physical.

Since the question is sometimes raised as to whether tasks may be achieved while the problem itself remains little affected, an analysis was made of ratings of task achievement in relation to problem improvement within each of the problem categories. Indeed, remarkable congruence was found between ratings of task achievement and of problem improvement in all categories except problems of interpersonal relationships. Rather than suggesting any deficit in the task-centered system, this finding may indicate that tasks related to such problems were not sufficiently well chosen so as to be expected to affect the problem. Such unsuccessful task selection might, in turn, account for a lower rate of problem resolution in the category of interpersonal relationships. However, the numbers involved in this category are too small to preclude more than a very tentative hypothesis.

Most of the workers in this program felt that the task-centered approach was especially appropriate for the population served. That is, since the program provided for focus on issues related to loss rather than an exploration and treatment of clients' problems generally, the model supported both workers and clients in adhering to these issues. Workers who approved the approach felt that many clients were attracted to the program by its clear focus and would not have participated in a more generalized program. Other workers felt constrained by the mandatory focus on loss and the short-term limitation as well as by the task-centered system. These workers would have preferred more leeway to deal with a breadth of family problems. However, these objections seem due more to a professional preference for long-term treatment than to dissatisfactions with the task-centered mode. One objection did relate to the task-centered approach; some workers expressed the opinion that to expect clients readily to identify problems and tasks and then to adhere to such foci might be appropriate for "neurotic, motivated" clients but not for more disturbed, disorganized, or resistant clients. However, many participants in this program were neither especially well-functioning in their general life situations nor, at least at first, especially well-motivated. Nonetheless, all but one family concluded their agreed-upon participation with at least some progress. This finding, which will be further supported by findings of the Mini-School Program to be reported below, suggests that the task-centered approach is useful with groups other than the neurotic and well-motivated. Indeed, it may be especially appropriate for such groups.

Those who find the approach useful only with well-functioning clients may not fully understand the worker's role in assisting clients to clarify issues of greatest importance to them. Some workers, despite orientation, seem to maintain the impression that clients are required to arrive with preformed ideas about problems and tasks. On the contrary, there is a necessity for worker activity in problem clarification that is exemplified in cases of many adults and especially among children. For example, it is rather typical for adolescents as well as younger children to state at first that they are at the clinic only because of parental insistence. In such instances, clearly no issues will be identified unless the worker engages the youth in discussion of whether, aside from his parents' concerns, he himself is troubled with some difficulty.

Some workers found the task-centered approach especially useful with children. They experimented with the use of a written contract, especially with older children, to engage the child in goal-setting, adherence to focus, and evaluation. First there is discussion of the child's concerns, then either the worker or the child writes down the problems and tasks. Often further discussion of the written version ensues, during which the child "edits" the contract. Children often bring their copies to interviews to remind themselves of what they would like to talk about. If the child does not bring his copy to the last few sessions, the worker gives him a copy so that the worker and client can review items together.

We do not know if changes in the particular problems treated will positively affect the clients' other life problems nor do we know how well clients' problems would have been resolved without treatment. Among the 23 families, 12 were recommended by their workers for further treatment in some other program, and of these, 9 indicated agreement with the worker's judgment by participating in further treatment. However, the use of further treatment does not indicate that the outcome was either favorable or unfavorable: in some instances it may indicate that little had been achieved; in others, that clients had utilized the program to identify problems requiring further assistance. Indeed, we found that one-half of those who accepted further treatment had mainly reported high levels of goal attainment while the other half had mainly reported low attainment. Aside from this issue, clients seemed to express their approval of the program's methodology both through reported levels of improvement and through their decision to continue, with but one exception, throughout their agreed-upon length of participation.

The MiniSchool Program

This intensive outreach program for severely emotionally disturbed children and their families has been in operation since February 1973. The program was funded by the Commonwealth of Massachusetts, Department of Special Education, to demonstrate an alternative community service for children who had been certified by state regulations to receive residential placement. These children had not been placed for a variety of reasons: unavailability of a suitable placement, parental refusal, or professional judgment that placement might be more detrimental than helpful to the family as a whole.

The program has two major objects as described in its proposal: (1) to improve overall functioning and organization of the family through mobilization and maximizing of ego strengths to a point where the child can remain in the home and make use of resources available in the local school system and community; (2) to coordinate efforts and maximize effectiveness of available supportive systems or persons (schools, social agencies, relatives, etc.).

The program was funded to provide a maximum of five months' service to each of the families who met the program criteria and had previously been seen at the clinic for diagnostic evaluation or treatment. Nearly all had terminated their contract without worker agreement. In order to obtain a complement of eight families, the most recently seen families fitting the criteria were called in and the program was explained to them. Hence no selectiveness was used to obtain the group aside from the necessity that there be a child certified for residence but not in residence. During this procedure, four families declined to participate before the total group of eight had agreed to do so.

Although a five-month period would not be considered short-term by the standards of the task-centered model, the chronicity and multiplicity of problems acknowledged by the families made five months seem short indeed. Another way in which the program differed from the model was in its mandate for intensive service. In contrast with a limit of a few in-person hours, this program encouraged extensive family and collateral contact, either at the clinic, clients' homes, or other agencies, especially schools. The amount of contact was limited only by clients' wishes as expressed in their contract with the worker and by the worker's available time.

Multiple contracts were made with family members, whether individual adults or children, or various combinations of adults and children. These contracts included agreements on problems, tasks, site of interviews, and frequency of contact. Despite differences from the model in terms of intensity and length, the task-centered approach seemed to us especially suitable since both program and approach emphasized mobilization and use of clients' abilities for problem solving. Of greatest importance was the likelihood that the mutuality emphasized in the model might have helped involve this group of clients, nearly all of whom had previously rejected traditional outpatient treatment.

An extension of the model, one which we have not previously seen reported, was the establishment of task-centered contracts with fellow professionals. These contracts were made in order to facilitate the second objective of the program, to assist in mobilizing and coordinating community resources and to enhance the families' collaboration with these resources. Hence, workers made contracts with the one or two professionals in the community most involved with each child, nine persons in all, and in all cases either a teacher or principal. It should be noted that the objectives of these contracts were clearly consultative rather than therapeutic in nature.

In reporting results of this program, findings with respect to client progress will be mentioned only briefly, since they have been described more thoroughly in another article (Cohen and Ewalt, 1975). Instead, results of a study of clients' views of the task-centered approach itself will be emphasized.

Briefly, with respect to clients' assessments of progress, findings were remarkably similar to those reported above for clients of the Limbo Program. That is, about 90 percent of problems and tasks were said to have improved or been achieved at least partially, about 40 percent to a substantial degree. This proportion of problem alleviation seems remarkable given the serious nature of the difficulties with which these families were dealing. This is not to imply that the serious emotional disturbances of the children (and sometimes of parents also) were basically altered. Nonetheless, persons afflicted with these severe difficulties felt that they had progressed with problems and tasks of primary concern to themselves. Equally remarkable is the fact that all of the eight families continued to participate throughout the five-month program. Both of these findings seem to speak well for appropriateness of the task-centered approach with this group of clients. Similar to clients in the Limbo Program, about half were desirous of further treatment, and this interest was unrelated to ratings of progress made during the MiniSchool contact.

In order to explore clients' opinions about the task-centered approach itself, a follow-up study was conducted with adult members in the eight families. Twelve of 14 potential respondents agreed to participate. These included 11 mothers and fathers and 1 grandmother, at least 1 respondent from each of the 8 families. Data were obtained through telephone interviews by a social worker otherwise unrelated to the MiniSchool Program, utilizing a semi-structured schedule.

Clients' experience with the task-centered approach as applied in the MiniSchool Program was reportedly as follows. All but one of the respondents stated that he or she had contributed to an agreement about problems to be discussed as well as tasks to be undertaken. All of these respondents thought that such agreements were "very helpful" as compared with "fairly" or "not at all" helpful. Ten of the 12 persons recalled deciding with the worker whether interviews would occur in the home, at the agency, or a combination of the two, and all expressed satisfaction with the arrangements. Eight of the 12 recalled that a time limit of five months had been established at the outset. All respondents said that if they were to obtain further counseling, they would prefer the same type of program rather than some other kind. This response may, in part, be accounted for by the intensity of the service received. However, clients' responses with respect to the contractual aspects of the task-centered approach were clearly favorable.

Similarly, school personnel were interviewed subsequent to the conclusion of the program with respect to the progress of the child and to the methodology of the program. Four felt the child's functioning in school had greatly improved; 3, somewhat improved; 2, not improved. No one thought the situation had worsened. All felt that, where improvement had occurred, it was due to the work of the program. With respect to program methodology, 8 of the 9 school persons recalled making contracts regarding problems and tasks for themselves. Seven of these 8 felt the making of such agreements was very helpful, 1, fairly helpful. Of the 8 who recalled having made task-centered agreements, 6 felt goals of these agreements had been substantially achieved and 2 partially achieved. These findings suggest that the task-centered methodology may be found useful in client-centered case consultation, as described by Caplan (1970), as well as in direct work with clients.

The Short-Term Treatment Program

The task-centered approach has also been applied in the clinic's ongoing, nongrant-funded, short-term treatment program. As organized at this clinic, the short-term treatment program includes clients who accept a disposition of three to twelve treatment hours *following* the initial diagnostic-interventive period of work with the client. Hence, application of the task-centered approach in this program differs from the model in that it represents the second, rather than the first, contract made between the client and the clinic.

The procedure for referral to the short-term treatment program provides that, if clients are desirous of further service of a short-term nature, the first clinic worker conducts the first step of the task-centered approach: exploration and identification of problems and tasks. If only one or two further visits are thought necessary, the first worker conducts these interviews. If three to twelve visits are planned, clients are often, though not always, transferred to a different worker in the short-term treatment program. This worker begins contact by reviewing the previously specified problems and tasks, and revising if necessary. Thereafter, the task-centered model is followed through to the mutual evaluation phase at termination.

This report covers 36 short-term treatment contracts implemented between December 1973 and July 1974, including contracts with 3 individual children, 17 individual adults, 11 married couples, and 5 other combinations of family members. The mean number of appointments planned for these cases was 7.7 and the mean number carried out was 7.1.

In terms of the number of appointments planned in comparison with the number of appointments carried out, in 21 instances the time plan was observed as planned; in 2 instances, 1 additional appointment was held; and in 13 instances, fewer appointments were held than planned, usually because intended goals had been achieved. However, only three cases varied from the plan by more than two visits. The range of duration of treatment was 1 to 28 weeks, with a mean of 12.5 weeks. Clients in this group were most frequently concerned with difficulties in role performance, less frequently with interpersonal conflict and reactive emotional distress, and infrequently with other problem categories. The distribution of problems encountered in the short-term treatment program, in accordance with the Reid and Epstein categorizations, and the proportion of each category thought to have shown partial or substantial improvement, are shown in Table 2.2

Table 2.2
Target Problems and Problem Change, Regular
Short-term Treatment Program

PROBLEM CATEGORY	NUMBER OF PROBLEMS	% OF ALL PROBLEMS	IMPROVEMENT RATINGS (% OF CATEGORY)		
			SUBSTANTIAL	PARTIAL	NONE
1. Interpersonal Conflict	13	18	38	54	8
2. Dissatisfaction in Social Relations	4	6	25	50	25
3. Relationships with Formal Organizations	1	1	—	100	—
4. Social Transition	5	7	20	60	20
5. Role Performance	34	47	29	68	3
6. Reactive Emotional Distress	14	19	29	71	—
7. Inadequate Resources	1	1	—	100	—

Comparison between our Limbo and short-term Programs reveals some differences with respect to problem distribution. Whereas reactive emotional distress was the problem most frequently found among Limbo clients, difficulty in role performance was most frequently found in the short-term program. This variance is probably explained by two differences in program characteristics. First, the Limbo Program served entirely clients new to the clinic who had recently experienced loss of a family member, whereas clients in the short-term program had already had a period of contact with the clinic and had not necessarily experienced a recent acute stress. Secondly, the short-term program primarily served adults who might be expected to be concerned with their role performance as parents whereas the Limbo Program included a large number of children whose problems infrequently involved role performance.

With respect to outcome in terms of problem improvement, although problems in both the Limbo and short-term programs showed at least some improvement in about 90 percent of instances, the mean percentage of problems rated *substantially* improved in the Limbo Program was much higher (63 percent) than in the short-term program (29 percent). Three possible explanations worthy of further exploration occur to us. Problems of greatest concern to persons under severe recent stress (as in the Limbo Program) may be expected to show some abatement more readily, with or without treatment, than the not necessarily acute problems encountered in the short-term program. Secondly, since many more children were involved in the Limbo than in the short-term program, perhaps these younger persons improved more rapidly, or thought they improved more rapidly, than the adults. Thirdly, since the short-term program was comprised of a much larger and more diverse group of workers who were not as closely supervised with respect to the task-centered approach, we have the impression that when progress was being evaluated, workers' rather than clients' judgments may have taken precedence in some instances and resulted in lower ratings of progress. Nonetheless, further investigation of likelihood of improvement using the task-centered approach among persons with acute versus longstanding problems, and among adults versus children, would be worthwhile.

In relation to the 72 target problems, 243 tasks were agreed upon.

Since outcomes for 12 of these were missing, this analysis is comprised of 231 task items. By the unique-repetitive dichotomization, 6 of these tasks were unique, 225 repetitive. Four of the 6 unique tasks were achieved. Repetitive tasks showed substantial improvement in 41 percent of instances; partial improvement in 49 percent; none in 9 percent. By our mental- physical-mixed categories, 71 tasks (31 percent) were mental; 137 (59 percent) were physical; and 23 (10 percent) were mixed. No differences were found between distributions of improvement ratings for mental versus physical tasks.

As in the Limbo Program, the mean for task achievement ratings was compared with the mean for problem improvement ratings. In this program, in contrast with the Limbo Program, more frequently tasks were rated substantially achieved than problems were rated substantially resolved. This difference was accounted for entirely by the problem categories of reactive emotional distress and social transition, progress ratings of problems and tasks in other categories being congruent. Again it is possible that the flaw of workers' sometimes rating according to their own judgment rather than the clients' could account for relatively lower ratings of problem resolution, though why this should affect only two categories is not clear. One speculation might be that in the reactive emotional distress category, workers' skepticism about improvement may be greater than with other categories, causing them to underrate improvement in comparison with clients' views. Since the number of problems in the social transition category is so small (5), it may only accidentally appear to have lower problem resolution than task achievement. It is still worthwhile to consider whether or not task selection for these two categories was sufficiently adept to be useful in modifying problems. A broader implication to consider, however, is that the task-centered approach may be expected to achieve a greater degree of problem resolution, in the clients' view, when clients are in acute distress (as in the Limbo Program) than when they have been dealing with problems for some time (as in the short-term program).

As in the other two programs reported, about one-half of all clients entered further treatment. This progression was to be expected for many clients since in 14 (29 percent) of the cases, use of the short-term program was specifically intended to prepare clients for other treatment modalities. Some of these clients felt the need to clarify problems on which they would work in further treatment, and others wanted to deal with certain fears or intimate concerns prior to entering group therapy.

Summary

The task-centered approach has been found useful and apparently effective in three treatment programs in a psychoanalytically oriented child guidance setting. Adults, adolescents, and younger children were included in all three programs. Effectiveness is suggested by the achievement of substantial improvement, at least in the clients' view, in about 40 percent of all target problems, and at least partial progress in another 50 percent of problems. Controlled studies are needed to assess the contribution of other factors to outcomes, such as the clients' capacity to improve on his own. A further indicator of the model's appropriateness is to be found in clients' continuance throughout their agreed-upon length of service: practically no clients discontinued without agreement in any of these programs.

Distribution of target problems was different from that reported by Reid and Epstein (1972) in their pilot studies, especially in that a far higher number of problems of reactive emotional distress were encountered. For that reason, it seems that the task-centered model is applicable to populations other than those with whom it was initially applied. This conclusion is supported by other studies in this volume, particularly the one reported by Brown (chapter 15).

A small follow-up study of clients' views of the model itself indicated strong approval of the methodology despite the fact that this study was conducted among clients who for the most part had previously rejected outpatient treatment. Application of the model to case-centered consultation was tested with a small number of school personnel. These persons also reported that they had found the approach acceptable and effective.

Suggestions were made for two types of additions to the model's categories. With respect to target problems, the category "lack of problem clarity" was added in order to assist clients whose very difficulty was inability to identify their problems. With respect to task categorization, it

leniency with her daughters and just as stoutly said Mr. Wick sometimes expected too much of John.

My role in the third session was to support the parents' recognition of the need for change in Mrs. Wick's way of relating to John. Her anxiety and overprotection was identified as an obstacle to her stated goal of helping John to accept his illness. In addition, we looked at other reasons for changing. Mrs. Wick recognized that John would eventually have full responsibility for himself and needed to be prepared. I spoke of the changing role of parents at adolescence, the need for them to encourage John's healthy normal drive for independence. Mrs. Wick voiced some of her fears and ambivalent feelings: wanting to be sure diabetic management was done right; fear that John might "goof up." I suggested that John could only learn through his own experience. I empathized some with her concern about mistakes.

At the end of these three sessions the target problems which emerged were:

1. Mrs. Wick's excessive overprotection of John.
2. Mr. Wick's excessive demands of John.
3. Mrs. Wick's anger and inappropriate guilt over John's illness.
4. John's depressed feelings.

In the third interview, we set up tasks:

1. Mrs. Wick was to permit John appropriate responsibility for managing the diabetes.
   a. John would do the diabetic management activities except meal preparation.
   b. Mrs. Wick would do the meal preparation.
   c. Mr. Wick would give John an insulin injection when John could not do so himself.
2. Mrs. Wick was to be considerate of John's proper need for freedom in general. Specific operational tasks to carry out this goal were not spelled out but were expected to flow from Mrs. Wick's increased comprehension of, and attention to, John's age-appropriate characteristics.
3. Mr. Wick was to remind Mrs. Wick to relinquish her controlling activities toward John.
   a. He was to be encouraging to her, rather than deprecating of her, in these efforts.

b. Both were to keep in mind that Mrs. Wick was in fact a good, adequate mother undergoing some change in her motherly behavior as a consequence of John's age and illness.

The next four interviews concentrated upon task implementation and dealing with obstacles. At the beginning of the fourth interview, Mr. Wick did not seem to be with us. After commenting on his mood, I determined the reason was a current conflict with his boss. I did not pursue that issue because it was not germane to the target problems. Noting his mood, however, apparently enabled him to continue to work in the interview.

We dealt with two areas: (1) progress in the tasks set last week, including John's greater freedom to involve himself in activities away from home. His parents were really pleased and I acknowledged their satisfaction and progress. (2) Mr. Wick's way of dealing with John's discouragement and resentment. When John expresses these feelings it makes Mr. Wick mad. He fears that encouraging him to do so is being overprotective and will make John a sissy—a baby—not a man.

In interview four, there was some interchange between the parents on their ways of dealing with John. Mrs. Wick felt that Mr. Wick was too strict. Mr. Wick was encouraged to think about how it must feel to develop diabetes at age 13; whether it was babyish to express legitimate feelings. Referring to the parents' description of John's independent behavior, I asked if that sounded like a baby. I suggested that each parent needed to move more toward a middle ground approach in order to achieve their goals: Mrs. Wick needed to change (as she had begun to do) her tendency to hold John back; Mr. Wick needed to modify his tendency to push John to be a man too soon and to make him ashamed of his legitimate feelings. If John understood that his father accepted his feelings, it might relieve him. Mr. Wick was thoughtful but skeptical. It was decided that John would join us next week (interview 5) so that he would know what we were working on and so that we could deal together with the issues discussed in this session.

The following week, family interaction around one simple incident demonstrated what we had discussed the previous week. A different perspective emerged. John told, with bitter feeling, of how he has to bring his sandwich to school. The other kids go to the gym for hot lunches and bring them back to the room where all eat together. This makes John feel different; he thinks the kids stare at him when he's eating. He doesn't like this; he doesn't like school. Mrs. Wick looked hurt; Mr. Wick brushed John's feelings aside, saying that he should ignore the others. John's frown spoke volumes. I pointed this out and asked for the parents' reactions. Mrs. Wick continued to look anxious and Mr. Wick said John is too sorry for himself. At this point, John clammed up.

I suggested to them how John might be feeling. Because of the diabetic diet, he had to bring his lunch. That was different from what he saw the other kids do. This really bugged John. He wanted his parents to know and accept his difference—not feel sorry for him or tell him he shouldn't feel this way. John nodded his confirmation. I suggested to John that it might bother him a lot more than it bothered the other kids. Who knows, they might be complaining to their parents about having to go all the way to the gym to get their lunches; why couldn't they bring a sandwich to school like John did? When we talked about the next session, I left it up to the parents and John as to whether he needed to come.

Three weeks intervened between interview five and six. John did not attend the sixth interview, because he had something to do with his friends. Mr. and Mrs. Wick were less concerned because he seemed happier, more comfortable, and more accepting of his illness. He used to dread going to school every morning but now he is "bouncy." He goes out with a smile on his face, and is again attending school parties. He told his mother, "You know, that social work lady told me right—half of them are bringing their lunch like me." (Possibly they always did.)

John made a step forward when for the first time he slept away from home at a friend's house. Mrs. Wick took his insulin to him in the morning. While supporting the positive movement, I also questioned the need for this. Did this foster independence? We thought together about other growth-promoting alternatives. Overall, the parents agreed that John was now more independent. Mrs. Wick told him, "I have to cut you loose, put you on your own."

The seventh session occurred one week later. The Wicks felt that their goal was achieved. We reviewed what had been accomplished and what they had done to effect change. The changes described the preceding week had continued. John no longer sat around "blue or down in the dumps." Mrs. Wick connected these changes with modification of her behavior toward John—she was now letting go. She felt "100 percent more comfortable" about the diabetes and about herself. She still got "slightly" depressed—like recently when John ran a "4 + sugar." Her immediate reaction was, "What did I do wrong?" However, she caught herself and decided this was the course of the illness. I strongly commended her ability to observe herself and interrupt her tendency to blame and punish herself.

Mr. Wick stated that John had been "too dependent on mommy." This was no longer true and he was satisfied. Both parents thought John was functioning now as independently as other boys his age. What still remained to be worked on was for John to draw up his own insulin and to have more practice in weighing and preparing his own food.

I summarized the feelings and behavior we had discovered. I underscored the changes Mrs. Wick had made, the support Mr. Wick had provided, the resultant changes in John, and the fact that they were all more comfortable. I pointed out that it was not clear what changes Mr. Wick had made in his behavior with John. The expectation was that both parents would continue to apply what they had learned, keeping in mind that they both needed to move more toward the middle. I mentioned the ups and downs in everyone's life and suggested that it only made sense for the Wicks to return to talk things over at any time they wanted to—not only about John, but about other members of the family or their relationship.

At the end of seven sessions, the family-planned goal and changes in the target problem were satisfactorily achieved through family work on the designated tasks. The main obstacles were the parents' polarized attitudes and behavior based on their own needs rather than on accurate perception of John's needs. Major treatment communications used were: (1) enhancing awareness of behavior which facilitated or interfered with task achievement; (2) cognitive explanations to encourage task-directed behavior and bring about different perspectives.

Finally, a word about my reactions in working with this model. Initially I felt restricted, as I had to discipline my inclination to explore areas not strictly connected to the target problems. I was also uneasy with the increased use of cognitive explanations since it was in contrast to my usual way of functioning.

This case represents some ways in which the task-centered treatment model may be adapted in a hospital setting where crises frequently occur and where emphasis is on treatment of the family, not the individual. In a crisis situation, that part of the "underlying problem" which affects the current stress is explored and worked through, when possible. This is illustrated by the time needed in the first two sessions with Mrs. Wick to deal with her strong feelings. A part of the "underlying problem" was extruded prior to introducing the task-centered approach. Including the involved family members helped to delineate the target problem, tasks, and obstacles.

In assessing the effectiveness of the task-centered model and its use in work with the Wick family, several questions emerge: (1) What accounted for the fact that more obstacles did not arise to interfere with the resolution of the target problem? (2) Could more work have been done with Mr. Wick's response to the situation? (3) Can factors be identified that would enable one to predict whether progress will be sustained? (4) In a more general vein, is this model applicable to work with individuals or families who have shaky ability to trust and minimum tolerance for self-observation?

Chapter 4

‧⌄

William J. Reid, D.S.W.

Process and Outcome in the Treatment of Family Problems

In the two preceding chapters, task-centered treatment of family problems was examined in a child guidance and a medical setting. The problems dealt with were primarily child-related. In this chapter, we turn to an application of the model in two family service agencies and will focus on its use with difficulties in marital relations. The chapter reports on a research study carried out in the agencies. The next two chapters will deal with aspects of the same project from the standpoint of participating practitioners.

Numerous questions prompted the project. Does the task-centered model offer a feasible and useful means of treatment of problems in family relations, particularly marital disorders? What are the areas of difficulty in applying this method to the treatment of such problems? How well would it be implemented in trials conducted by experienced practitioners with their own style of practice and with relatively little training in the model? How would family agency clients evaluate the approach? Such questions reflected the general purpose of the project: to test out the model under a particular set of conditions and to gather data that would serve as a basis for its evaluation and improvement.

In brief, the study consisted of trials of the model with 31 cases in two family agencies. Two obvious limitations were the small size of the sample and the lack of control or comparison groups. To compensate somewhat for these limitations, the findings from the present study are compared with three other bodies of data: (1) A cumulative data file of 89 task-centered cases carried by students at the School of Social Service Administration (SSA) as part of an ongoing research and development program (see chapter 1); (2) an experimental study which compared brief and extended casework of 120 families in another family agency (the Community Service Society of New York) (Reid and Shyne, 1969); (3) a nationwide study of services and outcomes for over three thousand cases from member agencies of the Family Service Association of America (Beck and Jones, 1973; Beck, 1974; Beck, 1975). Although these bodies of data must be compared continuously with data from the present study, they do provide some rough norms against which some of our results may be assessed. Comparisons will be made at points of meaningful similarity in respect to type of client, service, or measurement.

Agencies, Cases, and Practitioners

Two agencies, the Family Service of the Cincinnati Area and the Family Service Society of Hartford, agreed to participate in the study. Actually, each agency conducted separate subprojects, which are being combined for purposes of this report. Both were carried out according to guidelines supplied by the author with some variation between agencies. The same set of instruments was used in each subproject (see Appendix). Project data consisted of instruments and narrative case summaries completed by caseworkers, tapes of treatment interviews, and questionnaires completed by clients. The data were sent to SSA for processing and analysis.

The study sample consisted of 31 cases drawn from these two agencies. The bulk of these cases (n = 21) was taken from the Cincinnati agency. The Cincinnati cases were divided about equally between two MSW practitioners, both of whom had over ten years' counselling experience. The ten Hartford cases were distributed among six MSW practitioners whose counselling experience ranged from one year to more than ten years.

The practitioners, as a rule, were experienced in time-limited, short-term practice—in fact, the Cincinnati caseworkers, who carried most of the project cases, had been using this form of practice with the bulk of their regular treatment cases. None of the practitioners had had prior experience with the present task-centered form of short-term treatment, however. The amount of formal training in the task-centered model varied between the two sites. In Cincinnati, it consisted of the two practitioners reading instructional material, listening to a tape of a task-centered marital case, meeting with the author in two training sessions, and trying out the model on a small number of cases prior to the project. At Hartford, formal training consisted of the staff's reading instructional material and a two-hour session with the author. In addition, staff meetings concerned with applications of the approach were held at both sites.

The two agencies used somewhat different criteria for case selection. In Cincinnati the staff decided to restrict the project to cases of marital conflict. At Hartford, criteria were broadened to include other types of family relation problems as well as adjustment difficulties in adults. In both agencies, project caseloads were made up of consecutive referrals to project caseworkers, beginning with a specified target date and ending when a predetermined number of cases had been accepted. Because of variations among practitioners and agencies in collecting data on early drop-outs (usually cases that terminated before a second interview), it was decided to define a project case as one receiving three or more interviews.

The project served a total of 51 clients in the 31 cases. A client was defined as an individual who received at least one in-person interview in a project case. The great majority (90 percent) were married adults, although about a quarter were separated from their spouses. Over 90 percent were white. About two-thirds of the men had either professional or skilled occupations. A majority of the women (60 percent) were housewives. Two-thirds had at least high-school educations; over a third had at least some college. On the whole it was a youthful group: the median age for men was 31 years; for women, 20.

Target Problems

Target problems were categorized according to the problem classification scheme used in research on task-centered practice (see chapter 1). In all but four cases in the present sample, marital conflict was a matter of concern in one way or another. Application of the problem classification scheme revealed, however, a more varied and complex picture of the actual targets of intervention than might be suggested by use of the broad category of marital disorder.

Practitioners identified at least two target problems in most cases, three problems in about a third of the cases. A total of 69 problems were recorded for the cases as a whole. They summarized the problems in brief statements which were used as a basis for problem classification.

The most frequently occurring problem, not surprisingly, was "interpersonal conflict—marital," which accounted for a third—but only a third—of all problems. To warrant classification in this category, the target for change agreed upon by practitioner and client was the marital interaction itself—how husband and wife were behaving toward one another. Another third of the problems was divided about equally among three categories: *dissatisfaction in social relations, difficulties in role performance,* and *reactive emotional distress.* Many of these problems were related to marital conflict but reflected targets for change other than marital interaction itself. Thus, in one case a problem was defined as a woman's difficulty in being assertive in social relations generally, including her relation with her husband. This problem was better classified as one of dissatisfaction in social relations rather than interpersonal conflict. Similarly, some clients saw their problems in terms of their emotional distress about the marriage or in terms of specific inadequacies in their performance in marital roles rather than in terms of the marital relationship. The next largest category was problems of social transition (7 percent of all problems). These problems also frequently involved marital difficulty, but the emphasis was usually on a decision as to whether or not to stay with a spouse rather than on marital interaction as a target for change. The remaining problems were scattered over the other categories of the system. These included difficulties with formal organizations, inadequate resources, and behavior or personality problems not elsewhere classified. Again, some of these difficulties, such as low income and excessive drinking, were intertwined with marital conflict. In general, the classification system provided a picture of the particular problems worked on. In so doing, it perhaps shed some light on the range of specific target problems that make up "marital cases."

One of the requirements for target problems in the task-centered model is that they be relatively specific. To determine how well this requirement was met, the practitioners' problem descriptions were coded on a 5-point scale that ran from "global" to "very specific." A problem statement was coded as global if it described a generalized broad area of concern in abstract terms, for example, "Mrs. L was in conflict with her daughter, mother-in-law, and especially her husband." Problems were rated specific if they pertained to particular behaviors or circumstances: "Mrs. B was undecided whether or not to remain separated from her husband." It was found that 62 percent of the problems were rated as either specific or somewhat specific, thus suggesting some implementation of the problem-specificity feature of the model. This percentage compares favorably with the 59 percent of problems rated at the same level of specificity in 89 task-centered cases carried out by students at the School of Social Service Administration.

One feature of the model apparently carried out with a high degree of fidelity was reaching agreement with the client on target problems early in treatment (in the first two interviews). This was accomplished in over 90 percent of the problems. The corresponding figure for the SSA student cases was 74 percent, possibly indicating that the more experienced Cincinnati-Hartford practitioners could zero in more quickly on target problems.

Service Characteristics

DURATION AND AMOUNT

The task-centered model calls for an early agreement with the client, within the first two interviews if possible, on the approximate duration and amount of service. This agreement is usually expressed in terms of so many interviews, usually within a range of from eight to twelve, within a 3- to 4-month period. This phase of the model seemed to have been adhered to rather closely. In all but one case agreement was reached by the second session on the number of interviews to be held. In the majority of cases (58 percent) either 7 or 8 interviews were planned. In no case did the initial agreement call for less than 5 or more than 10 interviews. An exact number of interviews was specified in all but 2 cases, in which a range of 6 to 8 sessions was planned.

The *actual* number of interviews in each case corresponded quite closely to the number planned. In the 29 cases in which an exact number of interviews was agreed on, the majority (55 percent) received exactly the planned number; in an additional 34 percent of the cases, the actual number came within one of the planned number. In the remaining 6 cases, the planned number exceeded the actual in 2 or fell short of it in 2. Both cases in which a 6- to 8-interview range was projected finished within that range. For the project caseload as a whole, the median number of interviews was 8; 67 percent of the cases received from 6 to 8 interviews; the maximum number recorded for any case was 11.

Thus it is clear that in terms of planning and adhering to interview limits, the practice followed the model with a reasonable degree of fidelity. Interestingly enough, most of the deviation from the model was in the direction of fewer interviews being planned and conducted than the 8 to 12 called for in the model. In about a quarter of the cases, less than 8 interviews were planned *and* carried out but in no case were more than 12 sessions either agreed on or completed.

The interviews were generally conducted on a weekly basis. The median duration of treatment was 11 weeks, consistent with the 3- to 4-month time called for in the model. No case took longer than 4 months; over a quarter were completed in under 2. Here again the limits of the model seemed more than ample to accommodate to the reality of practice in the project.

TYPES OF INTERVIEW

Interviews were predominately with individual clients (60 percent of the total). The remaining 40 percent consisted of husband-wife joint interviews. When we consider only cases in which marital conflict was an issue, the percentage of joint interviews rises to 47 percent.

Three clear patterns of interviewing emerged in marital conflict cases: (1) the use of joint interviews as the primary or only service modality (11 cases); (2) one or two joint interviews interspersed with single interviews with husband and wife (4 cases); and (3) cases in which single interviews with the wife were the dominant or exclusive medium or treatment (8 cases). In terms of total interview hours (counting a joint interview as one hour for the husband and one for the wife), wives were seen for a total of 271 hours, husbands for a total of 181. The husbands' share of the total interview time was 40 percent.

USE OF TASKS

The main distinguishing feature of the model is the organization of treatment around tasks or problem-solving actions undertaken by the client. The practitioners were asked to record each client task on a special form (see the Task Review Schedule in the Appendix). A total of 144 tasks were recorded.

As noted in chapter 1, two levels of tasks are distinguished in the model. *General* tasks express a direction for the client's efforts but do not specify particular actions the client is to undertake. About a fifth of the tasks were of this type, for example, "the client is to find ways to improve social relations and become less lonely," or 'Mr. and Mrs. D are to work toward establishing greater independence from their parents." *Operational* tasks call for specific behavior on the part of the client. The remaining four-fifths of the tasks were of this type. An example of such a task would be, "Mr. and Mrs. E are to make a list of financial obligations and to examine them together."

The number of tasks per case varied considerably; the primary source of their variation was clearly the practitioner. One of the Cincinnati practitioners stood out in this respect with a median per case of nine tasks, most of them specific. The other caseworkers averaged one or two tasks per case. In the original model (Reid and Epstein, 1972) it was suggested that work be concentrated on a relatively small number of tasks. In subsequent work, it has been found that tasks are often used in much larger numbers when they are specific and limited.

Perhaps because of their complexity, cases involving marital problems have tended to produce greater numbers of tasks than other kinds. Thus an average of nine tasks per case, while still high by our current norms, is not seen as "out of line."

As its designation suggests, task-centered practice is meant to be focused on helping clients define and carry out agreed-upon tasks. How well did the caseworkers' approaches fit into this framework?

To answer this question, relevant project data including tapes of interviews, practitioner listings of major interventions, and narrative case summaries were analyzed. Analysis was selective and qualitative. Unfortunately, resources did not permit a systematic coding and quantitative analysis of worker interventions from tapes.

Despite these limitations, some tentative generalizations can be made. In keeping with the model, general tasks were used in most cases to direct the efforts of both client and practitioner toward the achievement of an explicit goal. The amount of attention given these tasks varied, however. In some instances it was extensive. Often, however, only a modest amount of worker activity was directed toward helping the client facilitate these general tasks; effort seemed to be concentrated instead on other issues and goals, in some instances cases relating to problems that perhaps had not "surfaced" when the tasks had been formulated, in others to events of the preceding week, and in still others to husband-wife interactions within the interview.

Another use of tasks was to provide clients with specific assignments to be carried out in the immediate future—for example, "to take a week-end trip together." In terms of the model such tasks should be derived from target problems or from more general tasks, they should be jointly formulated with the clients, and the strategy and tactics of their execution should be carefully gone over. These desiderata were met in some instances but not in others. For example, sometimes specific tasks were generated toward the end of interviews at the instigations of the worker with little discussion of the specifics of their execution. These tasks were not always clearly related to either target problems or more general tasks.

The model calls for reviews of task progress to be conducted at the beginning of each interview. This guideline was followed rather unevenly. Often client task progress was not explicitly discussed until issues relating to the task came up in the interview; sometimes tasks were not reviewed at all.

To get a somewhat more precise picture of the degree of task-focus in each case, we made use of the practitioners' recordings of key interventions. Practitioners were asked to summarize, in a single sentence, each intervention they thought was particularly important in the interview, such as, "I pointed out that their marriage would work better if they left the past alone." In the median (midmost) case, 37 such interventions were recorded. We then determined the percentage of interventions that seemed related to tasks recorded by the worker. Although this index is obviously a crude one, it did provide some estimate of the degree of task-centeredness in each case. If the model were followed with a high degree of fidelity, a large proportion of interventions regarded as central should be task-related. Degree of task-focus, as measured by this index, showed a considerable range across cases: from a low of 5 percent to a high of 75 percent. In the median case, 30 percent of the interventions were judged to be related to tasks the practitioners had recorded. In only a fifth of the cases were more than half the interventions task-centered. In a random sample of SSA project cases a median of 48 percent of the interventions were judged to be task related.

CONFORMITY TO THE MODEL: GENERAL OBSERVATIONS

On the whole, practitioners used tasks in a more selective and partial way than that envisioned in the model. On the other hand, practice in the project was clearly short-term and time limited. This aspect of the model was closely adhered to. Moreover, the workers' efforts were more highly focused on specific problems and goals than is probably customary in family-centered treatment. In this respect practice was certainly within the spirit of the task-centered approach.

Variation between model guidelines and actual practice would naturally be expected given the fact that practitioners received at most only a minmum of training in the model and, moreover, these guidelines sometimes called for approaches that were at variance with their accustomed practice styles. Practitioners seemed to resolve the variance by adapting the model, or portions of it, to their own styles. Thus the practitioners, generally schooled in expressive psychodynamic treatment, sometimes seized opportunities to involve clients in examination of underlying conflicts or interpreted meanings of interactions in the interview, even though such operations took them outside of the problem-task structure of the case. The end result tended to be a blend of model elements and their own established modes of practice.

Another reason for apparent "departures" may be found in the model itself. For example, the model offered only general guidelines for the treatment of marital problems. Procedures specific to this kind of problem constellation had not been well developed. Thus practitioners were expected to supplement or go beyond the often vague and scanty offerings of the model. And, of course, it is well they did.

Outcomes

Outcome data were obtained from practitioners and clients. Using rating scales, practitioners recorded changes in problems, progress on tasks, or other judgments relating to outcome (see Appendix). Clients were asked to complete self-administered evaluative questionnaires which were returned to agency personnel other than the practitioners. Questionnaires were returned for 81 percent of the cases.

THE PRACTITIONERS' PERSPECTIVE

A measure of problem change for each case was obtained by averaging the caseworkers' ratings across problems in each case. The rating scale ranged from 1 (problem aggravated) to 5 (problem no longer present). To assess the reliability of these ratings, an independent judge applied the same scale to tape recorded reviews of progress conducted by the practitioner in final treatment interviews with clients. His ratings correlated reasonably well (r = .64) with those of the practitioners. The practitioners' mean ratings of problem-change also correlated at about the same level (.68) with a corresponding measure of problem-change derived from the clients' questionnaires. These correlations provide some support for using the practitioners' ratings as an index of problem-change.

Using the practitioners' ratings as an outcome criterion, one finds that problems, on the average, showed some degree of positive change (at least slight alleviation) in 74 percent of the cases. Almost half (48 percent) received an average problem-change rating which fell in the "considerably alleviated" portion of the scale. No change was reported for 23 percent of the cases and in 10 percent (3 cases) the ratings indicated a worsening of the problem situation. The problem change ratings were not found to be significantly associated with such input variables as agency, worker, or type of problem.

The client's task achievement constituted a second measure of outcome. The amount of progress the client made in each task was rated by the caseworker on a four-point scale, the Task Achievement Scale (see Appendix). Although they overlap, measures of task achievement and problem change do relate to somewhat different phenomena. A problem can change for better or worse because of factors beyond the client's control. Thus a high (or low) degree of client task achievement may be offset by other factors contributing to problem change. For this reason task achievement may be a better measure of the apparent effects of the practitioners' interventions than problem change. It is also, of course, a measure of special interest in the present model.

Overall, some progress, or at least partial achievement—a rating of 2 or better—was recorded for 72 percent of the tasks. (The corresponding figure for the SSA project cases was 80 percent.) Moreover, 46 percent of the tasks were judged to have been substantially or completely achieved. As might be expected, tasks on which little or no progress was made tended to be concentrated in the less successful cases. On the whole, a fifth of the cases accounted for 75 percent of the failed tasks.

In addition to rating the client's achievement on each task, the practitioner also provided, on the same instrument, data on who originated the task (client or practitioner), whether the client carried out the task independently or in coordination with the task of another client (usually a spouse), and the degree of the client's commitment to the task (that is, his apparent motivation to work on the task). This information was to be recorded prior to work on the task. We were interested in learning which, if any, of these factors might influence task progress. Multiple regression analyses were conducted for the first two tasks in each case with the variables cited above entered as predictor variables and the amount of task achievement as the dependent variable. The

level of task specification (previously described) was also added to the
pool of independent variables. The only consistent statistically significant predictor of task progress that emerged from these analyses was
the client's initial commitment to carrying out the task (rated by the
worker on a five-point scale from low to high and generally defined as
the amount of interest and enthusiasm expressed by the client in working on the task.) The simple correlations between commitment and
task progress were .41 and .49. This result corresponds to findings that
have emerged from the analysis of SSA project cases. In those cases as
well, the initial commitment was the only significant predictor of task
progress that has emerged from this particular set of independent variables. In the present study, the characteristics or origins of the task did
not seem to matter much as far as outcome was concerned. What did
matter was the client's apparent willingness to work on it.

FROM THE CLIENTS' VIEWPOINT

As previously noted, data from client questionnaires were obtained
for 81 percent of the cases immediately following termination. Both
husbands and wives were asked to complete questionnaires when both
had been seen by the caseworker. A total of 33 clients responded, 20
wives and 13 husbands. The mean practitioner rating of problem
change for cases on which no client data were received was 2.6 (problems slightly alleviated), somewhat below the mean of 3.3 for cases on
which follow-up questionnaires were obtained.

Measures of overall outcome were obtained by asking clients: (1) to
rate change since beginning of service in the most important problem
they had wanted help with; (2) to indicate how they were getting along
now compared with when they began treatment. The two measures
proved to be highly correlated. They also yielded a similar picture of
outcome. In 72 percent (18) of the cases, clients indicated that the
major problem was at least a little better; in 14 of these cases (56 percent of the total) they rated the problem as either "a lot" better or no
longer present; also in 72 percent of the cases clients said they were
getting along at least a "little better" since service began, and in 45
percent of these cases the rating was "a lot better."

These outcomes appear roughly similar to those reported by Beck
and Jones (1973) for cases with three interviews or more. In that study,

77.8 percent of the planned short-term and 71.5 percent of the continued service cases were reported as improved according to the global outcome ratings based on clients' reports. It should be noted, however, that in the FSAA study, marital problems were found in about two-thirds of the cases as opposed to our study, where such cases amounted to almost 90 percent (Beck, 1975). Other data reported from the FSAA study suggested that favorable outcomes for marital cases were somewhat lower than for the second largest group—where the primary problems involved children (Beck and Jones, p. 154). Thus the outcomes for the present sample might have compared more favorably with those of the FSAA study if the comparison had been restricted to the marital cases in that study.

Clients' appraisals of the *helpfulness* of service offer a somewhat different perspective on outcome. In evaluating a brief, highly focused model, we are particularly interested in learning to what extent clients think they are helped with most of their problems. Forty-two percent said they were helped with most. However, an almost equal percentage (44) checked the statement "we were helped with *some* of the problems that were really bothering us but they didn't get to all of them." The remainder (14 percent) indicated thay were helped with none of their problems or gave equivocal answers to the question.

These findings suggest that a sizable proportion of clients (42 percent) thought they had problems that were not reached by service. These 13 clients seemed to fall into two subgroups. The largest (8 of the 13) also indicated that the one most important problem they wanted help with was "a lot better" and thought they had "considerably benefited from service"—(see next item below). The profile for clients in the second subgroup was less clear-cut, but they tended to report less progress on their main problem and to evaluate service helpfulness less positively. Thus, most of the clients who reported that the practitioner did not get to all their problems indicated that they had received subtantial help with their most important difficulty. Still, those findings raise questions about the adequacy of project services for some clients. Data to be presented subsequently will shed further light on this issue.

The second measure of perceived helpfulness was more general in nature: "On the whole how would you rate the helpfulness of service?"

To this question, 68 percent chose the two most positive responses: "I was considerably benefited" and "I couldn't have gotten along without it." An additional 21 percent said they were "slightly benefited." The remainder (11 percent) said they were "neither helped nor harmed."

Although global ratings of service helpfulness are probably inflated by tendencies for clients to give responses that are socially desirable and that justify their own investment in the program, they do provide some indication of the amount of benefit clients thought they had received. The total percentage of clients reporting some benefit from service, 89 percent, compares favorably with data from other studies on client evaluations of the helpfulness of counseling in family agencies. The identical item was used to assess the helpfulness of either brief or extended counseling in a study reported by Reid and Shyne (1969, p. 117). For cases in that study receiving three or more interviews (n = 109) some benefit was reported by 86 percent of the clients receiving short-term treatment and by 71 percent of the clients who received continued service. In the FSAA study the corresponding figures for cases with three or more interviews were 87.4 percent (planned short-term service cases) and 83.5 percent (continued service) (Beck and Jones, p. 136). Again it should be noted that these percentages might have been somewhat lower had they been restricted to marital cases.

Despite the positive evaluation of service, a substantial proportion of the clients (39 percent) still reported that they had personal or family problems that they thought they still needed help for. An additional 25 percent indicated they were "uncertain" about whether or not they had such a problem. This variable did not prove to be significantly associated with the client's appraisal of the helpfulness of service.

This is a puzzling finding. One might be tempted to say, at first glance, that it may reflect the insufficiency of the brief services provided in the study. Reid and Shyne (1969) asked clients a similar question at follow-up and found an almost identical percentage (38.7) of the clients in that study also felt the need of additional help for personal and family problems. Clients receiving continued service (averaging 8 months) were as likely to report this need as clients receiving brief treatment (p. 148). Moreover, over half the continued service clients (42 percent of the short-term clients) either expressed this need or had in fact obtained additional help following the termination of project services. Perhaps one cannot realistically expect casework, whether brief *or* extended, to completely resolve the kind of complex personal and family problems dealt with in these studies.

Client reactions to the early agreement on the limits of service and to the length of service were examined. All clients responding perceived that time-limits were agreed upon. The modal response (56 percent) was that this practice was "acceptable," indicating a more or less neutral attitude toward this aspect of service. Those reacting positively to the agreement on time limits ("saw it as a plus") outnumbered those reacting negatively ("didn't strike me as a good idea") by about 2 to 1. On the whole this component of service appeared to be unproblematic for all but a handful of clients. It would perhaps be unreasonable to expect that most clients would see it as a "plus," just as one would not expect students to have positive feelings about the fact that a course was set up for so many sessions.

Reactions to the actual length of service did point up a possible problem area in the model. While no client expressed the opinion that service was "far too brief," about a quarter would have liked a few more sessions. Of the 9 clients who held this view, a disproportionately high number (7) were wives. As previously noted, the client's opinion about length of service was not significantly associated with whether or not he thought he had a problem for which he currently needed help. Nor was it associated with his appraisal of service helpfulness.

These findings are similar to those reported by Reid and Shyne (1969). In that study a third of the clients had negative reactions to the brevity of service, again a higher proportion of wives than husbands (pp. 119–20). Again client reactions seemed uncorrelated with other measures of outcome. It seemed that many of the clients in that study wanted "a few more interviews" rather than a lengthy period of service but adequate data were lacking. In the present study the item on service length was designed to test this notion. It seems clear that the clients in the current sample who wanted more service wanted only a modest amount in addition to what they had received. We are still left, however, with the disconcerting fact that an appreciable proportion of the clients did not receive as much service as they wanted. One wonders if fewer would have been dissatisfied if the length of service had been at the upper rather than the lower range of the model. Hari (chapter 6) suggests another interpretation for these findings.

A final area of interest was the clients' assessment of the helpfulness of particular treatment operations called for in the model. Clients' reactions were elicited in regard to four operations that were both important in the model and could be described in a clear, brief manner: the workers' use of advice and encouragment; helping the client increase his understanding; focus on specific goals. The results are given in Table 4.1.

Table 4.1
Client Evaluations of Selected Treatment Operations

ITEM	PARTICULARLY HELPFUL	SOME HELP	NOT HELPFUL	DID NOT DO	N
Advice	15	13	1	4	33
Encouragement	15	8	2	9	33
Understanding	21	9	—	3	33
Specific goals	14	17	2	—	33

We note first that most clients thought that all of the techniques were used. Interestingly, the only operation that all clients perceived was the focus on specific goals or tasks. That as many as a quarter of the clients did not see their progress as having been encouraged by the worker is somewhat disconcerting. Without exception, these 8 clients also indicated that their single most important problem had not changed for the better. This lack of progress could have been a reason why encouragement might not have been given, but one also notes that almost all these clients had made some progress on at least one task, thus providing some basis for giving encouragement. Whatever encouragement might have been proffered apparently did not make much of an impression on these clients.

Of the four techniques studied, the practitioners' efforts at helping the clients develop understanding of self and others was regarded by the clients as the most helpful. Although they found concentration on specific goals and tasks to be generally helpful, this technique was less highly valued than the remaining ones. Given the wording of the item, the reference here is probably to use of the more specific rather than the more general tasks. In assessing these findings, it should be noted that the workers may possibly have been more experienced and skilled at imparting insight than in dealing with specific goals and tasks.

Implications for Model Development

A central purpose of the project was to obtain data that might help guide the development of the model. A number of findings of the study have served this purpose.

First of all the approach used in these trials seemed reasonably productive, judging from comparisons of present outcome data with the results obtained from trials of other approaches. At one level the study provides a measure of additional support to the rather large body of evidence that brief, time-limited methods are at least as effective, and probably more efficient than long-term service, for the treatment of problems in family relations (see Reid and Shyne, 1969, Chapter 8). It is difficult to determine from the data what the task structure added to the planned brevity of the model. Clients seemed to view the practitioners' use of specific tasks as helpful but placed more value on the advice and insight they received. We do not know what role, if any, might have been played by variations in worker skill in carrying out these various operations. It is also possible that the use of such techniques as advice and insight may have been enhanced by the task structure. Since indicators of the model's performance as a whole were generally positive (judging by the norms of other approaches) there is reason to suppose the task-centered version of short-term treatment does offer promise for this kind of client-problem configuration.

The findings have pointed to some aspects of the model that need further work. One concerns service duration. A quarter of the clients, mostly women, appeared to want more interviews than they received. A similar reaction was noted in a previous study of short-term treatment. Such findings create a dilemma. On the one hand a service duration of 8 interviews or so seems to sit well with the majority of clients and seems to accomplish as much, generally, as service of longer duration. On the other hand, one does not want to terminate before the client is ready.

One obvious solution is to be more "flexible" about service limits— for example, to set forth a range of interviews (say from 8 to 12) as the limit of service rather than a fixed number, or to be freer about suggesting extensions of the limits. This solution has its drawbacks, however. One can lose the mobilizing (goal-gradient) effects that result from working against a fixed point of termination. "Loose" short-term contracts run the risk of fading into open-ended patterns of service, with their various limitations.

But probably some way needs to be found to reach somewhat longer term contracts on a selective basis. Quite possibly there was not enough flexibility in the present study. Ideally there might have been greater variation in service length, and more extension of original con-tracts. The question is, "How can this variation be achieved when it is advantageous to do so, and be avoided when it is not?"

One possibility may be to build an "extension option" into the initial contract. This would call for a review of progress in the next to the last scheduled interview. The client would be given the option at that point of a 3 to 4 interview extension to work on specified problems or tasks, assuming there were such remaining. Other approaches need to be considered, including the invention of better ways of handling the clients' reactions to the end of service. Both Wise (chapter 5) and Hari (chapter 6) address themselves to the latter point.

It is obvious that a great deal of work needs to be done on the use of the model in the treatment of problems in family relations, particularly marital problems. One area of difficulty revealed in the present trials has to do with identifying and "sticking with" important, yet manage-able, problems. Although the practitioners were successful in locating key problems fairly early, there was a tendency in many cases for other problem areas to command attention as the case proceeded.

Another type of difficulty, related to the first, was in devising feasi-ble tasks that might substantially alleviate a significant relational prob-lem. Some tasks were too general to accomplish this purpose ("to im-prove communication") and some others seemed somewhat peripheral to relational problems. In still other instances, tasks called for restitutive behavior the client was not ready to carry out. For example, a task that simply called for a quarreling couple to quarrel less might fall in this category. The model itself offered no specific guidelines for problem analysis or task construction in respect to relational difficulties.

A way to correct such shortcomings in the model might be, I think, to place greater emphasis on the identification and analysis of interactional patterns or rules that might give rise to specific problems (Haley, 1963). Once the patterns have been clarified, then tasks might be developed to alter those patterns. Thus if a target problem concerned mutual avoidance between marital partners, the practitioner would attempt to determine the pattern of interaction leading to the avoidance—what the partners might be saying or doing to one another that might cause them to go their separate ways. Initial tasks might then be directed at the alteration of those actions; subsequent tasks might be concerned with their doing things together. This modification would call for more extended analysis of problems prior to task formulation and for the use of tasks to alter rules controlling interactions among family members. This approach might be combined with a more rapid development of tasks to correct less serious or less complex problems. There still seems to be some advantage in getting family members to undertake at least some kind of problem-solving action at the very beginning of treatment.

Implications for Model Dissemination

In one sense, the project was an experiment in the dissemination of a service model. Our experiences may be instructive to a field, such as social work, in which models by the score are being developed, exported, and applied in one fashion or another.

Dissemination of a new treatment approach to an agency may occur in various degrees, from an intensive and lengthy program of inservice training to a one-day workshop. Our training endeavors, particularly in one agency, probably exceeded the norm. Moreover, we were transmitting reasonably well explicated methods to receptive, sophisticated practitioners who were actively interested in learning and using them and who made, as far as we can determine, a most conscientious effort to put them into practice.

Yet even under these favorable conditions the treatment design exercised only a partial influence upon the activities of the practitioners. What was implemented was not so much the model as a blend of its methods and the practitioners' pre-existing technical repertoires. Perhaps that was all that could have been expected. If any lesson is to be learned, it may be this: it is perhaps unrealistic to think of a treatment model as being disseminated and implemented in its entirety. It may make more sense to view the practitioner as having his own model of practice which he may modify in response to offerings from other approaches but does not surrender. To put it somewhat differently, one can better disseminate specific techniques than systems of practice. We were certainly successful in transmitting the former. The practitioners did put much of our technology to use within their own practice styles and, we think, did so most effectively.

References

Beck, Dorothy Fahs. 1975. "Research findings on the outcomes of marital counseling." *Social Casework* 56:53–81.

Beck, Dorothy Fahs, and Jones, Mary Ann. 1973. *Progress on family problems: A nationwide study of clients' and counselors' views of family agency services.* New York: Family Service Association of America.

——1974. "A new look at clientele and services of family agencies." *Social Casework* 55:589–99.

Haley, Jay. 1963. *Strategies of psychotherapy.* New York: Grune and Stratton, Inc.

Reid, William J. 1973. "Improving accountability through a research-based service design." In *Accountability: A critical issue in social services.* Edited by W. T. Hall and G. C. St. Denis. Pittsburgh: Graduate School of Public Health, University of Pittsburgh.

Reid, William J., and Epstein, Laura. 1972. *Task-centered casework.* New York: Columbia University Press.

Reid, William J., and Shyne, Ann W. 1969. *Brief and extended casework.* New York: Columbia University Press.

Chapter 5

Frances Wise

Conjoint Marital Treatment

The treatment of marital incompatibility presents a particular challenge to the casework staff at Cincinnati Family Service. Troubled husbands and wives come to us daily. As new methods are suggested, we are eager to test their applicability. Therefore, we welcomed the opportunity to participate in the task-centered treatment project.

The purposes and design of the project as well as pertinent details on case selection and staff have already been presented (Reid, chapter 4). This chapter will present the experiences and impressions of one of the workers who used the model with ten cases involving marital discord.

Initial Phase

After a case was assigned, I called to make an appointment within a short interval. In my telephone call to the family, I tried to speak to both husband and wife in order to urge them to come together. As a result, nine of the ten couples had a joint first interview, and eight continued jointly. At the time of application, all nine of these couples were living together, though five had been separated just before the application. In the tenth case, it was only the husband who wanted help; divorce was already in process. None of the clients described the problem as an interactional one, but rather referred to the partner's behavior as the upsetting factor.

All but one couple were in their twenties or early thirties. Six couples were married less than ten years; only one of the couples was childless. All husbands were employed. Eight had blue-collar jobs, the other two had professional occupations. Three of the wives worked. All were charged a fee ranging from $3.00 to $25.00 and all fees were paid. Most couples described long histories of marital conflict with separations.

At Family Service, our conviction about the effectiveness of time-limited treatment has made us comfortable about setting service durations. It has been our experience that when the worker accepts the effectiveness of time limits, she handles them without conflict. In the research cases joint maritals were seen for eight interviews, a plan outlined by the end of the first interview. In one case, the contract was extended by one interview because of a crisis. The case in which only one client was treated continued for six interviews by plan. The time-limited orientation is another way the client is helped to face reality because treatment is geared to the here-and-now.

As delineated in the model, the initial phase consists primarily of clarification of the most important problems as the clients see them and reaching a decision on the areas of work. In each case, in the first portion of the interview, the behavior of one of the spouses was presented as the most painful problem by the more vocal of the pair. Excessive drinking, lack of attention, and infidelity were among the complaints described. Since all agreed that they wanted help with marital discord, which necessarily involved both of them in the difficulty, the next step was to refocus on interpersonal problems.

In marital work it is difficult to focus on interpersonal targets since the husband and wife have come as injured (or penitent) parties. The clients were nevertheless encouraged to direct themselves to the problems of the marriage as opposed to complaints about each other. In response most referred vaguely to "difficulties in communication," but soon the specific problem areas began to emerge. It was always necessary to examine the problems in terms of the marriage. The question was: how is it a problem between you?

The first interview was tailored to elicit the problems (up to 3) on which the couple wished to work. It was hard to get agreement on the problems because of the client's desire to talk about symptomatic behavior. Thus, a wife wanted to do something about her husband's infidelity or his alcoholism. My effort was to reorient her toward the question: What is the effect of his behavior on the marriage?

It seems to me that the worker must distinguish between symptom and problem. A symptom is the outward evidence that something has gone wrong. In marriage a sudden episode of violent quarreling may signal that there is a problem within the relationship. A problem is an impasse; the husband and wife are confronted by a situation to which they cannot adjust. Thus the worker first hears about or observes the symptom. It may be the husband's infidelity which reflects a problem within the marital relationship. Since the couple has come to the agency together to look for help for the marriage, not for themselves as individuals, the worker phrases her question: How is his behavior affecting the marriage? This is the same approach I use when one spouse is an alcoholic. What are the problems that the alcoholism causes in the marriage? With the focus on interaction, problem areas in the marriage will usually surface.

While I heard the details as the clients presented them, my professional ear listened for the underlying character structure. Thus, a wife may identify the problem as her husband's forgetfulness or his lack of affectionate understanding. This is the reality as she sees it. But I would try, through questions, to see deeper into the dynamics that have moulded this woman into a disgruntled wife. She may reveal herself as a person who has always felt emotionally starved. Her problem, then, could also be categorized in terms of character dynamics; for example, difficulties in the areas of giving-getting and of closeness-distance. Again, the challenge to the caseworker is to recast the problem so that the clients understand how it is reflected in the relationship. Thus in this example, one might say that the wife's need for understanding and closeness is being frustrated by her husband's inattentiveness.

Use of Tasks

When the problems have been described in interactional terms, what can the clients do about them? The couples struggled to suggest possible avenues of action. When they could not come up with any ideas, I found it helpful to universalize ("this is what some couples do") or to suggest possibilities which the clients could pick up and develop. It is my conviction that the tasks had to be related to an understanding of the clients' dynamics in order to be meaningful. For instance, a compulsive wife who was overwhelmed by loss of control when her husband walked out was helped to regain control by developing the tasks of visiting a lawyer and setting up a financial plan.

The worker pressed for interactional or reciprocal tasks. If one client suggested a change, what could the other do in return? If the wife was to stop leaving dirty dishes in the sink after dinner, the husband's reciprocal task might be to come home on time so that the meal could be served at a convenient hour. Each spouse was encouraged to suggest the other's assignment. The kinds of tasks ran a gamut of choices: budgeting, excursions together, examining educational opportunities, new methods of dishwashing, handling discipline differently, affectional greetings. It was surprising how often clients had not thought of simple solutions which might have been obvious to an observer. The reason, of course, was the intense degree of emotional involvement between them that obscured any rational examination of their situation.

In the discussion of the tasks, the projected assignment was broken down into manageable segments. For instance, if the couple was to go on an excursion together, part of interview focused on the details of the trip: the selection of the place, phoning for reservations, etc. If one theme ran through all the tasks, it was the effort to help the clients gain a feeling of achievement which, in turn, would enhance their self-confidence.

Did the clients do the tasks? Reid's findings for the project as a whole holds for these cases: most tasks were accomplished to varying degrees. I was struck by the fact that many clients at termination evaluated the state of the marriage in a way that reflected the amount of task effort. Thus, in two situations where the task work had been minimal, the wife (the initiator) expressed a desire for separation. Both of these couples had been previously separated. The husbands were compulsive individuals who could not offer sufficient gratifications to their wives who, perhaps because of their oral character structures, needed excessive "closeness." Each waited for the other to "give," in terms of the task; neither moved, hence the impasse. Divorce became the solution. As these examples suggest, the character structure of the participants was a factor in task accomplishment. When each partner was enmeshed in severe characterological problems, neither was energized for task work. These were persons who had never really succeeded in establishing a relationship; therefore there was no marriage bond.

In using task-centered methods, one must be aware of transference reactions, especially of tendencies of clients to view the practitioner as a parent figure. The very nature of a task suggests the parental relationship. The client may once again see himself as a child receiving instructions about his chores. The partner who has assumed the parental role in the marriage may try to form an alliance with the worker. The awareness of these ramifications underscores the need for the clients to develop their own tasks rather than having them assigned by the worker. It was often quite difficult, however, to get the clients to take the initiative in choosing tasks. Task selection demands a slow, careful, problem-solving approach. The worker leads but does not direct and always refers the clients back to the question: What do you think you can do to relieve the problem between you?

Limitations of the Model

As we proceeded in the project we recognized problems in using the model with certain types of clients. Clients whose defense structures are rigid may be unable to agree on problem areas. Each spouse will blame the partner for the marriage failure. At best, problems are defined in broad areas such as "difficulties in communication," but then cannot be delineated. Both husband and wife may have such severe emotional problems that growth seems blocked. Such a couple were the B's.

At first glance, they seemed like young, attractive new parents whose way of life had been changed by the arrival of a baby girl, now seven months old. Both were in their twenties. Mrs. B, blond, bubbly, dressed in a chic pants suit, seemed flighty. Mr. B, an engineer, was tall, slim, black-haired. He was both reserved and tense. He had worked for a large manufacturing company for three years. He had been a navy flyer and "washed out," but claimed he had done so because of his wife's objections to his flying. I became uncomfortable with his inappropriate laughter, the sardonic expression around his mouth. At first his wife talked uninterruptedly. In subsequent interviews the husband would insist, "Let me talk," and then went off into long discourses. Mrs. B's response was always quick and spontaneous. Mr. B was slow, seemingly contemplative. He maintained he was being thoughtful but it was hard to follow his discourse.

Mrs. B had called for an appointment at the suggestion of her obstetrician. The doctor thought that Family Service could help with the marital problems caused by Mr. B's disinterest in his family. Actually, the physician had never seen Mr. B, but referred them upon hearing Mrs. B's distress. Neither had had any previous help. The month previous to the application they had separated. She had gone back to her parents' home and had returned when her husband agreed to come for counseling.

In the first interview they could not come to any agreement about problems. It was almost impossible to maintain a problem focus. I suggested they come back the next week each and bring a list of three problem areas. Mrs. B's list was on lined paper, in large handwriting, three pages long. It sounded like a "Dear Abby" letter. It described her husband as keeping her at arm's length. She looks for togetherness but there is only his separateness. With examples, she refers to his lies, his violence, his calculating behavior.

Mr. B's list, printed precisely in neat letters on lined graph paper, was divided into two pages—on the first, problems in the marriage which he defined as his wife's criticisms of his behavior, and on the sec-

ond page, the four better attributes of his wife and the five poorer attributes. In contrast to her pleas for closeness, his statements (except for
a reference to her not fixing his breakfast) were pleas for distancing and
expressed fear of being overwhelmed by a close relationship.

The couple chose "communication" as the problem on which they
wanted to work. They could not suggest tasks. With support and direction from me they agreed on some changes in listening and in conversation. After the first interview there were many cancellations and several times they were late by as much as a half hour. (They came to the
last interview almost on time.)

The tasks were never accomplished. The explanation was always the
same. Mr. B, despite his wife's warning, waited until the last minute
and then it was "too late." Mr. B procrastinated; Mrs. B did not set
any limits; each looked to the other "to give"; neither could make the
effort. In one interview we used the time to practice the task the
couple had suggested and not done: discuss vacation plans. The next
time they had gone no further.

I saw Mrs. B as a narcissistic young woman whose tremendous
needs could never be met by her tight, ungiving husband, a compulsive person fighting for distance in order to avoid a close relationship.
His defense system was fragile, with some evidence of paranoid ideation. In the last interview, Mrs. B decided that she would leave her
husband and go back to her home town, seemingly confirming an earlier decision. Neither was interested in any individual help: the problem, each thought, was all in the partner. It seems to me that task-
centered methods should be abandoned and another approach substituted in cases where the early interviews indicate that one or both
partners have been too emotionally traumatized to be able to develop a
relationship with one another.

Another problem that the model may present is that task performance may encourage acting out in clients with weak ego structures.
The acting out, in turn, provokes another marital crisis. This can best
be illustrated by a case in the project, the H's.

There is an Alice-in-Wonderland quality about Mrs. H. She has long
blond hair, fair skin, blue eyes. She talks in a lilting voice, plays the
ingenue role. Her husband is blond, well-built, stolid, nonverbal, perhaps limited intellectually. He may have been brain-damaged in an ac-

cident. He is plodding, slow to speak, has been manager of a dairy department for several years. His wife enjoys philosophical and religious discussions which he cannot follow. She has found a companion in a young single male. The couple has four boys, five to eleven years.

The initial tasks were mainly in the area of changes in communication and financial planning. When it became clear that Mrs. H was looking for feminine confirmation from her husband, tasks were developed to help them to be more affectionate toward each other. As a consequence they had sexual relations without bothering to take the usual precautions and Mrs. H became pregnant.

The couple came in with this crisis in the seventh interview. The immediate problem was the pregnancy, and they needed to come to a decision about an abortion. Because I felt it was necessary to see them through this period, the contract was extended to nine interviews. Later, to help her deal with her feelings about the abortion, Mrs. H was referred to another caseworker for individual help.

This experience has alerted me to the need to explain to the client the implications of the task. My own understanding of dynamics should have alerted me to the possibility that the task could trigger unplanned behavior. For instance, Mrs. H was an impulsive woman who had never been able to discipline herself. Knowing this, I should have helped the H's build some limits into tasks calling for freer expression of affection; perhaps they might have been encouraged to discuss their birth control methods.

Uses of the Model

Task-centered methods proved particularly useful in certain circumstances and with certain kinds of couples. In some instances, the approach served to cut through a client's ambivalence and encourage decision making. Thus, nonperformance can be motivation for change. Faced with the challenge of performance a client may have to face his own ambivalence, thus forcing a decision he has been avoiding. For example, a decision to separate may be reached after a client realizes he cannot carry out tasks necessary to resolve problems in the marriage.

In the project and subsequently, we have found that the model can be used well with couples who are striving to return to a previously stable marital relationship. The Whites were one of the research families who accomplished the tasks they set up for themselves. Each spouse had individual problems which would always interfere with the marriage, but this method helped them get back to a previous adjustment which had been satisfying to them. When they applied, Mr. White acknowledged that he had thought of divorce. By the end of the contact there was no further mention of separation.

Mr. White is a tall, lean man, with close-cropped, sandy-colored hair. His manner is precise and rigid. His father was a German soldier, and he fits this stereotype. He relieves his tension with a high-pitched, raucous giggle; the sharpness is disconcerting. He appears emotionless, but the undertone of anger is unmistakable. Mrs. White, in contrast, is black-haired, tall, and slender, with vivid coloring. Her large mouth flashes with strong white teeth. She is reserved but more poised than her husband. She speaks with a slight accent, is Danish, and shows traces of a discomfort with English. Her father had been an army officer; she met her husband on one of his furloughs during World War II. They lived together, but were married before his tour of duty ended.

Mrs. White called to make an appointment. Her husband had accused her of flirting. They wanted an appointment to ascertain if her husband's accusations were justified. Throughout the eight interviews, Mr. White attempted to put the worker into the position of judge. In the last interview, he referred to his disappointment that the worker did not delineate who was "wrong," and who was "right."

The tasks began with efforts to improve Mrs. White's housekeeping. She complained of his rigid, demanding attitude. It made her feel like a child with the need to use disorder to rebel against his perfectionistic standards. Soon, however, Mrs. White had arranged a schedule: the house was neat and the dishes were not left in the sink. Her husband supported her with recognition of her efforts.

The couple had problems in child rearing, and agreed to work on several tasks related to mutual handling of discipline. The clients were to decide together on the consequences of unacceptable behavior. The parent observing the behavior would tell the child that the other parent would be consulted, and together they would determine the consequence. Both parents would then discuss the decision with the child. Each parent was committed to follow through.

The Whites described problems in showing affection, neither feeling secure in the relationship with the partner. One of the tasks was to set aside time before dinner when the two would be together. As a result, new methods of affectional interchange cut through the uncomfortable teasing that each employed.

The last interview occurred after the Thanksgiving Holiday. Mr. White was proud of his wife's dinner; they had invited his family and Mr. White thought his wife's organization of the meal was superior to his sister's way of handling it on a previous occasion. The couple had completed eight interviews. We have had no further contact.

Task-centered treatment may be used to advantage in conjoint work with other types of marital pairs. Immature, impulsive couples who are action-oriented may make good use of this method especially when there is gratification in the marriage. Young marrieds often find it of help, since for them, it incorporates an educative experience.

When only one spouse seeks service, this model can well be the choice if the client is in an emotional crisis and is looking for quick relief. Clients who have lost a spouse through separation often define the presenting problem as marital, especially if both come together for one interview when the marriage is in the last throes of dissolution. A frequent cause of the break-up is infidelity. With the recognition that there is no real marriage, one spouse discontinues and the other wants further help. The deserted mate who is depressed can be helped to feel better. Task performance is energizing. In the project, and subsequently, we have seen many clients mobilize toward starting a new life through their own efforts in task performance, supported by the caseworker. In the course of accomplishment, client self-esteem improved.

Our Modifications

In the two years since we completed the research project we have continued to use the model. We have found it has been helpful to add our own variations to fit individual situations. When we have seen couples whose marital relationship has only been recently strained, we have added to the problem exploration the further query, "Why is it a problem now?" If the marital relationship has been upset by an emotional crisis which the clients deny, appropriate tasks can be delineated and accomplished much more easily after the crisis has been clarified. For instance, a husband and wife who have started quarreling may not be aware that the marriage of their last child is indeed a "loss" they have been denying. Tasks that again make them feel needed may readjust their relationship. More generally, we make greater use of an understanding of underlying dynamic factors in the clients' personalities and marital interactions than the model seems to call for. In the second interview, we usually obtain a brief history of the marriage. Through the history the client is often helped to recall forgotten positive aspects of the relationship, which in turn helps us identify the healthy parts of their personalities.

We have dealt with terminations in a little different manner. In addition to the summation of accomplishments, exploration of future activities, etc., we have helped the clients recognize any uncomfortable feelings about termination, acknowledging their negative emotions as well as the positive feelings that come with accomplishment. Thus, termination can be considered a corrective emotional experience, helping the client to deal with endings that are always a part of life experience.

Chapter 6

~•~

Veronica Hari, M.S.S.

Instituting Short-Term Casework in a "Long-Term" Agency

It all started eight years ago at Family Service Society, Hartford, Connecticut, when, in order to do something about shortening the waiting list, a tentative suggestion was made to the ten MSW workers that time-limited therapy be tried. During lulls in the noisy and shocked cries of "unprofessional," "short-changing the client," etc., agency statistics were pulled for the previous ten years. They showed that, planned or not, most clients came for an average of five interviews, i.e., most did *not* come for endless, open-ended therapy. Further shock waves—"just can't be so," "the statistics must be off"—and then some beginning realization that the ambivalently held ego-ideal, so to speak, of the workers was that of the psychoanalyst and that, somehow, "status" work had come to be equated with analysis, which was long-term. Then came a beginning acceptance that we were *not* analysts; that, although our practice was based on psychoanalytic theory, our goals and techniques were different.

However, it was obvious that workers' longing for professional status via long-term therapy was not going to change overnight and that, until there was some change in attitude, short-term therapy would never get off the ground. Therefore, a study of caseworkers' reactions to participation in a time-limited therapy was initiated in 1966.[1] Each worker would carry three cases randomly selected from intake. Court, school, or public welfare referrals were excepted since these were viewed as authoritative, i.e., not self-referred, and it was assumed it would take longer to involve these clients in a working relationship than clients who were self-referred. Selected clients were to be seen for a total of eight interviews, including intake. A series of questionnaires was administered to each worker at predetermined points in the eight-month study, including an attitudinal questionnaire that listed these responses: (a) interested, (b) angry, (c) enthusiastic, (d) apprehensive, and (e) discouraged. At the end of the intake dictation, the worker was to include a statement covering the following headings: (a) presenting problem, (b) underlying problem (including clinical diagnosis, if apparent), (c) tentative therapy goals, and (d) tentative therapy plan.

At the completion of the project, the staff concluded soberly that open-ended practice is easier than short-term practice,[2] because short-term therapy, when well done, makes much greater demands on the workers. It requires more, not less, professional skill than does long-term therapy, since the worker must establish a working relationship with the client and diagnose much more quickly than when a long-term approach is used. The establishing of the worker / client relationship and the making of a diagnosis are dependent on the worker's emotional investment of himself in the treatment process, his understanding of the latent (dynamic) meaning of material the client presents, and the worker's capacity for eliciting and dealing with the client's negative feelings. These factors are not related to the number of interviews or to the passage of time. However, if the worker is convinced that all of this

---

[1] We were fortunate to have consultation on this study from Howard Parad, then Dean of the Smith College School for Social Work, and from Roger Miller, Director of Research at the School.

[2] A similar reaction was obtained from practitioners in the Reid and Shyne (1969) study in which brief and extended forms of casework were compared.

does take a long time, then long-term treatment will ensue, since clients proceed at the pace set by the worker.

However, Rome was not built in a day, and workers quickly resumed the open-ended approach with most of their clients once the attitudinal study was completed. Then, in 1969, some workers began to complain about carrying cases two years or so, where nothing seemed to be happening but where, somehow, the client would not voluntarily terminate and the workers could not *make* them terminate. One might say that the famous "hostile-dependent relationship" had been established—between worker and client this time—and that it was proving to be its usual unproductive self. It also became clear that when workers left the agency, most of their caseloads were, at that point, closed out. In order for cases to be transferred, a transfer summary was required which had to include, in specifics, what the ongoing work with the client was to be. Therefore, the question arose: if cases in large numbers got closed at the point when workers left the agency, why weren't they closed earlier on the basis of sound professional considerations?

We then decided to review the literature on termination—and found that there was very little on the subject (this was in 1969). It was interesting to us that our field work students that year had had, as a classroom assignment, the same task—to review literature on termination—and had come up with a similar dearth of same. So then, we had another piece of the answer to the question, "Why the opposition to time-limited therapy?" It wasn't just that long-term therapy was equated by the workers with high status because of its origin with psychoanalysts (excluding Freud—who never did do long-term therapy); it wasn't just that open-ended treatment is, for a variety of reasons, easier to do than short-term. It suddenly occurred to us that dealing with "endings" in a dynamic way was where we were all "stuck"—that our own "separation anxiety" was getting in the way. I should add that one of the cornerstones of our agency's approach to therapy is the belief that the worker's input is crucial. R. D. Laing (1971) expresses it as follows:

We are intervening in, and changing the situation *as soon as* we are involved. As soon as we interplay with the situation, we have already begun to intervene willy-nilly. Moreover, our intervention is already beginning to change *us,* as well as the situation. *A reciprocal relationship has begun.* The doctor and the still predominantly medically-oriented psychiatrist use a non-reciprocal static model: history comes after the complaint; examination comes after the history; *after* this, one makes a tentative or if possible *definitive* diagnosis; thereafter comes "therapy." Diagnosis is *dia:* through; *gnosis:* knowledge of. *Diagnosis* is appropriate for social situations, if one understands it as *seeing through the social scene.* Diagnosis *begins* as soon as one encounters a particular situation, and never ends. The way one sees through the situation changes the situation. As soon as we convey in any way (by a gesture, a handshake, a cough, a smile, an inflection of our voice) what we see, *some* change is occurring even in the most rigid situation. (p. 40)

We found ourselves rereading Jessie Taft's "The Time Element in Therapy" (1937) and being especially affected by the following:

Time represents more vividly than any other category the necessity of accepting limitation, as well as the inability to do so, and symbolizes therefore the whole problem of living. The reaction of each individual to limited or unlimited time betrays his deepest and most fundamental life pattern, his relation to the growth process itself, to beginnings and endings, to being born and to dying. (p. 12)

We were suddenly and *un*avoidably confronted with the fact that our need to *avoid* endings—acted out in our prolonging therapy unendingly, so to speak—was related dynamically to our own "unfinished grief work" in terms of past losses, and our own difficulty in looking at the reality of the ultimate ending, death.

We read also Norman Paul's "The Use of Empathy in the Resolution of Grief" (1967), with its powerful opening paragraph:

Rage, terror, profound sadness, helplessness, acute loneliness, and despondency are among those feelings that both children and adults find most difficult to bear; all are associated with the state of grief. Through the expression of grief and empathic responses among family members, each member can be freed from these painful feelings for the pursuit of more constructive activities. (p. 53)

Also impressive was C. Murray Parkes's statement (1965, p. 24) that, "Grief may prove to be as important to psychopathology as inflammation is to pathology."

It has been interesting to us to discover that, in by far the majority of clients to whom we have offered time-limited task-centered therapy, recent and early losses are the predominant dynamic underlying current dysfunctioning—loss of a job, loss of a spouse by death or divorce, loss of a healthy child (families who have physically or mentally handicapped children), loss of health (including terminal illness)—and that a beginning working-through of the underlying grief reaction can be precipitated and facilitated by a time-limited approach.

We undertook (in 1970) a one year's planned short-term project, using Reid and Shyne's (1969) study as a model for selection of cases, although our sample was confined to marital cases. By now, workers were much further along toward accepting the validity of the time-limited model for both the clients and themselves, in terms of improved service resulting from workers' increasing awareness of the need to sharpen diagnostic and therapeutic skills. Included in the year's project were 196 families. Of all clients, 91 percent reported that the service had been helpful (37 percent felt it had been very helpful, 24 percent moderately helpful, and 30 percent slightly helpful).

Measured client characteristics included *age* (50 percent were 20 to 30 years of age, 47 percent were 31 to 50 years of age); *education* (44 percent had high school or less, 50 percent had two or more years of college); *race* (86 percent were white, 13 percent were black). The average number of interviews per client was 5; average length of service was 7 weeks. Of the total of 683 interviews, 71 percent were joint marital, 5 percent were with total family, 22 percent were individual. By the time this project was ended, the majority of staff was completely sold on the validity of offering time-limited therapy to clients, and the waiting list was, by now, of manageable proportions.

We became interested in developments in methods of short-term treatment. As a way of pursuing this interest we volunteered (1973) to participate in the task-centered project previously described by Reid (chapter 4). Our use of time-limited treatment had by that time been extended to include parent-child situations where the child's maladjust-

ment seemed clearly reactive to family tensions. Kaffman (1965) had indicated that such a time-limited approach could be effective "provided
that the emotional conflict was not totally internalized." In such parent-
child situations, we were offering twelve rather than eight interviews,
on the assumption that it might take longer to facilitate the use of less
destructive defensive systems when scapegoating of children is involved than when a couple presents marital dysfunction as the symptom which brings them to the agency. Twelve interviews, rather than
eight, was also based on Kaffman's time limit of three months.

For the task-centered project, then, we included both marital and
parent-child situations. We then decided to take a chance and include
"individual personality adjustment" situations which, until then, were
on our list of "this needs long-term treatment."

At first we were dismayed by the very tight structuring in the use of
interview time as required by the model, and somehow felt it would be
difficult to apply in the delivery of a nonconcrete service such as psychotherapy. However, in retrospect, we realize that it was a further in-
valuable aid toward the never-ending professional task of sharpening
diagnostic and therapeutic skills, with the objective of improving service to clients and increasing accountability for the ever-shrinking voluntary dollar. Whether we like it or not we are now living in what has
been called a "Prove-It" era. The task-centered model is a functional
one, in these times, in that it lends itself, much more than does the
open-ended, less structured treatment, to program monitoring and
evaluation; for example, client self-report data become more useful if
the client is reacting to an explicit, well-structured technology which
he can comprehend.

The approach also encourages workers to share their professional
thinking with clients, when appropriate. It is more likely in such circumstances that valuable professional input will be used creatively with
clients, rather than being consigned to the case record, where it becomes the subject of interesting debate between fellow workers or between worker and supervisor but practically never between worker and
client.

We had had no training in the model prior to beginning our project
and, since we are a good distance from Chicago, we were forced to answer for ourselves, in group discussions, most of the questions that

arose before and after we got under way. Another factor was our limited experience with research, i.e., we had each, in the far distant past, written a thesis as a requirement for obtaining our graduate degrees, but we had no research department or research worker in the agency; neither is the staff really "research-minded." As with many social workers, there exists almost an antipathy to research, viewing it as a kind of unwanted and unwarranted scientific intrusion into our particular "art form"—therapy. Therefore, one of the bonuses of undertaking the project was that we were forced, at least in part, away from our rather stand-offish attitudes toward research. We were required, at very short notice, to change our whole, highly-individualized style of doing clinical social work, and we experienced considerable strain as we strove conscientiously to structure project interviews in a way that seemed completely foreign to us. I think Reid gives recognition to this in chapter 4: ". . . these guidelines sometimes called for approaches that were at variance with their accustomed practice styles."

Immediately prior to each project interview came the anxious self-reminding of what was required by the project instruments, e.g., "I must fill out the Task Review Schedule," and this tension carried over at least to the initial part of the interview. Then somehow, one's particular "professional self" took over anyhow; one was, so to speak, "lost" in the interaction with the client. Then the interview was over and *then* came the project-related anxiety once again in the concern over, "Did the interview proceed in such a way that the project instruments can be completed?—And if not, what do I do now?"

Another, and perhaps the most important, source of tension and professional learning was having to deal with the issue of termination in the first interview. In instructional material provided for project staff by Reid (1973), he states: "If the caseworker accepts the theories about the nature of problem change and the mobilizing effect of time limits advanced in the book, he should be able to set and stick to these limits with conviction. If he does not, then he should probably not be using the model." However, in the present volume (chapter 4) he seems to have softened this position, suggesting "an 'extension option' might be built into the initial contract." Apparently this modification was prompted by the finding that "a quarter of the clients, mostly women, appeared to want more interviews than they received."

This finding came as no surprise to us. In our judgment most clients come for help with the conscious or unconscious expectation that the therapist will cure *all* their pain and *all* their problems forever. In the beginning phase of treatment, the client is often in the position of a young child expecting all the answers from an omnipotent, omniscient parent. Hopefully, the client then moves into the middle phase of treatment (unless the therapist acts out his or her own omnipotent, omniscient fantasies with the client) as the therapist helps the client to face the harsh reality that there are no absolute answers to his problems—there is only a choice of struggling with or retreating from it. From there, the client moves into the most painful and anxiety-provoking stage of all—termination, with its reality of "separation without resolution" (Mann, 1973, p. 4).

Perhaps one might conclude, then, that in the situations where project clients were wanting more interviews than they had received, they had not been helped adequately to deal with the dynamics of termination. Interestingly enough, in relation to Reid's observation that it was mostly women who wanted more than the specified number of interviews, Mann (1973, p. 34) points out that

> time as a limited commodity is portrayed as Father Time, with a beard and scythe; limitless time, immortality, is invariably presented in the figure of a woman. Time always represents the reality principle. . . . By contrast, the attributes of the pleasure principle, the primary process and timelessness, are related to the mother. Ambivalence in respect to time is exemplified in our images of finite time as Father Time and immortality as a woman.

In staff group discussions during the course of the project, the workers expressed the opinion that clients were often ready to discontinue after the fifth interview because they "feel much better and don't need to come any more." We speculated in three directions about the possible reasons for this. Was it (1) because the client did not need more help at that point in time? (2) because clients were beginning to sense that planned termination was in sight, and wished to discontinue to avoid "separation anxiety"? or (3) because we had "goofed" and clients were politely saying they were not getting from us what they needed? Certainly there is evidence of clients' "increased coping capacity" (the general goal we have for agency clients) after even one therapeutic interview, so one thought is that even fewer than eight interviews could constitute effective treatment. The impression we had that maybe fewer than eight interviews could have been used relates to one of the findings from the study as a whole: as Reid observed in chapter 4, "Interestingly enough, most of the deviation from the model was in the direction of fewer interviews being planned and conducted than the eight to twelve called for in the model."

One of the surprises we had in our use of the model was the considerable interest shown by the clients in cooperating with us in its use. We had projected onto clients our own hesitance about using the model. In fact, however, they mostly seemed pleased and flattered at being selected to engage in a research project associated with the University of Chicago.

Another result of our participation in the task-centered treatment project was that the clients who came to the agency asking for help with individual personality problems (as against those who presented marital or parent-child problems) appeared to use the approach effectively. Prior to our project, we had offered such clients only open-ended treatment; we have now added such "individual personality adjustment" situations to those for which a time-limited, task-centered approach can be valid. Our list of clients-and-their-situations-for-which-only-long-term-treatment-should-be-offered is shrinking rapidly! The staff has gradually and painfully moved to the position where they are now more comfortable, in spite of the greater stress, in doing time-limited, task-centered work. As one highly-skilled and creative worker said recently, "I'm to the point where somehow I have difficulty doing long-term work." In fact, at this time about 90 percent of the agency's clients are being seen on a time-limited basis, although we continue to work on developing sound criteria for offering long-term service so as not to fall into an all-or-nothing frame of mind.

It should not be overlooked by administrators that sound, short-term, task-centered work takes a greater toll on workers' energies. In long-term work, one sees fewer clients, so one has to go less frequently through those taxing early interviews when one struggles to "build an emotional bridge" to the client which, if it is to be helpful, must be tailored individually to each client. By the same token, one has in long-term work to go less frequently through "endings," i.e., the termination process which, if one has had a real emotional investment in the client, is a strain not only on the client but also on the worker.

Incidentally, one of the advantages for administrators of this modality is prompt payment of fees by clients when treatment has ended. We have had a very noticeable lack of delayed payments and bad debts with clients receiving planned brief treatment, as compared with clients receiving open-ended treatment.

We still have many miles to go in coming to grips with remaining "resistances" to use of the time-limited, task-centered approach. The resistances show themselves, especially with beginning workers, in some equation of "short-term" with "superficial," and "long-term" with "deep"; in workers' distress that they cannot in eight or twelve sessions to a "total" job of reconstructing clients' personalities; and in their alarm that clients may still have "problems" at the end of brief treatment (as if any form of treatment could solve all problems).

Slowly, however, the whole concept of the helping process is turning around from the medical "cure" model, to something which says that people need professional help when they get "stuck" for a variety of reasons and have feelings that they do not understand, and that most people *want* short-term, clearly-focussed help that gets them "unstuck" and flying on their own again as soon as possible. Amongst ourselves, as we have discussed the pros and cons of time-limited, task-centered therapy, we have become convinced that in a Future Shock age involving, as it does, endless change—a constant process of loss, of giving up the old before one can invest in the new—this approach is the treatment of choice for the majority of our clients.

References

Kaffman, Mordecai. 1965. "Short-term family therapy." In *Crisis intervention: Selected readings.* Edited by H. J. Parad. New York: Family Service Association of America; pp. 202–19.

Laing, R. D. 1971. *The politics of the family and other essays.* New York: Pantheon Books.

Mann, James. 1973. *Time-limited psychotherapy.* Cambridge, Mass.: Harvard University Press.

Parkes, C. Murray. 1965. "Bereavement and mental illness: Part 2, A classification of bereavement reactions." *British Journal of Medical Psychology* 38:13–26.

Paul, Norman L. 1967. "The use of empathy in the resolution of grief." *Perspectives in Biology and Medicine* 11:153–72.

Reid, William J. 1973. *Summary of task-centered model and case examples.* Chicago: School of Social Service Administration. (Mimeographed.)

Reid, William J., and Epstein, Laura. 1972. *Task-centered casework.* New York: Columbia University Press.

Reid, William J., and Shyne, Ann. 1969. *Brief and extended casework.* New York: Columbia University Press.

Taft, Jesse. 1937. "The time element in therapy." In *Dynamics of therapy in a controlled relationship.* New York: The Macmillan Company; pp. 3–23.

Chapter 7

Eleanor Reardon Tolson, A.C.S.W.

Alleviating Marital
Communication Problems

The major purpose of the study reported in this chapter was to evaluate the effectiveness of a set of task-centered methods, the Task Implementation Sequence (Reid, 1975), in alleviating specific problems in face-to-face communication between marital pairs.[1] It is assumed that such problems are a common source of difficulty in marriages and that they contribute to other difficulties (referent problems) in the relationship. That is, if marital partners cannot talk to one another in a mutually satisfying and effective manner, the quality of their marriage is diminished as a result, and they can be expected to have difficulty in working through problems of common concern in respect to children, finances, sex, and so on.

[1] The study is reported in full in Tolson (1976).

Previous Research

Literature pertinent to the study at hand appears to be scant. In an exploratory project reported by Carter and Thomas (1973), twelve couples were tape recorded while discussing two predetermined topics. From these discussions the researchers prepared a written statement describing their communication strengths and problems and making recommendations. After sharing this analysis with the couples, the researchers requested that they discuss one of the previous topics again. The experimenters selected four problems for the purpose of examining the effects of intervention and concluded, "The results for the two cases reported are encouraging with regard to the efficacy" of this technique (p. 108).

Two studies by Richard B. Stuart (1968 and 1971), are tangentially related to mine. The sample in the first study was composed of five married couples. The wives' major complaint was a deficit in communication and the husbands' complaint was a deficit in sexual activity. The wives specified the kinds of communication which they wanted from their husbands. The husbands were rewarded with tokens when they engaged in these communicational acts. The tokens could then be exchanged for physical contact ranging from kissing to intercourse. The weekly intercourse rate increased from an average of zero to over three times per week; the daily conversation rate increased from less than one hour to almost five hours. Tape recordings were made for all (7) treatment sessions with two couples. When these were analyzed to determine the number of positive and negative statements made about the spouse, they revealed that verbal behavior became "markedly more positive" (p. 225).

In the second study, Stuart attempted to increase the number of positive statements made in the interaction of four mother-son pairs where the son was a delinquent. A signaling device called SAM was utilized whereby each of the conversationalists could signal the other by means of lights. Positive or negative statements were indicated by the lights. During the first four sessions, the therapist signalled to each after a positive or negative speech. During the last five sessions, the mother and son signalled to one another. The increase in positive statements ranged from 20 to 47 percent.

One study (Reid, 1975), tested the effectiveness of the proposed treatment strategy. The design was implemented and the data gathered by twenty first-year students enrolled in the task-centered sequence. Each student treated a control and an experimental case. In both cases, they developed a task which was intended to alleviate the target problem. In the experimental case, they then utilized a package of procedures, the Task Implementation Sequence (TIS), which included planning task implementation, establishing commitment, resolving obstacles, modeling, rehearsal, planning recording of task progress, and summarization. In the control case nothing further was done following task formulation. Significantly more experimental than control clients completed the task. While this work supports the efficacy of the TIS, none of the experimental cases were married couples with communication problems and so its success with this kind of sample and problem is yet to be demonstrated.

Study Plan

I decided to test the efficacy of the TIS as a method of treatment for marital communication problems in a single case. A multiple baseline design was used in an attempt to isolate the effects of treatment. The logic of the design, as I used it, called for collection of baseline data on a set of problems followed by treatment of each problem in sequence. If each problem showed greater change following treatment than during the baseline period, then one could infer that the change was the result of treatment as opposed to other factors, such as spontaneous recovery or external circumstances. The layout of the design in the present study is presented in Table 7.1. During Phase 1, baseline data

Table 7.1
Multiple Baseline Design

COMMUNICATION PROBLEM	PHASES				
	I WEEK 1	II WEEK 2	III WEEKS 3,4	IV WEEKS 5,6,7	V WEEK 30
1	Baseline	Treatment	Follow-up	Follow-up	Follow-up
2	Baseline	Baseline	Treatment	Follow-up	Follow-up
3	Baseline	Baseline	Baseline	Treatment	Follow-up

was obtained on all communication problems. During Phase 2, the TIS was employed with respect to the first problem. During Phase 3, the TIS was used to work on the second problem, and so on. Once a problem had been treated the couple was left to work on it largely on their own, as attention shifted to the next problem.

The Case

The study was conducted as a part of treatment of a marital pair, the T's. The couple, both college teachers, had been married fourteen years and had three children, ranging in age from four to thirteen. They were referred to me as an independent practitioner from an out-patient psychiatric clinic where Mr. T had called requesting marital treatment.

The bulk of the study was conducted during the first portion of treatment (in seven interviews over a nine-week period). Treatment, largely task-centered, continued for about five months with focus primarily on child rearing and sexual problems. No further attention was given to the communication problems dealt with during the first nine weeks. At the conclusion of this period, follow-up data on these communication problems were collected.

Problem Identification and Data Collection

During the first seven weeks, communication problems were identified and monitored by having the T's tape-record three 7-minute episodes of face-to-face communication each week, one immediately after the session and the other two at home at approximately two-day intervals.

I tentatively identified the problems after listening to these tape-recorded segments. The unit of analysis used in problem identification was the "speech," which consisted of what each partner communicated while he or she "held the floor." Problems selected for treatment consisted of (1) interruptions, which were defined as occurrences in which one partner began to talk before the other had finished his speech, or in which both partners talked simultaneously; (2) monopolization, defined as the occurrence of speeches in excess of eighty words [2]; (3) topic changes, which were defined as a partner's making shifts or digressions from the topic of the other partner's preceding speech.[3] It was found that the frequencies of all problems could be determined from typescripts with a satisfactory degree of reliability.[4]

Data revealing the frequency of occurrence of the problems was shared with the T's, along with examples of each problem. The problems were introduced in sequence: after the first problem was identified, treated, and had begun to decrease in frequency, the second problem was introduced, and so on. Although I assumed more responsibility for problem identification than is suggested by the task-centered model, the T's did agree that each of these problems was a source of difficulty and in fact selected the third (topic changes) from a list of several problems which I prepared. Exploration of other problem areas of concern to them were deferred until later in treatment— another deviation from procedures called for by the model.

Treatment

The treatment of the identified communication problems consisted of an application of the TIS. My use of this approach in the present case is outlined below.

Establishing rationale and commitment. In Reid's articulation of the TIS, this step pertains to establishing rationale for the commitment to implementing the task. In this study, this activity was applied to the problem rather than the task. This was necessary because the problems were not originally identified by the T's and, thus, motivation for alter-

[2] The eighty-word criterion is arbitrary but has the following justification: speeches of that length "stand out" in the Ts' dialogue. Less than five percent were of this length in the initial baseline period. A review of a variety of typescripts of family communication suggest that speeches over eighty words in length are generally uncommon in dialogues among family members.

[3] As might be expected a fairly elaborate set of criteria needed to be developed to decide which speeches reflected topic changes. (See Tolson, 1976).

[4] Reliability coefficients for the three variables based on duplicate coding of transcripts of conversations between Mr. and Mrs. T were as follows: interruptions, $r = .85$, monopolization, $r = .97$, topic changes, median percent of agreement $= 83$.

ing them could not be assumed. My attempt to help the T's develop a rationale for and a commitment to modify the communication problems differed somewhat from problem to problem.

The first communication problem, interruptions, was addressed in the second interview. It was described as a manifestation of the struggle for control in which the T's were engaged. Support for the existence of a struggle for control was provided by reminding them of some information they had shared during the baseline or intake interview and by current behavior: namely, that they had difficulty locating any specific problems but were, nevertheless, not getting along with one another. This was supported by explaining a little of communication theory: that a message, in addition to containing content, defines a relationship (Watzlawick, Beavin, and Jackson, 1967). Their frequent interruptions were a way of arguing about who held the floor, or the control, in this relationship. Thus, the attempt to build commitment to alter the seemingly trivial problem of interrupting was based on a theoretical explanation. Monopolization became more of a problem after the T's had made some progress on reducing their rate of interruptions. Although one might expect the length of their speeches to increase if they interrupted each other less, the amount of increase, particularly in Mrs. T's speeches, could not be accounted for by this reason alone. The rationale presented for working on monopolization was that if one symptom of the control struggle was simply replaced with another, no progress would have been made. Emphasis was placed on the effects of a monopolizing speech, such as the feelings aroused in the listener (impatience and anger) and the loss of content.

Less time and effort was spent on increasing the T's commitment to modifying the third communication problem, topic changes. This problem was addressed in the fifth interview. By this time the T's had already observed that conversations which began with the purpose of solving a problem dwindled to haggling over unrelated or tangentially related matters. They were reminded of this.

The attempts to develop a rationale for working on the communication problems and, hence, increase the T's commitment to modify them, differ along what would seem a logical, albeit unanticipated, progression. The progression appears to be based on the ever-increasing knowledge of the clients. In the initial phase of treatment, problem rationales were based on theory. In the middle phase, they were based on a combination of theory and behavioral repercussions for the T's. Late in treatment, the rationale came from the shared experience between therapist and clients. Mr. T, who was primarily concerned about difficulties in their face-to-face interaction, seemed more committed to working on the communication problems than Mrs. T, who seemed to think the difficulties lay more in their attitudes and feelings toward each other and in other problems, although it was hard for her to be specific.

Task formulation. This activity began once the problem had been specified and the T's acknowledged that the problem seemed worth altering. (For the first two problems acknowledgement came in response to a direct question. For the third problem, it was implied by the act of selecting the problem from a list of problems.)

The activity of formulating a task was begun by a direct question: "What do you want to do about this?" Usually very little additional input was required. Suggestions for a task for each problem were prepared in the event that the T's were unable to develop one. The T's seemed to have trouble constructing a task for monopolizing so one was suggested. The T's eventually rejected it, however, and constructed their own.

The tasks designed to alter the number of interrupting and monopolizing speeches consisted of each making hand signals to the other when he or she wished to speak. The task for altering topic changes was for each to paraphrase the idea of the other's preceding speech in order to achieve continuity in their dialogue.

A guide to evaluate the potential effectiveness of a task was developed with the T's. It consisted of the requirement that the task differ sufficiently from normal interaction so that it would be noticed and yet was not so absorbing that it would be difficult to use or would interfere with the ongoing conversation. This guide was necessary to facilitate arbitration of their individual responses to the problem of task development. Mr. T, originally, tried to avoid formulating specific tasks and wanted to cope with the problem "when it comes up." Mrs. T, on the other hand, tended to plan complex tasks which seemed, in themselves, to contain whole new areas for debate. This guide was not anticipated but developed while watching the T's attempt to formulate the first task. It was articulated at that time.

Analyzing and resolving obstacles. The tasks developed were interactional; that is, they were designed to effect reciprocal change. Tasks of this sort with couples experiencing marital difficulties present special problems and potential obstacles. First, the relationship is one in which each individual is unlikely to respond positively to attempts by the other to influence his behavior. Thus, it is important to try and design tasks which would avoid, to the extent possible, the arousal of negative feelings. Second, the individual employing the task is likely to become discouraged if using the task doesn't result in some benefit. (This also applies to clients whose tasks are not interactional, but with individual clients one seldom has the opportunity to directly influence the behavior of others in his environment.) This potential obstacle is overcome by planning not only the task but also the response.

The T's needed only a little help in overcoming these two potential obstacles. With regard to interruptions, Mrs. T directly asked Mr. T if he would become angry when she used the hand signal. He said he would not. Mr. and Mrs. T talked about responses. They discussed questions such as, "Do I stop speaking immediately or do I finish my sentence?"

A couple with less foresight might be helped to eliminate these obstacles by considering two questions: What feeling is the task likely to arouse in this particular responder? What behavior is the task intended to stimulate in the responder?

Modeling, rehearsal, guided practice. The T's began practicing the tasks within the interview without prompting. Since two of the three tasks were nonverbal, the amount of practicing could not be assessed from tapes of the interviews. (Evidence of practicing exists on the tape, however, in the form of inappropriate-sounding laughter from all concerned. The laughter is induced by the hand signals rather than psychoses.)

Planning client recording of task progress. A form had been devised for the purpose of assessing the frequency with which the tasks were utilized. This was given to the T's and its usage was explained.

Summarization. The task, including when it was to be employed and the response it was to evoke, was restated at the end of the interview in which it was formulated.

Results

Data on change in the three communication problems are presented in tables 7.2 to 7.4 below.

Table 7.2
Percentages of Interrupting Speeches, Mr. and Mrs. T.

PHASE	WEEKS	CONDITION	MR. T.	MRS. T.	COMBINED
I	1	Baseline	67	47	57
II	2	Treatment	26 *	30 *	28 *
III	3,4	Follow-up	23	35	29
IV	5,6,7	Follow-up	17	29	25
V	30	Follow-up	20	28	24

Table 7.3
Percentages of Monopolizing Speeches

PHASE	WEEKS	CONDITION	MR. T.	MRS. T.	COMBINED
I	1	Baseline	4	3	4
II	2	Baseline	9	13	11
III	3,4	Treatment	4 *	8 *	6 *
IV	5,6,7	Follow-up	4	10	7
V	30	Follow-up	13	9	11

Table 7.4
Percentages of Speeches Containing Topic Shifts

PHASE	WEEKS	CONDITION	MR. T.	MRS. T.	COMBINED
I	1	Baseline	49	52	50
II	2	Baseline	34	34	34
III	3,4	Baseline	36	53	45
IV	5,6,7	Treatment	28 *	47 *	31 *
V	30	Follow-up	21	30	26

* Point at which TIS was applied.

The pattern of results revealed in the tables suggest that the TIS had an immediate impact on the communication problems. All problem measures show some degree of positive change from the preceding baseline period after the TIS was applied (starred cells), although problem occurrence was not always reduced below earlier baseline measures. In all instances effects persisted at least one phase beyond the treatment phase.

Effects seem to be the most clear-cut in respect to interruption, which showed a dramatic decrease after the TIS was introduced; the effects persisted through all subsequent phases. Monopolization has a more complex pattern. As was noted, an increase in lengthy speeches was expected as a result of a decrease in interruptions; thus the Phase 2 baseline for monopolization was apparently influenced by the experimental intervention. Percentage of long speeches declined again after the TIS was used but still remained above the initial baseline. It may be that the "optimum" percentage of lengthy speeches is closer to the percentages observed during the treatment phases than to the initial baseline. In appraising these findings it should be noted that the second baseline period contained several instances of excessively long speeches, 180 words or more. Speeches of this length did not recur after treatment started. The relative frequency of the third problem, topic changes, is less following treatment than for any of the baseline periods (with the exception of the Phase 2 baseline for Mrs. T).

Comparing the two partners, one finds that Mr. T's communication problems showed the greater amount of change immediately following treatment and, for the first two problems, a greater degree of persistence in the phase following. With the exception of the first problem, Mrs T made relatively more progress than her husband between the end of the treatment period and the final follow-up. In face, in respect to the third problem, Mrs. T showed more positive change during the five-month follow-up period than she did immediately after treatment.

Finally, decreasing amounts of change were achieved during the treatment periods as we moved from problem one to problem three. Examining the data for Mr. and Mrs. T combined, we see that a 68 percent reduction in interruption occurred between the baseline and the treatment period; the comparable reduction for problem two was 45 percent and for problem three, only 12 percent. The same pattern can be discerned when data for Mr. and Mrs. T are analyzed separately.

Evaluation of Impact and Practice Implications

The TIS appeared to be an effective means of reducing specific communication problems. In respect to two of the problems, changes were still evident approximately five months after the problems had been treated. At the same time, the study demonstrates the importance of viewing efforts to change such problems in systems terms. Decrease in interruptions may have contributed to the increase in monopolization during the second baseline period and to its lack of persistence in the posttreatment period. This may be an example of "symptom substitution," a much discussed but little documented phenomenon. The finding suggests that clinicians who try to affect specific problems in marital interaction need to be aware that their efforts may lead to possible negative side effects in other parts of the interactional system. At the same time these effects need to be appraised in the light of gains achieved. In the present case, it may be argued that some increase in monopolizing speeches was outweighed by the benefit resulting from the decrease in interruptions, which had been a serious obstacle to any meaningful dialogue. Also it is possible that longer speeches are less of a source of strain if they are related to the topic at hand; and there is evidence that the T's conversations were becoming more focused with alleviation of their problem of topic changing.

The differences between the partners in speed and amount of problem change may have been related to differing orientations and motivations. Mr. T frequently stated his belief that working on surface interaction was the place to begin. The problems he identified in his marriage concerned face-to-face interaction and the type of treatment which he believed possessed the greatest likelihood of success was one which focused on behavior, especially interaction. Mrs. T, however, was eager to move on to other kinds of problems. While she acknowledged the interrelatedness of feelings and behavior, she believed that changes in feelings must precede changes in behavior. As Mrs. T's communication behavior did change more slowly and erratically than

Mr. T's, it is likely that the attributed sources of their discomfort and their beliefs about the most effective treatment approach combined to determine the degree of their motivation for working on communication problems. This, in turn, may have affected changes in the frequency of the problematic communication behavior.

One treatment implication is obvious and supports the task-centered treatment model: work on problems selected by the client is more likely to bear fruit. A second is somewhat more subtle: it may be strategic to use methods which the client believes will successfully solve the problems. Perhaps we should spend less time and effort persuading clients of the efficacy of our methods, and instead offer them referrals to therapists whose methods are in harmony with the clients' beliefs. The versatile therapist could, of course, employ the method most compatible with the client's notions.

The progressive decrease in amount of change in the problems may be accounted for, in part, by Mrs. T's growing resistance to exclusive focus on communication problems. Another partial explanation may be found in the fact that the definitions of the communication problems became less and less distinct. Interruptions are largely an "either-or matter," and both parties are aware or can easily be made aware of their occurrence. Monopolizing is a matter of degree and is affected by the content. If one partner is talking at length about an issue of interest to the other the listener is less likely to define this speech as monopolizing than if the speaker is talking about something which seems irrelevant. Topic changes are a matter of definition as evidenced by the fact that it takes trained raters to achieve reliability when measuring their frequency. Certain lessons can be learned from the foregoing: when communication problems are the focus of treatment, the problems should be defined as explicitly as possible. Efforts should be made to select problems, whatever their type, in a way that maximizes the motivation of each partner. Depending on time constraints, the latter can be done by alternating the focus of treatment between problems identified by each spouse. Thus, a specified number of weeks could have been spent working on communication problems (of primary concern to Mr. T), and then a specified number of weeks working on problems identified by Mrs. T. The alternative would have been to balance the time in each interview between the problems of each partner.

In conclusion, task-centered methods appear to have promise as a means of bringing about positive change in specific marital communication problems. There is need for further work of this kind guided by a systems view of marital interaction. In so doing, it will be necessary to develop systematic connections between treatment of separate communication problems and between work on such problems and work on other aspects of the marital relationship.

References

Carter, Robert D., and Thomas, Edwin J. 1973. "Modification of problematic marital communication using corrective feedback and instruction." *Behavior Therapy* 4:100–9.

Navran, L. 1967. "Communication and adjustment in marriage." *Family Process* 6:173–84.

Reid, William J. 1975. "A test of a task-centered approach." *Social Work* 20:3–9.

Stuart, Richard B. 1968. "Token reinforcement in marital treatment." In *Advances in Behavior Therapy*, Vol. 6. Edited by Richard D. Rubin et al. New York: Academic Press.

—— 1971. "Assessment and change of the communication patterns of juvenile delinquents and their parents." In *Advances in Behavior Therapy*, Vol. 8. Edited by Richard D. Rubin et al. New York: Academic Press.

Tolson, Eleanor Reardon. 1976. "An evaluation of the effectiveness of the task implementation sequence in alleviating marital communication problems." Unpublished Ph.D. dissertation, University of Chicago.

Watzlawick, Paul; Beavin, Janet H.; and Jackson, Don D. 1967. *Pragmatics of human communication*. New York: W. W. Norton.

Chapter 8

~.~

Wilma Salmon, M.S.W.

A Service Program in a
State Public Welfare Agency

The Division of Family Services is part of the Louisiana Health and Human Resources Administration, the state agency responsible for public welfare services. The Division, which has local offices in each parish, is responsible for social services to families and children, and to adults. Personnel consists of approximately 1,000 direct service workers, 120 supervisors, and support staff.

Program Developments

In 1973, the service program of the Division was separated administratively from the payment of public assistance. This development provided impetus to the restructuring of the service program, since its staff no longer had to be responsible for handling public assistance grants. Management by objectives became a central theme in this reorganization. In this approach to administration, specific objectives were delineated. Program inputs were designed to achieve the objectives and the program's success in achieving them was carefully evaluated. Since the task-centered model seemed to fit well into this approach, it was selected as a major means of providing direct client services.

A case management system was devised to manage the flow of services. Case managers were to do intake, problem identification and assessment, service planning and implementation, and monitoring of service activities. Case managers and clients were expected to identify barriers to the client's social functioning or, in task-centered terminology, to identify target problems. A structured, time-limited service was to be planned, aimed at barrier removal and attainment of the desired, specified goals. Teaching teams from the state office went to each of the 10 service areas in the state to train managerial and supervisory staff in the case management system and the task-centered model. Subsequently, selected managerial and supervisory staff introduced the management system and task-centered casework to the total staff.

During the orientation sessions it was recognized that one of the most significant ways the task-centered model differed from our traditional approaches to casework was its emphasis on time. This aspect made us aware of our reluctance to terminate unproductive worker-client relationships. In the training, we attempted to demonstrate the task-centered approach, emphasizing identification of target problems, problem exploration, task formulation for both client and worker, and the setting of time limits for task accomplishment.

We took note of Reid and Epstein's usage of the term "task" to identify what the client is to do. We decided, in addition, to state to the client and write into the contract tasks to be undertaken by the worker. Worker tasks were defined as specific actions the worker would take on the client's behalf, such as locating a service or securing some resource. By this means, it was hoped, clients could be given a clear conception of what their workers planned to do. Rooney (Chapter 12) followed a similar practice. The agency has prepared a form for written contracts with clients, introduced also into the training of staff in the task-centered approach. Reid and Epstein advocate use of oral contracts. It was our thinking, however, that in a large agency dealing with great numbers of clients and staff that the written contract would assist in clarification, standardization, and monitoring of activities and results.

The Foster Care Program

My responsibility was to direct programs concerned with community-based care. One program, foster care for children, provides the best illustration of our efforts to implement the task-centered approach. Five objectives for the foster care program for 1975 were developed by the state office, as follows:

(1) From January 1, 1975, to December 31, 1975, completion of contracts with all foster children 13 years or older. Each contract was to include a plan in at least one of four areas: education and training; living arrangements; jobs; and personal plans.

(2) By October 1, 1975, approval of a stipulated number of foster homes suitable for the foster children under care according to the types expected to be needed: regular, receiving, group, and special homes.

(3) Starting January 1, 1975, through December 31, 1975, for each child who entered foster care, plans were to be drawn up to cover the child's first year of placement, and to specify the future care objective from among three options: returning to family, adoption, and long-term foster care.

(4) By October 1, 1975, approval of a stipulated number of adoptive homes available for black children.

(5) By October 1, 1975, completion of general procedures for staff to use in making decisions to place any child outside his own home. These procedures were to identify the crucial circumstances to be assessed in any such decision.

The rationale for these objectives was based on findings about children "adrift" in foster care (Maas and Engler, 1959; Jenkins, 1967; Fanshel, 1971; Sherman, Neuman, and Shyne, 1973). The major conclusion drawn from these studies was that the longer a child remains in foster home placement, the greater the likelihood that he would be in placement for extensive periods of time. Accordingly, maximum effort to plan for early discharge from placement could usually be expected to enhance the possibility for the child and parents to be reunited in their own home.

The statement of objectives was distributed to local area offices and staff meetings were arranged for discussion. These meetings focused on three areas: (1) a general explanation of management by objectives; (2) explanation of each objective currently in the plan, and of the responsibilities of the worker, supervisor, and administrator for meeting the objectives; (3) discussion of the Reid-Epstein task-centered model as a means for carrying out the stated objectives, emphasizing specific, action-oriented, time-limited activities.

The staff groups who met in these discussions were small enough to permit a lively exchange of ideas. Many doubts about the task-centered approach were expressed. There was question about the freedom and willingness of the "captive" clientele in foster care to express their own ideas and wishes for what work should be done. There was a belief expressed that staff and clients would not be able to conceive of anything specific enough to include in a contract. There was anxiety about the consequences should workers not meet the contracted agreements due to lack of time and resources. Fear was expressed about the possibility of legal action by parents who would "hold you to the contract." There was skepticism about the ability of emotionally disturbed parents or mentally retarded persons to make or keep contracts. It was predicted that if contracts were made between workers and children an awkward situation would develop with foster parents who were "left out."

Many positive reactions to a task-centered approach were expressed. Staff liked the clarity of stating what specific action parents could take to enable the return of their children. It was thought that the contract provided stability for the parent in the face of the everyday reality of changes in workers and shortage of staff. Some staff thought the task-centered approach could demonstrate to "captive" clients the agency's interest and understanding of their wishes to reduce the discomfort of their status. Staff recognized how the task-centered model required them to let clients know what they could expect of the worker and agency and what was expected of clients. The whole approach seemed in keeping with present emphases in child welfare on the rights of children, natural parents, and foster parents. It seemed possible that parents of limited ability could make and keep appropriate contracted agreements. Such agreements might help maintain a child in foster care when it was needed. The prospect was raised that the agreements could be accomplished through conferences which included children, foster parents, and natural parents.

Implementation of the Task-Centered Approach

In April 1975, task-centered casework was introduced statewide. Although no systematic study of the task-centered program has yet been attempted, it is the overall impression of state staff that the two most difficult areas for line staff have been the determination of priorities among problems and the explicit formulation of tasks to be performed by the client and worker. There appears to be widespread acceptance by staff of the usefulness of focusing on specific goals and objectives and the setting of time limits for task completion. It does not seem clear at this time whether the model has increased client participation in treatment plans. We do expect a continued conflict of values between the expressed wish of the client and the protection of the interests of others as the worker sees them, especially for "mandatory" clients, i.e., cases under care in the state system as a result of court adjudication.

Two examples of contracts with parents whose children are in foster care may be helpful in illustrating our current mode of utilizing task-centered treatment. In the first situation, the mother worked as a "go-go" dancer. Two years earlier the juvenile police had picked up her children when they were found alone at night. The mother, who was separated from her husband, lived in the show business area, frequently changing jobs and living arrangements. From the beginning of placement she voiced her desire to get her children back; but she and the three agency workers assigned to the case over the two-year period had never been able to get together on a plan.

The tasks agreed upon by the client and worker in the contract were geared to the achievement of the mother's wish to regain custody of her children. Tasks were specific actions which could establish in court the mother's ability to resume care of her children: a steady job, regular housing, reliable child care plans in the mother's absence. The contract also expressed the agency's commitment to request the court to return custody if each objective were attained and maintained for six months without the client's having added additional barriers to the return of the children.

Tasks for the parent were to: (1) secure a stable job, (2) secure and maintain a two-bedroom apartment adequate for the children, (3) visit the children regularly, (4) contribute toward their support, and (5) keep the agency abreast of any significant changes in her situation. Tasks for the worker were to: (1) regularly discuss and evaluate progress in achieving the tasks, (2) recommend return of custody to the mother if tasks were achieved and maintained for six months, (3) arrange visiting schedules with children in the foster home. One item of this agreement was renegotiated. The mother failed to contribute money to support the children. A change was made to permit her to have a bank account into which she would deposit the monthly support money to be used for meeting the children's needs upon their return to her custody. This agreement, as amended, was kept.

The mother accomplished the tasks. At present, her first child has been returned to her custody with a tentative date set for the return of the second. She commented, on reading the written agreement, that this was the first time she had known what the agency expected her to do before she got her children back. Each of her previous three workers had told her something different.

The second situation involved a young mother who had been in foster care herself. She was a teen-aged, unmarried mother whose daughter was initially placed in foster care while she was in a state training school. When this mother was released from the institution, she married a young man with a drinking problem and a poor work record. When the couple had been married six months, the court returned the daughter to the couple, with agency supervision. During the supervisory period the worker found the child abused. The court placed the child in foster care again.

The mother began pressing immediately to have her daughter back. Her husband agreed, since he wanted to keep his wife happy. He denied he had any problem or needed any help, although he was still drinking and had an erratic work record. He seemed interested in his son who had been born during the marriage. The couple verbalized an understanding of the criteria for the child's return but were unable to follow through on anything concrete. A task-centered contract was made with the mother only since the husband acknowledged no need for help. As in the previous case, the contract called for specific steps the mother would need to take to regain custody of her child.

The mother's tasks were to: (1) secure a regular and adequate source of income; (2) continue to use family planning; (3) obtain two- or three-bedroom housing; and (4) attend the Mental Health Clinic. Tasks for the worker were to: (1) arrange an appointment with the Mental Health Clinic; (2) provide continued foster care and family counseling. The client did not accomplish the tasks, but sought return of the child directly from the court.

A copy of the written contract between the mother and the worker had been forwarded to the judge in a case status report. At the hearing the judge produced the contract and asked the parents item by item if they had completed the agreement. The parents acknowledged failure to follow through. The judge denied their petition for return of the child. Even though the mother failed to complete the tasks, the model furnished a test of her capacity to take action deemed necessary to provide a suitable home for her children.

The task-centered approach has proved useful in direct work with adolescents in foster care. Some case examples are presented below. Glenda, 17 years old, came into foster care from a large, poor family. Her mother died when Glenda was 12 years old. Her aged father could not provide adequate care. She had an out-of-wedlock child at 14, surrendered to the agency for adoption. She had a second- out-of-wedlock child at age 16. This second child she steadfastly refused to surrender. Her second baby was placed in foster care. Glenda's expressed objective was to get out of foster care herself and assume custody and care of her baby. She was hostile in her contacts with the agency worker. She was stubborn and antagonistic in the foster home. Her father died while Glenda was in foster care. She maintained contact with two older brothers who were living independently.

A contract was tried in this situation, based on the worker's accepting Glenda's goal for herself and baby. The intention was to secure an agreement containing concrete steps necessary to reach her objective of having her child back. Glenda and her worker together defined the immediate need to look at her school and vocational interests and possiblities in order to enable her to find a job and become self-supporting. Glenda's wish to see her child more often and get to know her was agreed upon. This contract was seen as a beginning step. It resulted in the reduction in hostility toward the agency worker and a decrease in negative, provocative behavior in the foster home. Because Glenda was a ward of the court, and because of her youthfulness and lack of skills for independence, additional contracts were to be planned over approximately the next year and a half. Glenda pinpointed the following target problems: (1) inadequate clothing and other school supplies; (2) no vocational plans; (3) no job; and (4) not being sufficiently acquainted with her baby. The initial contract took account of Glenda's own priorities. Because Glenda's care was "mandated" to the agency, it was necessary to be explicit with her that the agency expected to make further contracts for the duration of its legal authority.

Joan, a 14-year-old foster child, was thought to be unhappy in her placement. She was doing poor work in school, especially in math. She was angry and critical in her attitudes toward others. She avoided speaking directly to people. She never revealed her thoughts to others. The foster father was particularly annoyed because Joan constantly referred to him in the third person, as "he." When the caseworker started a task-centered sequence with Joan, the girl was sullen, but accepted some responsibility for her behavior. They arrived at a contract with specific tasks for both Joan and the worker. Joan chose three target problems to work on for the immediate future: (1) poor math work; (2) her unfair criticism of certain people she disliked because of race, appearance, dress, and especially physical handicap; and (3) not speaking directly to other people, especially the foster father.

Audrey, a 14-year-old child in foster care, considered "severely disturbed," had a volatile temper and habitually incurred the disapproval of others. She was the youngest of six children, all of whom had experienced several placements. Her natural family was in a chaotic condition. Her divorced parents constantly quarreled with each other. The children were given to frequent outbursts. An older sister had been in a state mental hospital. Audrey's fear of ending up like that older sister seemed to be the impetus to work on her problems with her caseworker. Audrey's target problems were (1) worry about the instability of her natural parents; (2) poor school work; (3) cursing other people; (4) fear of going to jail or a state hospital; and (5) inability to modulate her temper. The general tasks with which work was begun were ((1) to listen to herself when she started to get scared or angry, and to take up the problem with an adult as soon as possible; (2) to talk to the person she was angry with instead of cursing at him; and (3) to attend school every day.

John, 18 years old, had to make plans for his future as his graduation from high school was near. He had come into foster care at age 14, after being shuffled from one relative to another for a period of two years following the death of his mother. He had a congenital deformity of his arm and shoulder. John had done well in high school and wanted to try college rather than attend a trade school or secure employment. John and the worker agreed that immediate concrete steps had to be taken to achieve John's goal of college entry. John's tasks involved "footwork" that was necessary to confirm his interest sufficiently to justify the agency's approval of financial support for college. John's target problem was a lack of plans and financial support for college. Beginning tasks were: to get a catalog and application from a nearby college; to send a transcript of high school grades and ACT test score results to the caseworker; and to set up appointment for a precollege physical examination.

Review of these cases indicates that workers conduct considerable discussion with clients and guide them to formulating appropriate target problems and tasks. The teen-agers in these examples range from a seriously disturbed child to a well-adjusted high school graduate planning for college. The contracts vary widely in their specificity and in the kinds of action to be taken with problems enumerated. We have as yet no reports on, or evaluations of, how the work with the adolescents proceeded beyond the initial phase.

Conclusions

Our experience with the task-centered model has just begun. Nothing has occurred to discourage the agency in its continued use. We are attracted to task-centered casework since we believe its successful use would be one way to move away from treatment plans traditionally imposed on clients in public agency social services. We find this approach quite compatible with our desire to implement management by objectives. The task-centered model, once staff is trained in its use, would increase our capacity to be accountable and would enable us to be more specific about service goals and about progress made toward achieving them. Eventually, we should be able to analyze and classify the various task-centered activities that caseworkers carry out, and to use this information for better understanding of our manpower needs. For these reasons we expect that the task-centered approach will become an increasingly important part of our social services system.

References

Fanshel, David. 1971. "The exit of children from foster care: An interim research report." *Child Welfare* 50(2):65–81.

Jenkins, Shirley. 1967. "Duration of foster care—Some relevant antecendent variables." *Child Welfare* 46(8):450–56.

Maas, Henry, and Engler, Richard. 1959. *Children in need of parents.* New York: Columbia University Press.

Sherman, Edmund; Neuman, Renee; and Shyne, Ann W. 1973. *Children adrift in foster care.* New York: Child Welfare League of America.

Part II: Children and Adolescents

Introduction

As noted in chapter 1, there is no clear-cut distinction between the problems of children and their families. Papers in this section deal with problems in which the primary contracting client was a child or adolescent.

Epstein's report of a task-centered school social work project provides a framework for the model's approach to children. The problems addressed are limited to the boundaries set by the child's perception of his problem—what the child understands is the trouble, and what he can do to alleviate it. Usually, in the school settings, the children's perceptions of their problems correspond to the opinions of teachers and parents. The children, however, tend to focus their concerns in a literal manner. They describe their difficulties narrowly. The adults involved—parents, teachers, social workers—usually perceive the child's problems as broader in scope.

The school social work project deals with these dilemmas by respecting the differences. The child is helped to specify his problem concretely in his own terms. Conferences with teachers and parents concentrate on eliciting and recognizing their concerns, which are both similar to and different from those of the child.

Helping adults alter their objectives for the child is often the first step in problem alleviation. Negotiation is called for to resolve conflicts about emphasis and goals among the child, parents, and teachers.

What the adults want from the child is often obtainable if they give him a reasonable portion of what he wants and feels he needs. The practitioner is the broker. The bargaining pivots on what shall be given, what shall be received, and the worthwhileness of the exchange to both parties. The bargaining consists of deciding who shall do what, and how often.

The practitioner is responsible for exploring, analyzing, and organizing the meaning of the child's target problem within its social context: classroom and school environment; family and neighborhood; peer relationships; the child's and parents' intellectual and personality attributes; their economic status, culture, and ethnicity. Only those areas with the most possibility for effecting the alleviation of the problem are selected for close attention. The model precludes attempts to intervene in the social context in opposition to, or in an altogether different direction from, the child's acknowledged problem. This proscription is qualified when the child's difficulties are a hazard to his well-being. Nevertheless, teachers, parents, and social workers concentrate on those target problems on which the child has agreed to work.

The report on the school social work project illustrates concrete and achievable objectives. Its goals are designed to help the child perform better at school (Costin, 1972). One would normally expect such goals to be achievable, as in fact they are, judged by the outcomes reported. The goals consist of alterations in observable behavior and attitudes.

Adaptation of selected techniques from other models is illustrated in the cases reported in both Epstein's and Rossi's papers. The general problem-solving approach of the practitioner in the case of Mattie (Epstein) illustrates broad exploration of the child's social context (Perlman, 1970). However, the task-centered approach restrained exploration of the father-daughter relationship, despite "clues" which might suggest problems. The sense of the task-centered model is that explorations about possible problems occur only if a client or family member explicitly identifies a source of concern and expresses a desire to do something about it. In Rossi's case, the social context is confined to the classroom. In this case, also, there are hints about attitudes in the child which could be construed as needing correction. Neither the child nor the mother proposed such areas for work. Both children in these cases made progress: one became able to talk in class; the other improved her achievement in school subjects. The new behaviors were of importance in the children's lives, fulfilling the purpose of treatment.

These case reports raise some questions about appropriate scope of exploration. These questions are not fully resolved. The task-centered model provides wide latitude for the practitioner to initiate the discussion of issues he believes the client should consider. The practitioner in Mattie's case made modest efforts to broaden the scope of treatment, but neither the child nor family responded to these efforts. Rossi made no efforts of this type. The fact that both children benefited is more important than notions about the desirable parameters of exploration.

The next two papers deal with adolescents in their school lives. Garvin's essay highlights the compatibility of the task-centered model with the development of the teenager. As viewed in this paper, the adolescent's world demands that he locate himself among the various roles available in achieving adulthood. The task idea is natural to this age group, consumed with finding out about occupations and people, and making decisions about what to do after high school graduation. Garvin's analysis of strategies for selecting target problems, and constructing and implementing tasks, is cast in terms of task-centered group work. This mode takes advantage of the adolescent's developmental tendency to emphasize peer relationships.

While Garvin presents directions for theory and strategy for group work with adolescents, Rooney is concerned with the development of specific techniques of group treatment with such clients. Rooney constructs guides for structuring the content and sequence of individual interviews with potential group members, develops criteria for homogeneity of target problems among group members to facilitate task selection and achievement, and suggests ways to develop norms to maintain the group. Rooney reports, also, on the use of "consulting pairs" in the task-centered group work model. In this technique group members are paired off and instructed to help one another through discussion of problems and tasks. He describes a structure for training, identifying, and directing the work of these dyads, and also for relating the dyads to the work of the group as a whole. Particularly interesting are techniques evolved for obtaining supports from authorities. These supports enable group members to extricate themselves from entrapment in the labeling and punishing systems of the school organization.

The four papers just discussed take as their central theme problems in the performance of children in school. Their problems might be construed as reflections of actual or potential psychopathology. That hypothesis, however, is eschewed in favor of an "interactionist" (Vinter and Sarri, 1965) or "ecological" approach (Hobbs, 1975). The child's problem is viewed as part of a system which influences his daily life.

Assessment and intervention are concentrated on the exchanges between the child, the settings in which he participates, and the significant individuals who interact with him. Change in any part of the system, or in several parts, can improve the system's action and the child's situation. The experiences with the task-centered approach discussed in these four papers are consistent with the position suggested by Hobbs (1975, pp. 113–20): "Behavior is a function of these four factors: what a child knows how to do, what is explicitly or implicitly expected of him in a given situation, what is important to him, and what he perceives to be the probable consequences of alternative behaviors" (p. 119). The treatment strategy derived from this view involves: revising and expanding the child's present competencies; revising the perceptions of significant adults and authorities about the child; changing their priorities and expectations; changing the child's priorities; providing resources to aid in the adult's ability to sustain the child in a manner compatible with the child's own interests; restructuring exchanges between the child and others to increase rewards and decrease punishment, frustration, oppression, discrimination; removing the child from the discordant situation if necessary and possible; and combining all these strategies, as necessary and feasible.

The goal of such intervention strategies is to provide a critical amount of assistance for the child and for the important people in his environment. Achieving a less harmful situation in the present ought to enhance children's developmental opportunities to some degree.

The papers by Bass and Hofstad are explorations of ways of applying task-centered methods in the juvenile corrections field. A great deal of social treatment has an overt or covert social control aim. Although social control and treatment tend to have dissonant objectives, social control aims are usually contained in the theories and mechanisms of treatment practice with involuntary clients. To extirpate social control features from social welfare seems literally impossible. Techniques have been developed to influence clients to submit or engage to some degree in treatment. These activities usually achieve far less voluntary engagement than hoped for (Kittrie, 1971). The dilemma is no more prominently displayed than in the field of juvenile corrections. Punishment has long been regarded as an ineffective means for reforming wayward youth; but "treatment" of juvenile offenders has not been a profitable venture either, possibly because of limited resources and limited technology. Bass and Hofstad illustrate program innovation constructed from the bottom up. Both experiments had basic acceptance by the administrations but were designed and implemented at staff initiative. The details of practice were arrived at empirically. Bass and Hofstad relied upon case-by-case observation and experimentation, rather than building a total program based upon theory or, more likely, upon untested hypotheses. The authors were generating hypotheses while they tried out and adapted the task-centered model to their settings. Their efforts are systematic and could be subjected to research evaluation given the necessary resources.

Bass studied runaway adolescent girls who were in detention. He interviewed persons in various parts of the total system: detention home, court, family, and the runaway girl. He exploited the sense of crisis experienced by all the participants because of the circumstances of detention. He did not concentrate on the runaway episode but on changes which could enable the girl to go and stay home. He relied upon reciprocity or exchanges between all participants to arrive at negotiated tasks. His authority was real and undisguised. He used his power to command bargaining and he arbitrated disputes. The target problems were selected by the girls and their parents. They were problems needing resolution in order for the girls to go home. Bass took advantage of the parents' push for change. The child was often passive. The tasks which emerged had to do with the parents' developing a new behavioral repertoire which could influence the child. Bass is not a Pollyanna. His cases have mixed outcomes. But the economy of his approach is commendable.

To apply the task-centered model in a juvenile corrections setting in the way Hofstad has done, one must accept as a given that youngsters are under strong institutional constraints to change their behavior; if they do not, punitive or undesirable consequences may follow. The offender is given the choice: to try to change or face the consequences. The consequences must have been determined through proper judicial procedure, and the choice clearly understood by the client. If he chooses to act differently, it becomes possible to work within a task-centered framework. Problems acknowledged by the client can be formulated, and tasks to resolve the problems can be developed. Hofstad suggests how this adaptation can be made. At the same time he identifies procedures, such as the court's assigning tasks to the youngsters, that may do violence to the philosophy and methods of the model. Hofstad and Bass had some unsolved design problems because the court determined the length of time available for treatment sequences, regardless of any duration plan contracted with the adolescent client and his parents. The issue arose prominently when the judicial authority ordered a time span for probation which exceeded reasonable limits for brief treatment. Such problems are technically solvable by introducing timed segments into a long-term involvement. The target problems may vary from one segment to another, interspersed with periods of planned monitoring. This technical solution is complicated. Basic questions about juvenile court policies are involved and need study.

Hofstad raises questions (all of which arise from time to time in other settings) concerning: (1) possible inappropriateness of the model in "serious" cases; (2) technical difficulties in specifying tasks concretely enough to enable measurement of progress; and (3) incomplete achievement of tasks. "Seriousness" depends to a great extent on ideology, on what conditions induce apprehensiveness in authorities. If "serious" means dangerous, one is hard put to identify the treatment of choice. No approach is predictably best for diminishing danger. There is not even clear consensus about what behaviors or conditions signal danger. Hofstad's description of technical difficulties in task specification are common in work with the task-centered model. Most social treatment practitioners have not been trained in specific observation and formulation of problem conditions. Some are trained to obscure detail in favor of a "whole picture" captured by lenses of broad personality theories. We are presently working on developing guides which can aid practitioners in achieving greater technical specificity in problem formulations (Reid, 1975).

Concerns about unfinished task achievement are partly technical and partly ideological. We are developing and testing interventions which hold promise for enhancing task achievement. These include: increasing commitment to the tasks, helping clients rehearse and practice task behavior, breaking tasks into small pieces to increase the likelihood of success, and so forth. The ideological issue has to do with longing for the "big cure." This myth dies slowly; but die it will with more sophisticated understanding that treatment is a prosaic undertaking. It deals with concrete bits of life. It is not a mission to create "self-actualization" or neat adherence to ideal norms.

It is apparent from this group of papers that children and adolescents can identify pertinent target problems. They can be committed to task-structured work to reduce problems. The practitioners who evolved the programs discussed in this section reveal two important attributes: (1) a strong respect for the capability and integrity of children and youth; and (2) a dedication to the strictures of an empirical approach to developing treatment methods which can demonstrably improve the lot of children.

References

Costin, Lela. 1972. *Child welfare: Policies and practices*. New York: McGraw Hill Book Company.

Hobbs, Nicholas. 1975. *The futures of children: Categories, labels, and their consequences*. San Francisco: Jossey-Bass Publishers.

Kittrie, Nicholas N. 1971. *The right to be different: Deviance and enforced therapy*. Baltimore: Johns Hopkins Press.

Perlman, Helen Harris. 1970. "The Problem-solving model in social casework." In *Theories of social casework*. Edited by Robert W. Roberts and Robert H. Nee. Chicago: University of Chicago Press.

Reid, William J. 1975. "A test of a task-centered approach." *Social Work* 20:3–9.

Vinter, Robert D., and Sarri, Rosemary C. 1965. "Malperformance in the public schools: A group work approach." *Social Work* 10:3–13.

Chapter 9

~~~~~~

Laura Epstein, M.A.

A Project in School Social Work

The Task-Centered Schools Project is part of the larger Task-Centered Treatment Program conducted since 1970 at the University of Chicago's School of Social Service Administration (see chapter 1). The perspective of the project is that learning problems and associated conduct problems of school children are derived from a configuration of psychosocial factors. Not only do the child's personality, behavior, and family circumstances influence adaptation to the demands of learning, but also school practices and conditions determine the characteristics of his problems (Costin, 1969a, 1969b, 1972, 1975). The objectives of the project are to provide opportunities in clinical practice for students and to further research and development of the task-centered model (Epstein, 1975). Because the task-centered model concentrates on reduction of present target problems as they are perceived by the school children and their parents, the schools project therefore intervenes in specified classroom and family conditions which have immediate impact on the pupils' lives while in school.

Overview

Work began in 1971 in one elementary school. By 1975, seven schools had become associated with the project. This paper describes work in elementary schools between 1971 and 1974. Some aspects of the project's work in high schools can be found elsewhere (Rooney, chapter 12).

Between 1971 and 1974, about 250 children in four public elementary schools were provided task-centered treatment. All the schools were located adjacent to the University in neighborhoods which are predominantly black and working-class. The overwhelming majority of the children served by the project were from black, working-class families, about a quarter of whom were receiving public assistance. Approximately 14 students had field placements each year in the four schools which provided a hospitable climate for task-centered practice and research (Korbelik and Epstein, 1976).

Service Objectives and Organization

The immediate objective of the project is enhancement of pupil learning. The project is not identified as a program of distinctive "clinical services" but rather as part of the educational process. The problems for which the schools, children, and parents want services are related to difficulties in learning. Interaction between pupil characteristics and school practices, especially teaching practices and school conditions, establish the climate in which school problems occur. Physical and social factors may amplify pupil malperformance, such as: illness or chronic health problems, unsatisfactory peer relationships, level of family care of the child, economic stress, substandard housing, and unsatisfactory relations with parents and siblings. Clinical pathology is considered causative only when the problem condition cannot be located within the social context.

After the target problem is identified by the child (with the assistance of the practitioner), the exploration takes into account the following: what and how the child is being taught; what institutional factors are stressful and inhibit learning; what physical-social factors are producing and maintaining the problem; and what clinical pathology might be contributing to the problem (if the problem cannot be explained by the preceding considerations).

Pupil "malperformance" is a label signifying deviance. The term means that valued norms have been violated. It does not convey information about either the nature of the problem or its solution. "Malperformance" is not a unitary phenomenon. It is not primarily attributable to the pupil. What "malperformance" means depends upon the standards, criteria, and practices by which academic success and desirable conduct are evaluated. These criteria vary between schools and change over time (Sarri and Vinter, 1974; Hobbs, 1975). This position has been received with mixed reactions by school personnel. Many believe in theories which consider family and individual pathology to be the locus of difficulty. Some teachers place a high value on their pupils receiving open-ended psychotherapy, which the project will not provide. But most teachers have been favorable to the task-centered approach, and school administrators have valued the practical problem-solving that has resulted from the project's work.

Teams are the basic organization of personnel for providing school social work services within the project. The field instructor has no office in any of the schools and is rarely on site. Social work students in a given school form a team and select a team leader. Teams from the separate schools then form a consortium, a team of teams. Teams meet with and without the field instructor. There are regularly scheduled sessions with the field instructor and also individual conferences. Team meetings can be formal or informal. They carry out administrative monitoring, case consultation, research supervision, program development, and mutual aid.

Agreements are made with both school principals and the regular social service department in regard to the characteristics of the project service. Teachers' and parents' councils are involved in the service planning to various degrees, depending upon the customary manner in which the school involves teachers' and parents' councils in other matters. The project agrees to accept referrals of individual children and groups of children from teachers and principals. However, the project does not accept requests to work in other areas because of its particular curriculum concentration, social treatment practice. The project has, for example, been asked to help parents prepare grant proposals and conduct recreational and enrichment programs. Also, practitioners have sometimes wished to organize in the community to influence particular school practices. In principle, these curbs on the project's activities are artificial. They might not exist if the course design were of the "generalist" persuasion and if it included conceptual and skill content to support a broader program.

Treatment Practices

Direct social treatment services are developed in three overlapping stages.

1. The first stage, *program focus,* occurs at the start of each academic year with the new group of incoming social work students. This stage consists of conferences with school officials to identify clusters of pupils who are thought to be presenting some designated set of problems. At different times, particular schools have special concerns, such as an age group, a particular teacher's pupils, a particular economic group, a school-wide learning problem, a particular type of behavior problem, and so forth. During an orientation period, students observe school conditions. Some develop an interest in exploring a particular problem, which they may do in collaboration with school officials. The first stage has become primarily an orientation device. It offers new students in a new school year the opportunity to gear up. Within a short time student-teacher pairs emerge. One or two students begin working regularly with one or two teachers. These pairs generate their own referrals and problem concentrations.

2. *Problem-reduction* is the major activity with individual children and their families. This stage is one of direct treatment, using individual, family, and group sessions within the task-centered model. On the nonresearch cases (80 percent of the total), students may use an eclectic mixture of procedures. The course content provides them with a comparative framework to do so. However, the influence of the task-centered model is strong, so that all cases are handled in their essentials according to the basic procedures of the task-centered approach.

3. *Advocacy.* This term, as used in the project, means interventions in the community and in the school's practice; but its extent is restricted. Resource procurement of tangible benefits available in the

community is always done: securing public assistance, tutors, medical care, and the like. It is standard practice to intervene with teachers to change specified class conditions. Our efforts do seem to alter teachers' perceptions, teachers' practice, and classroom climate to a limited degree, often enough to relieve a critical stress on the child. In task-centered work these basic interventions at classroom level are essential for an individual child's task accomplishment to go forward. The target of intervention is nearly always a problem which is occurring, at least in part, because of undesirable interactions between the child and classroom conditions. When a child is asked in an initial interview what is wrong, he nearly always describes a dissonance between himself and the school climate. Parents do the same. Teachers usually point to pathology in the child or his family. The task-centered model requires that the interventions adhere to the child's formulation of the problem. The practitioner is forced into the interactional field of a classroom. However, much of the children's dissonance with the school, and the teachers' distress with the children, are traceable to school-wide practices, such as suspensions and assignments to special educational level classes (Educable Mentally Handicapped, Trainable Mentally Handicapped, etc.).

The treatment procedures, based upon the general task-centered model, varied over the four years as techniques developed with experience and as adaptations were made to the school setting. Practice had to become accommodated to the special requirements of these children's status as pupils in an educational institution. What was learned during this process may be in part transferable to other settings. The major technical developments which occurred in the model as used in the schools can be summarized as follows: (1) the process of targeting problems became more concrete and behavioral in character; (2) tasks became more numerous and incremental; and (3) our practice theory for the middle phase of treatment became better articulated.

Targeting Problems in the Initial Phase

This procedure posed three types of difficulties: a tendency to fix upon the first problem statement of the client, sparsely connected to the problem-context; a tendency to assume that the referral source's problem identification was the "real" problem, distorting exploration with the child client; and a tendency to infer the existence of psychopathology from diagnostic information of poor quality and to concentrate only superficially on the client's own problem formulation.

Guidelines were developed to increase the specificity of targeting problems with the children and significant others. Certain preliminary explorations were deemed necessary before the problem could be targeted in a meaningful way. Immediate conferences with the teacher or other referral source became standard practice. These conferences were designed to obtain from referral sources information about the problem situation, to clarify explicitly what they expected, and to obtain from them an agreement to undertake some actions to be planned mutually in order to help the child alleviate his problem. Another preliminary step was to have a brief, introductory session with the child. This procedure was intended to begin to familiarize the child with the social worker and the task-centered treatment process, to ascertain in a general way what were the child's perceptions of his problem, and to inform him that parents would be contacted to secure their agreement to treatment and their assistance in problem reduction.

Next, there followed an introductory session with the parent, parents, or guardian, with the child himself often present. This session was held in order to obtain parents' views on the child's problem, to establish the initial form and content of their participation in problem reduction, to explore the family context of the problem, to assess generally the wider social context of the problem from the parents' viewpoint, and to obtain parents' agreement to treatment and to participating in research. These steps usually made possible an assessment of the social context and a decision about the location of the most feasible point for intervention.

Most children are overwhelmed by the introduction into their lives of a school social worker who is an adult authority, noticeably on close terms with school officials, and a stranger to boot. Therefore, the first interview, which is normally used for the purpose of identifying target problems, was divided into a set of two or three interviews. This set permitted time to be spent on helping the child to feel comfortable, determining what problems the child wanted to work on and what problems mattered most to him. The use of familiarizing techniques reduced strangeness and enhanced role induction, and consisted mainly of friendly overtures. They were intended to reveal to the child what kind of person the social worker was. The child could make up his mind whether the practitioner was good or bad, for or against him, clever or a dolt, candid or manipulative. Games, outings, and treats made up the familiarizing program. Opportunities occurred for the child to state or act his wishes, opinions, attitudes toward the work at hand, and to reveal his problems gradually, to the degree he could and would. Children who verbalized sparsely could be helped to express themselves via behavior, as in play and games. Some children could be taught to increase the quantity of their verbal responses. Some children had no reluctance to speak out and needed very little, if any, of these familiarizing techniques.

Formulating problems and ranking them according to priority are activities in which client and practitioner collaborate (Reid and Epstein, 1972, pp. 38–72). With children, it is often necessary for the practitioner to be active in directing consideration of problems and priorities. He may suggest a rationale for working on a problem; suggest ways of formulating it and propose an order of priority for proceeding with a set of problems. With a high degree of practitioner activity, it is necessary to be scrupulously attentive to obtaining the child's response. Practitioners can be highly active in initiating these discussions of problem rationale, formulation, and priorities, but they must provide opportunity for children to react to the practitioner's suggestions. They should reduce their initiative when the child does begin to express his own desires more clearly.

Practitioners have needed to learn to direct children, teachers, and parents to define a problem behaviorally. What follows serves as a basic guide. The target problems should be stated in words which depict what the behavior is, not why it exists, or what can be inferred from it or what it ought to be. The behavior can be depicted as doing, feeling, thinking. The depiction should begin with what the client does; or, if responsibility is ascribed to others, what they do. What is done should then be amplified by concrete information about when it occurs and the circumstances in which it occurs. It should be possible to observe these behaviors or their consequences. The problem should be qualified by whether the behavior represents an excess in action (e.g., "talks too much"); or a deficit ("doesn't talk enough"). What the client and others think and feel about this behavior has to be ascertained but is not part of the behavioral definition. Target problem formulations which emphasize acting are usually most accessible to intervention, best understood by clients and referral sources, and lead to the most demonstrable results. The best formulation of a target problem is: He does this where (location) so-and-so many times (frequency) and when (antecedents). For example: "He is inattentive and attention-seeking" is not a problem but a complex and ambiguous conclusion. The problem should be stated in such terms as: "He does not listen when the teacher gives assignments; he brags in a loud voice to certain boys on the playground; he comes to the teacher's desk frequently and gets her mad."

A number of adaptations were made to guide task formulation. Tasks became more numerous than originally postulated. Tasks appeared as many distinct increments, the total of which approached attainment of a "general" task. The accumulation of small task increments was expected to achieve problem reduction. Incremental or operational tasks were often temporary. They led to other tasks. Tasks were dropped when completed or when attempts to activate them failed or became irrelevant because other tasks appeared more potent. For clients who did not readily formulate tasks, it proved desirable for the practitioners to formulate them, to alter and to assign them, always provided the client was given ample opportunity to consider these changes. It appears that client commitment to a task may be a more powerful factor in task achievement than whether or not the client initiated the task formulation directly.

Children especially (but also adults) sometimes reveal substantial ambiguity in developing tasks to fit a problem. The patterns observed with children responding to task suggestions are: "maybe: maybe this—maybe that"; "don't know"; "somebody else has to do it." The "maybe" situation can be handled by the practitioner's giving advice on the most desirable alternative; or by trying out the alternatives sequentially or concurrently. The "don't know" situation, if it does not change with exploration, needs a practitioner's initiative, that is, a strong recommendation on a suitable task. The "somebody else" situation is dealt with first by attempting to see if the other person can or will change. Many parents and teachers to whom a child ascribed his problems were cooperative and made changes which helped reduce the problem. If those efforts fail, then is the time to evaluate how much responsibility the child client may have to assume to get desired alleviation of the problem.

Children assumed responsibility for problem solving through tasks that for the most part were specified in terms of concrete behavior the child wanted to undertake. Some tasks called for one-time action: "to complete and hand in a composition," "to approach Diane and start a conversation with her," "to attend a club meeting," "to ask teacher to change seat" (to get away from bothersome peer). Other tasks asked the child to engage in repetitive actions: "not to interrupt other children when they recite in class"; "to spend a half-hour each night reading aloud to his mother and to make a list of all the words he can't read"; "to walk away when Darrel starts to mess with him." Interviews with children, typically about a half-hour in length, were largely devoted to devising and planning the implementation of such tasks, to rehearsing and practicing content the child was to do, and to reviewing task achievement. When appropriate, teachers and parents were asked to help the child carry out the task through either participating directly in the child's work on the task or providing rewards for successful task behavior.

In the middle phase, obstacles to task achievement include the client's lack of skills, his fears, the practitioner's becoming discouraged, errors in targeting the problem, and intractability of the target problem. If the client does not know how to go about doing his task work, he has to be taught: through explanation, demonstration, rehearsal, role play, and the like. The practitioner may help him review his beliefs about a situation to develop a more efficient and realistic appraisal of circumstances involved in his problem. Fears which appear to inhibit task work may be associated with lack of skill. Fear may be present because the client believes he is unable to proceed, instilled by previous experience of failure and by knowing that others believe he is incapable. Fears may be heightened by present stress. For this condition the child needs to acquire accurate knowledge of himself and others in order to pursue the task.

Grinding away at small bits and pieces of tasks, detailed reviewing of accomplishments and difficulties, and a strong hold on the focus of attention is not easy work. Some practitioners become discouraged in task-centered work with children. Our observation is that this type of discouragement, often associated with slowing of effort, is related to inexperience, and a deeply held belief in (or fantasy of) the "big cure." Some practitioners become discouraged because they believe that problems have old and tenacious underlays which should be examined and reconstructed as a matter of principle. Reactions of this sort usually give way with experience.

Sometimes the target problem has been erroneously identified. As soon as this becomes clear, the practitioner attempts to reformulate the problem and recycle the treatment sequence. A few additional sessions may have to be added. Work already done can be expected to be relevant because of the way human problems are intertwined.

Sometimes the problem proves intractable. There are situations which do not respond to social treatment technology, to state the obvious. Fanshel (1962) has analyzed this condition succinctly for a child welfare practice:

> There are many areas in which child welfare workers are dealing with extremely complex and pernicious social and personal problems where it would be unreal and naive to expect a high level of success . . . considering the relative paucity of research that has thus far been brought to bear upon them. . . . There also appears to be a relative lack of sophistication among the professional staff members themselves about the fact that an agency is not in a position to take complete responsibility for the eventual outcome of a child's life. Children coming into care have been exposed to a variety of pathological conditions affecting family life, and it is unreal to assume that we have evolved the techniques that make it possible to assure the restoration to normal functioning for every child (pp. 491–92).

Aside from sheer lack of knowledge, there are many situations where social resources either do not exist or are in such short supply that the problem cannot be alleviated. However, the idea of an intractable problem lies partly in the eye of the beholder. There has in the past been a tendency to disparage "limited goals," those accessible and prized gains which counteract a piece of a larger difficulty. Attending diligently to such parts of problems, and assuring that the practitioner and the client are concentrating on the same narrowly defined issue, can have an impact perceived as beneficial to children, teachers, and parents. Rooney (chapter 12) reaches a similar conclusion in respect to task-centered work with adolescents.

There are some additional observations about the middle phase of task-centered treatment which bear brief mention. While some children quickly "zero in" on a problem important to them, others slip and slide through several problem identifications. This occurrence may be the child's response to faulty technique. The practitioner may have explored the child's concerns inadequately. He may have adopted a "hidden agenda." His attention may not be congruent with the client's focus. On the other hand it is characteristic of human problems that they appear differently over time. The model makes a provision for recycling the sequence to adjust to changed perceptions of the problems and the development of altered tasks.

Another area of difficulty in the middle phase are instances where the client has ascribed the problem to others—parents, teachers, peers, usually. When the other persons cannot and do not change after a reasonable effort to influence them, this type of target problem needs to be altered. The child needs to assume more personal responsibility. Having witnessed and participated in the effort to change the other, and having now some understanding of why that desired change cannot be expected, the child's target problem can be reformulated with new tasks.

It is not uncommon to uncover factors in the social context which impair the client's capacity and opportunity to achieve problem reduction. Where these conditions are even the least bit manipulable, and often they are, it is necessary for the practitioner to take direct steps to modify them.

Research Cases

During the period 1971 to 1974, data were collected on 35 research cases involving task-centered treatment of children under 13 years of age. The cases represent the work of approximately 25 student practitioners. These clinical trials were conducted to obtain a more systematic picture of treatment operations and outcomes. Since the model was applied with greater thoroughness in these cases than others, a review of the data obtained from them should be particularly instructive. Students recorded data on problems and tasks on special forms (see Appendix) and tape-recorded selected interviews to permit independent checking of their observations. In addition, follow-up interviews were conducted with children (and, if the problem was home related, with parents) shortly after they had terminated service.

Because the clients were not specially selected their characteristics were similar to those served in the project as a whole: all but three were black, and with few exceptions families were either low-income and self-supporting or receiving public assistance. Half the children were in the 8–10 year age range; the other half 11 or 12. Almost all were referred by teachers or other school personnel largely for problems in academic achievement and in classroom or other school behavior.

In terms of our own classification system two categories accounted for most of the problems: role performance (as a student), 40 percent; and dissatisfaction with social relations, 43 percent. The former category consisted largely of problems in academic achievement, although it also included classroom behavior difficulties. The latter group consisted of a variety of problems concerning the child's relations to others, mostly peers, teachers, and siblings. Specific concerns included getting into fights, being teased or bullied, being treated unfairly, and not having enough friends. When one examines problems in each case regarded as the most important to the client, one finds that 45 percent were classified as dissatisfactions in social relations and 31 percent as problems of role performance. When problems of lesser importance to the client are examined, dissatisfaction in social relations accounts for 41 percent of the problems and role performance 48 percent.

The emphasis on problems in social relations is greater than one might expect from reasons for referral and reflects the model's stress on concerns as perceived by the children themselves. Problems uppermost in the children's minds were more likely to be in the area of social relations than in academic performance or classroom behavior, which in turn appeared to be of more concern to teachers. The shift in emphasis to the latter in the problems of lesser importance to the child suggests that trade-offs were being made, with some children perhaps agreeing to work on problems of particular concern to the teacher once it had been decided to work on problems of special importance to them.

The cases received a median of nine interviews, mostly with the children, although there were interviews with one or both parents, or joint parent-child interviews, in the majority of cases. In addition there were contacts with teachers in almost all cases with a median of three contacts per case. The median duration of service was eleven weeks. Only three cases were extended beyond the 12-interview limit of the model; none of these went beyond 17 interviews.

Outcome data obtained from practitioners were in the form of ratings of problem change and task progress. These ratings were based on the practitioners' interviews with clients, parents, and teachers and, where applicable, on their observations of the child. The reliabilities of these ratings were assessed by having judges listen to samples of interviews in which the practitioner reviewed problem change or task progress with the client. The degree of correlation between practitioners and judges was reasonably good ($r = .68$ for problem change, .71 for task progress).

For the cases as a whole, 75 target problems were formulated. Practitioners rated almost three quarters of these problems (73 percent) as showing at least some degree of alleviation; for almost half (49 percent) problem change was rated as considerably alleviated or better. Almost 90 percent of the cases had average problem change ratings which indicated at least some overall improvement.

The cases yielded a total of 92 recorded tasks. Half (54 percent) were judged to have been either substantially or completely achieved; another 19 percent were at least partially achieved.

Additional analysis was undertaken to determine correlates of problem change and task progress. Problem change was not found to be strongly related to other factors, although there was a tendency for certain problems of social dissatisfaction (those in which the child saw the locus of the problem in his own behavior, e.g., "I can't make friends") to have somewhat better outcomes than other problem types. The only variable significantly related to task progress was the practitioners' ratings of client commitment or willingness to undertake the task, a relation also reported by Reid (chapter 4). These findings seem to reflect the importance of client motivation to work on the problem or task.

Independent follow-up interviews were obtained from 29 children and parents, or 83 percent of the sample. Clients were asked to state the major target problems worked on. In most cases (69 percent) there was substantial agreement (perfect agreement in almost half) between the clients' statement of the problem and the practitioners' formulation. This finding suggests that the model achieved some success in establishing an explicit, shared understanding of the focus of service. Of the clients interviewed, 93 percent indicated that they had made at least some progress on their problems; 64 percent reported either considerable progress or that the problem had been completely solved. A statistically significant though not high level of agreement between client and worker ratings of problem change was found ($r = .30$, $p < .01$). On the whole, the clients were quite positive in their evaluation of service: 83 percent thought they had been considerably benefitted from service or "could not have gotten along without it."

The findings on problem change, which are comparable to those reported by Ewalt (chapter 2) and Brown (chapter 15), suggest that a good deal can be accomplished in work on limited problems through helping clients take specific actions to solve them. They also indicate there is room for improvement. That about half the problems treated were judged (by the practitioners) to have been considerably alleviated is encouraging; but we hope to be able to do better with further developments in methods of problem formulation and in the technology of task planning and implementation.

The Case of Mattie [1]

Many of the observations presented thus far are illustrated by the case described below. The case also illustrates a current direction in the project toward greater involvement of parents in school-related problems.

[1] Judith Mendels was the practitioner.

Mattie, 11-years old, was referred by her sixth grade teacher, who believed the child was not achieving up to potential. Mattie agreed but believed her problem to be less extensive than stated by her teacher. In math and social studies Mattie said the teacher moved too fast over the subject matter. Mattie had asked the teacher to go more slowly in math but she did not. The child saw no need for assistance from the social worker. Her parents helped her and she was conscientious about studying. She was, however, afraid of failing. She agreed to try a conference with the teacher.

The practitioner met with Mattie and the teacher together. The teacher elaborately described inattention and failure to follow directions. Mattie explained her fear of the teacher's angry responses when she asked for help. The teacher interpreted Mattie's reluctance to ask for help as due to internal personal problems. Mattie revealed that she was distracted by her stepfather at home when doing her homework. He did not like her and preferred her siblings. They all fought a good deal. When Mattie and the practitioner were alone after the conference, Mattie said she might like help in getting her stepfather to stop interfering with her studying at home. It remained open how best to proceed. The client was not willing to have a family conference.

In the next (third) interview, Mattie said the problem was cleared up. She spoke to her stepfather. They made a plan for him to protect her from interruptions while studying at home. One more interview was set to be sure of the improvement. The practitioner insisted upon this. At interview 4, the arrangement with the stepfather had broken down. Nine different ways to get protected time for studying were discussed. The practitioner initiated most of the suggestions. All but one was rejected by Mattie. She finally accepted the practitioner's suggestion to have a family conference about arranging home study time.

Interview 5 was in the home and included Mattie, her mother, her stepfather, and her two sisters. The practitioner focused the conference on ways the family could help Mattie overcome her school difficulties. The parents were observed to be capable and sensitive people. No evidence appeared to support Mattie's belief that the stepfather behaved provocatively to her, although a good deal of teasing and provocation was observed among the three girls. A schedule of play, work, and household chores was worked out. The mother believed that Mattie's teacher was overly demanding and frightened the child. If no progress were forthcoming with the schedule, the mother would negotiate with the school to transfer Mattie to another room or another school. At interview 6 (one week later), Mattie reported progress. She had begun to observe that sometimes her stepfather was playful and sometimes serious. His reactions were dependent on events and were not capricious. Thereafter, the child was seen briefly at weekly and then biweekly intervals for 10 or 15 minutes, at school. The agreed-upon schedule was being observed without mishaps.

Six weeks after the family conference, a more extensive interview (7) occurred. The home schedule had been observed. The parents and Mattie monitored the homework plan. Mattie took the initiative, when necessary, to speak to her stepfather if she thought he became too playful. He responded appropriately by desisting, although he needed to be reminded of the agreement. Treatment was discontinued. Mattie's grades had improved. She had learned some direct ways of talking with her stepfather so she felt less exploited by him. The family had demonstrated their caring about her. The teacher was somewhat satisfied.

A Few General Observations

The experience of the schools project has generated many interesting ideas about the whole area of direct treatment of children and interventions with families and schools around children's problems. Issues such as the appropriateness and usefulness of diagnostic labels, of variations in children's responses at different developmental stages, of the relative influence of the child's personality and external conditions on the way a problem is perceived by the child and by adults in the social network—these and other issues are raised. Without being able to explore the many questions of interest related to task-centered treatment of children, the project's experience is that children can and do understand how to use the services and most receive at least some benefit from them.

146   Laura Epstein

References

Costin, Lela. 1969a. "An analysis of tasks in school social work." *Social Service Review* 43:274–85.

—— 1969b. "A historical review of school social work." *Social Casework* 50:439–53.

—— 1972. "Adaptations in the delivery of school social work services." *Social Casework* 53:348–54.

—— 1975. "School social work practice: A new model." *Social Work* 20:135–39.

Epstein, Laura; Lee, C.; and Rooney, R. 1975. "Social treatment for multi-problem families: Analysis of issues and recommendations." Paper prepared at the School of Social Service Administration, the University of Chicago. (Xeroxed; available from the senior author.)

—— 1975. "The task-centered project: Social treatment for families, individuals, groups." (Xeroxed.)

Fanshel, David. "Research in child welfare: A critical analysis." *Child Welfare* 41:484–507.

Hobbs, Nicholas. 1975. *The futures of children.* San Francisco: Jossey-Bass Publishers.

Korbelik, John, and Epstein, Laura. 1976. "Evaluating time and achievement in a social work practicum." In *Teaching for Competence in the Delivery of Direct Services.* New York: Council on Social Work Education.

Reid, William J. 1975. "A test of a task-centered approach." *Social Work* 20:3–9.

Reid, William J., and Epstein, Laura. 1972. *Task-centered casework.* New York: Columbia University Press.

Rose, Sheldon. 1972. *Treating children in groups.* San Francisco: Jossey-Bass Publishers.

Sarri, Rosemary, and Vinter, Robert D. 1974. "Beyond group work: Organizational determinants of malperformance in secondary schools." In *Individual Change Through Small Groups.* Edited by Glasser, Sarri, and Vinter. New York: Free Press.

Chapter 10

~.~.·~.~.·~.~.·~.~.·~.~.·~.~.·~.~.·~.~.·~.~.·~.~.·~.~.·~.~

Robert B. Rossi, M.A.

Helping a Mute Child

This paper is a presentation and analysis of a single treatment case, conducted by the author, which made use of the technology of applied behavior analysis within the task-centered treatment system. It illustrates how task-centered treatment has been extended to a very young, almost nonverbal client and demonstrates how behavioral methods can be used to facilitate problem specification, task formulation, and implementation of tasks.

The case, conducted in an inner-city ghetto school, began with a referral from the client's second grade teacher who explained that she was worried because the client, seven-year old Daniel, had not spoken during the six months he had been in her second grade class nor in class the year before. Despite his muteness, the teacher felt that he got along well with the other children. Evaluation of his written work showed that he was performing at an appropriate level. She said that he once had read for the vice-principal, but only after a great deal of prompting when they were alone. She mentioned an incident which occurred earlier in the year when Daniel had urinated in his pants during class, apparently because he was not able to ask to leave the room.

During the next three days, as a continuation of the referral process, I observed the client in various classroom situations as well as during the lunch period. During these observation periods, totaling about four hours, the client did not speak with anyone. Besides the direct observation of the client's behavior, a concurrent analysis of his school environment showed that the teacher and students in his class often modified their behavior when interacting with Daniel. Because Daniel's teacher liked him, she would often rephrase questions so that Daniel could answer by shaking or nodding his head. If she was referring to an answer on the blackboard or in a reader, she would frame the word or let Daniel point to a correct answer. When his teacher asked the class a question, Daniel would often raise his hand but would not answer when called upon. The other children in the class would often answer the questions for him.

After completing my observations, I met with Daniel. Although he would not talk with me in the classroom when his teacher introduced us, he would repeat words for me very softly when we were alone in my office. I told him who I was and that I would be willing to help him learn to talk in the classroom. When asked if he would like to talk in class, he nodded yes. I explained what we would be doing in the sessions and that he would be getting candy for talking. While I named several types of candies, Daniel nodded at those he liked. These would later be used as reinforcers. I told him he could think about it and that if he wanted we would begin working in a few days. This was a brief twenty minute session.

In our second session we reviewed the earlier session and I began problem exploration by asking if there were any situations where he could talk. He told me that he talked at home and that he was the youngest—age 6—in a family with two older brothers, an older sister, and his mother. I discussed his inability to speak in school and how this affected him. He agreed again that he would like to work on the problem of talking and mentioned the candy. As a test to see how loudly he could speak, I sat in a chair facing away from him and gave him a piece of candy when I heard him ask for it. I then successively moved the chair further away after each reinforcement until I was approximately 30 feet away and still able to hear him. We then role-played a situation in which he would say "Hello, Mrs. Kelly" when we entered his classroom after our session. As we walked back from the session, we repeated the role-play as we got closer to the classroom. After a final rehearsal in front of the classroom door, he was able to enter and say "Hello, Mrs. Kelly" (the name of his teacher). No classmates were in the room at the time.

After this session I met with Daniel and his family in their home. His mother was eager to show me that he was not "retarded" and that he would talk. She had Daniel talk over the phone in front of me. She told me that she wanted him to talk in class, but she could not force him to do this. I explained how I would be gradually encouraging Daniel to talk in school. She said that she did not know why he would not talk, but it had been a problem ever since he had entered nursery school at the age of four. She said that Daniel sometimes talked about school when he returned home and also told me that Daniel would turn seven in two days and he had promised her that he would begin talking in school on his birthday.

Our third session took place three days after his birthday. Daniel had not begun to talk in school. We contracted for the general task of talking with friends and teachers at school. When I asked him whom he would best like to talk with in the class, he replied, "Carol." He would not agree to try to talk with her in the classroom but did agree—with a big smile—to let her come to our next session. I asked him for the names of other children he would like to talk with and obtained a list of seven girls and boys from his class. During this session we played a game in which I pretended I could not see him nod or shake his head and, therefore, needed to hear him say "yes" or "no" in order to unstand him.

During our first three sessions together, I had continuously reinforced loud, clear responses with verbal approval, smiles, and candy, the latter being the most successful reinforcer. When he failed to respond verbally, I would cock my ear. This functioned as a discriminative stimulus to cue Daniel that he had to talk to receive a reinforcer.

At the beginning of our fourth session, Daniel spoke to me in Carol's presence. She immediately exclaimed, "He talked! I never heard him talk before." Because they had sat next to each other for the whole year, I took this as a confirmation of my baseline observations. When asked to say "Hello" to Carol, Daniel would only look at her. I then had both of them answer easy questions—such as, "How many fingers am I holding up?"—while they sat next to each other in chairs facing me. Next, while they continued to look at me, I had them say "Hello" and then "Hello, Daniel" and "Hello, Carol," respectively. Finally I had them turn their chairs toward each other and Daniel was able to say "Hello" and then "Hello, Carol" while he faced her.

At each point in this process, when the steps were too big for Daniel, he would just stare at me and remain motionless. Sometimes his mouth would quiver when he was not able to respond. At that point, smaller steps were substituted until he could perform the task.

After the interaction between the children was established, I asked them to rehearse a short conversation in which Daniel asked Carol for a pencil—something he frequently did nonverbally. We talked about how handy it would be for Daniel to talk in class. Carol related how once Daniel was not allowed to accompany her on an errand because he could not say "Yes" when the teacher asked if he would like to go.

We contracted for two operational tasks outside our session: (1) that when we returned to the class Daniel would ask Carol for my pen, which she was holding, and return it to me, at which point I would leave, and (2) that they would play the game that they could not understand head shakes. Daniel was not able to complete the first task because the class had all moved into the next room for music class. Carol reported that they had played the game, but that Daniel had only spoken once.

Our fifth session was held in the back of the classroom, in an attempt to generalize to the classroom environment. Daniel, Carol, and I sat about 15 feet from the nearest seated classmate. Daniel began talking with Carol and me while throwing worried glances over his shoulder at the rest of the pupils who were busy filling out workbooks. During our conversation, Lee, a classmate, wandered back near us. Daniel would not speak when Lee was near or when he saw him facing us. I had Lee join us, but Daniel would not speak. I directed Lee to slide his chair back about 10 feet until Daniel would speak, then forward 5 feet until Daniel would not speak. Lee immediately caught on to the process and actively began a series of adjustments back and forth while we talked. Eventually, Daniel would say the names of colors to which Lee pointed. When Lee stated that Daniel never talked, I pointed out that now he was talking and that this was something new for him. Daniel talked with Lee and Carol until they were talking without much prompting from me. They agreed to have Sabrina join them. She also exclaimed that she had never heard Daniel talk before. Daniel smiled proudly at this. We rehearsed the task where Daniel would ask for the pen. They returned to their seats and Daniel carried out the task. His voice was inaudible to everyone but Carol.

In our seventh session the number of children present was raised to five and a teacher's aid was included. Again, slow steps of introduction had to be used. The new people were introduced gradually and the requirements of speech were gradually shifted from simple tasks, such as naming colors, to actual conversations. Candy reinforcement was used less and less during the session and by the end had been completely phased out. On the way back to the classroom after the session, Daniel spoke with two boys who initiated a conversation with him.

The eighth and final treatment session took place a week later in the classroom. Daniel remained in his regular seat. With some prompting, he was able to answer "No" to a question from his teacher as she left the classroom with about half the class. While they were gone, I had Daniel read for two classmates who sat next to him. When the teacher reentered, Daniel would not read for her. I motioned her to walk around behind Daniel. He then began to read to me while the teacher looked over his shoulder. When stuck on a word, the teacher corrected him from behind. He turned his head slightly and looked back at her from the corner of his eye but continued to read. At that point I walked to the back of the room while Daniel continued reading. His teacher then went to the blackboard and pointed at a word which he pronounced for her.

The next day I observed Daniel in class. He was in a reading group with four other children and would read when called upon. Following the reading session the teacher stated that she felt the problem was solved and things were going well.

In a session a week later, I reviewed the treatment program with Daniel. On our way to my office, he said hello to several teachers and children who made a point of greeting him. When asked if there was anything else he wanted to work on, he mentioned that his gym teacher had given him a spanking because he had been fooling around in gym class and that several bullies had given him trouble on the playground the day before. These problems were discussed but we agreed that they did not warrant an extension of our contract. Daniel was very talkative in this session, speaking in long sentences without prompting. He appeared to be making progress on his own after the treatment sessions.

Our final session was a follow-up interview in his home. His mother said that one day Daniel had come home beaming and stated proudly that he had talked in class. I summarized the progress which he had made in sessions. After we agreed that the problem was alleviated, she related an incident in which she had tried to force him to talk. She had been called in by his nursery school teacher three years before because Daniel would not speak. She said she thought that he would talk in her presence, but when he did not, she ended up by giving him a spanking. This also failed to remedy the situation and she had felt guilty about the punishment. When I mentioned that we had never discovered the reason for his muteness, she suggested that perhaps he thought he talked like a girl because his voice was high. Daniel agreed with this but said that he had changed his mind after he began to talk in class. While his mother was satisfied with this explanation, she did not feel this was the whole reason. She concluded that she did not think he would have trouble talking in the future.

Follow-up checks during the rest of the school year showed that Daniel continued to talk during class, lunch, and play periods. No incidents of muteness were reported by his teacher.

This case, involving a young, almost nonverbal client, is typical of a number of client types and problem areas into which task-centered treatment has expanded. For many such cases effective use can be made of behavioral techniques within a task-centered practice framework. Techniques of this kind are being used increasingly within treatment systems, including the task-centered model, which are not ordinarily identified as "behavioral." For example, such methods as behavior rehearsal, modeling, guided practice, and environmental interventions to facilitate execution of particular behaviors are now an accepted part of task-centered technology (Reid, 1975; Tolson, chapter 7; Brown, chapter 15). Using the case of Daniel as an illustration, my intent is to elucidate a set of methods, including variations of those just mentioned, that are widely used in behavioral treatment and that appear to have particular utility for task-centered work. The methods to be discussed are: (1) obtaining a preintervention baseline and conducting a behavior analysis; (2) achieving successive approximations of desired task performance through guided, reinforced practice; (3) temporarily restructuring the environment to facilitate task performance; (4) helping the client work on tasks in the natural, as opposed to the "office," environment.

Baseline and behavior analysis. These procedures involved direct observation of the problem behavior (muteness), observation and analysis of the antecedents and consequences of that behavior in the environment in which it occurred, and concurrent observations of the behavior of peers and teacher in the classroom. The data obtained provided direct confirmation of the original referral information as well as an evaluation of the problem in its natural environment. The analysis was necessary for determining what relevant contingencies in the environment were maintaining the problem and also provided a preintervention assessment of the severity of the problem to which a postintervention assessment was compared. In this particular case, direct observation by the practitioner was possible because the problem behavior occurred frequently and was unaffected by the observer's presence. In other cases direct observation by the practitioner may not be possible because the problem behavior is "covert," occurs infrequently, or is affected by the presence of the practitioner. As a result it may be necessary for the client or another person in his environment to take a baseline. The baseline might include recording occurrences of the problem as well as a description of the situation or conditions in which it occurs.

Successive approximation through reinforced practice. This procedure was instrumental in helping the client to achieve the general task of talking in class. Successive approximations of this task varied along three major dimensions. The first included variations in types—i.e., girls, boys, teachers, practitioner—and number of people present during the sessions. This involved eliciting from the client a list of those people in whose presence he was least fearful of talking. The second dimension involved variation of the characteristics of speech required in each session. This dimension included the variations in: (1) loudness, from almost inaudible to normal volume; (2) length, from speaking in single words to speaking in long sentences; (3) spontaneity, from talking only with considerable prompting to self-initiated conversations. The third dimension included variations in the situations in which talking was required. This involved generalization of speech in the practitioner's office to the hallway and the classroom. The size of the increments along each of these dimensions was determined by Daniel's performance at each point in treatment. When Daniel failed to perform a specified task, the task was then broken down into a more easily performed task. This procedure made it possible for Daniel to succeed at each step of treatment. By this means, task performance progressed from infrequent, inadequate speech in limited situations to adequate, conversational speech in all school situations.

This process functioned as an integration of a basic sequence in the task-centered model: problem specification, formulation of tasks, overcoming obstacles to task performance, and evaluation of outcome. Each successive step involved an initial redefinition of the problem (e.g., speaking in the presence of three people but not four), which in turn indicated a new subtask, (speech in the presence of four people), as well as an intervention to facilitate overcoming obstacles to task completion (successive positioning of the fourth person's chair). The observed degree of task-completion provided outcome evaluation, which in turn resulted in redefinition of the problem. Thus client progress involved a continuous cyclical process of evaluation and intervention through the above mentioned four components via the behavioral methods employed by the practitioner.

The procedure enabled Daniel to practice task behavior in a nonthreatening environment, another factor that may have contributed to his progress. Reinforcements (candy and approval) provided incentives for the behavior and the practitioner's coaching helped him develop skill in carrying it out.

Restructuring the environment. Besides the changes in dimensions described above, the key characteristic of this technique was the active participation of peers and teacher in helping Daniel. This case emphasizes the desirability of involving others to help the client achieve specific tasks. Although the client's tasks are central, the coordination of tasks performed by others can be instrumental in producing problem reduction, a point also made and documented by Ewalt (chapter 2).

Intervention in the client's natural environment. The role of the practitioner was expanded from its usual limits in task-centered practice to include work with the client in his natural environment, that is, in the classroom. This strategy required the coordination of in-session and out-of-session tasks. Although frequently the problem and the client's situation dictate whether in-session or out-of-session tasks are emphasized, these two types of tasks can supplement each other, as in the present case. While out-of-session tasks more closely approach and sometimes function as "real life" situations, in-session tasks have the advantage of closer observation and direct input from the practitioner during task performance. Direct evaluation of task outcome by the practitioner is also easier for in-session tasks. In Daniel's case, I was able to take advantage of both in-session and out-of-session tasks by accompanying the client from "office" sessions into the classroom environment to observe and aid in task completion; I also gradually brought in elements of his "real world" environment into our sessions by bringing additional participants into the sessions.

Because gradual transitions from in-session to out-of-session were used, the transition from behavior rehearsals and modeling was also a gradual, systematic process. During the treatment sessions, there was not a clear-cut line where behavioral rehearsal stopped and actual task performance began.

Besides constituting a shift away from the traditional use of "office" sessions, Daniel's case also involved a move away from once-a-week sessions to sessions which were flexibly spaced. For example, three baseline observations were taken daily, followed two days later by a session with the client. Sessions also varied in length from twenty minutes to an hour.

Because the task-centered system involves the client's performance of a specified task directly related to problem reduction, these four methods were easily integrated into treatment. Typical task-centered interventions such as exploration, structuring, enhancing awareness, and encouragement were used throughout the treatment sessions.

A particular strength of the task-centered model was its stress on involving the client in defining the problem, securing his commitment to work on it, and spelling out agreed-upon problems and goals in a contract prior to treatment. These elements, which are being used increasingly, though by no means universally, in behavior modification, may help mobilize the client's own problem-solving efforts and help assure that treatment is used to help the client achieve his ends. This is more useful than bringing about conformity to imposed norms.

One possible drawback to the task-centered approach is its demand that the number of treatment sessions be limited and determined in advance. Although Daniel's case was completed in eight sessions (not counting the preintervention baselines and the follow-up sessions), it is quite possible that it could have required more sessions. How many might have been needed was difficult to determine at the beginning of treatment. Although the task-centered model makes allowances for extensions of treatment where circumstances warrant, additional work needs to be done, as Reid points out (chapter 4), in achieving a better fit between the planned brevity of the model and the requirements of certain kinds of cases.

As the task-centered model has evolved it has incorporated, as it was designed to do, new methods to broaden its range of application and to increase its effectiveness. Behavioral techniques have already contributed to the model and will continue to do so, particularly at the level of improving its technology for helping clients carry out the specific operational tasks which are so often at the cutting edge of change.

Chapter II

~~~~~~

Charles D. Garvin, Ph.D.

Strategies for Group
Work with Adolescents

Social workers who work with adolescents have frequently utilized group methods because of their awareness of the role of the peer group during this period. Thus, workers in correctional agencies developed "Positive Peer Culture" (Vorath and Brendtro, 1974), detached workers reached out to gangs, residential workers drew upon natural groupings in their settings, and school social workers attempted various types of support groups.

Despite the presumed potency of the group as a vehicle for facilitating adolescent growth, theorists and practitioners alike were not without some concerns regarding the function of the peer culture. As one writer indicated, "the youth subculture is a segmental and ritual pattern which many youth enact in the spirit of a game while still retaining private standards and goals at variance with it" (Turner, 1964, p. 146).

Workers nevertheless cherished the rapidity with which adolescent groups developed cohesiveness, the strength with which group norms were upheld (if they were "pro-social"), and the willingness of adolescents to take emotional risks as they revealed their activities, even their fantasies, in early stages of group development. Adolescents, they found, communicated in groups with an openness not usually developed as quickly in adult groups.

Task-centered group work with adolescents holds the promise of utilizing the many assets which group experience in general offers for this age group, while avoiding some of its negative aspects. Individuals can profit from the support the group provides, the gratification of acceptance from peers, and the stimulation to explore new ways of coping. More important, however, is that in task-centered work, these processes are used for the purpose of accomplishing tasks related to individualized life goals.

An example of this from a school-based, task-centered group was the situation of John M. He wished to pursue a career as a dancer, even though he was cognizant of the ridicule which some of his peers might direct at him for a "female" occupation. Nevertheless, because of the kinds of contracts and norms which emerge in task-centered groups, he reported on progress in securing training and was complimented by other members for his persistence in this regard. They even had suggestions on how he could respond to his critics.

Performing tasks comes naturally to adolescents since they must engage in planful action in order to embark on new roles. For example, the adolescent may seek out information about an occupation, may volunteer or take employment in institutions related to work aspirations, or may take aptitude tests and discuss results with appropriate resources. A large subset of tasks relate to completing school requirements in furtherance of a career. Those who drop out of school have analogous tasks to secure training or apprenticeship opportunities.

An array of tasks also confronts adolescents as they resolve questions of sex identity, intimacy, and heterosexual or even homosexual interactions. These tasks include affiliating with social groups, learning skills for approaching and maintaining relationships with peers of both sexes, and determining the quality of the relationships for which they are ready.

Many of the tasks which adolescents undertake must also be used to manipulate aspects of the environment including the family, the school, and the criminal justice system. Adolescents who are successful in pursuing life careers must secure changes in family rules, must at times help institutions to accommodate to their needs, and must avoid some of the dehumanizing effects of organizations in our society. This can be accomplished by tasks framed in such a way that adolescents take responsibility for personal changes, when necessary, but also learn how to secure changes in the situation. Thus, many adolescent tasks are accomplished in order to secure accommodations from the environment.

Thus, in a group in a child guidance clinic, one member chose the task of setting up a discussion with her mother about curfew hours. She also selected the subtask of discussing with her mother feelings of frustration in the discussion rather than breaking off the dialogue. Another adolescent, who felt certain school rules were very unfair, chose the task of writing a petition to the school asking for a rule change and asking other students to endorse the petition.

One of the strengths of the task approach is that it is not limited to a particular set of techniques. Thus, the practitioner can develop or draw upon intervention strategies appropriate to the client group while still adhering to the task-centered framework. He can make use of task-centered methods to help clients identify tasks related to problems, carry through on these tasks, and evaluate both the degree of task accomplishment and the degree of problem reduction. The purpose of the remainder of this paper is to suggest such strategies for task-centered work with adolescent groups. The concept of strategy means a unified series of actions carried out by the worker to achieve a specific result. Thus the use of role play, a problem solving discussion, or a demonstration is a strategy. For purposes of analysis, as well as consistency with the model, we will discuss strategies in relationship to (1) problem selection; (2) group composition; (3) group formation; (4) task specification and (5) task implementation.

Problem Selection

As has been suggested elsewhere (Garvin, 1974) task-centered group work should start with an initial interview with the potential group member so that members can begin to select tasks quickly in the group setting—a necessity for short-term groups. With adolescents, the major focus of such interviews should be to facilitate the choice of group as opposed to individual treatment and to explain the rationale for task-centered work. While an overview of problems can be secured, unless a referral has been made and *accepted* for very explicit problems, adolescents will be strongly influenced on choice of problem by the expectations of other group members (see Rooney, chapter 12). This can create a problem for the practitioner in view of the strong commitment of task-centered workers to self-determination.

For example, in one adolescent group, in a residential setting, an adolescent originally talked with a worker about discussing in the group his problems with finding a girl friend. During the first meeting, he perceived the members as socially sophisticated and likely to be skeptical about his problem. For this reason, he indicated he wanted to work on a problem relating to school achievement.

Several strategies are suggested here to deal with the issue of self-determination in problem selection with adolescents. One is to borrow from *Positive Peer Culture* (Vorrath and Brendtro, 1974, p. 36) the successful idea of a "vernacular of problems." This consists of short lists of problems developed for the specific client population and using language easily understood by youth. Some examples of the terms from "Positive Peer Culture" are "low self-image," "aggravates others," "alcohol or drug problem," and "inconsiderate of self." Such lists accomplish several purposes. One is to identify for the adolescent a suggested range of possible areas for selection of tasks. Implied, also, is the idea that these problems are solvable through accompanying tasks. Finally, the terms used serve to facilitate the members' communication with others in the group and with the group worker regarding the choice of a problem. By presenting a range of categories, the expectation is expressed that the individual will choose the most meaningful one. Youth engaged in task-centered work can, of course, expand the list to meet their own needs, but if the lists are composed by members of the group, they may help most clients in the setting with identifying and choosing a problem on which to work.

The problem categories developed by Reid and Epstein can initially serve as a basis for developing categories for presentation to adolescent

(Reid and Epstein, 1972). Thus, arguments with parents and battles with other teen-agers are suggested by "interpersonal conflict," and "lack of friends" is related to "dissatisfaction in social relations." Many adolescent problems in school can be specified under "difficulties in role performance." Again, because school is such a central institution in adolescence, "problems with formal organizations" can be related to tasks to change school rules, tasks to create new school opportunities (e.g., new courses), and tasks to create new social situations (e.g., occasions for more interactions between ethnic groups or sexes).

In any case, it will be useful in many task-centered adolescent groups to have a discussion in the first session about how the group will affect each member as he or she seeks to select problems and define tasks. The worker can recognize, with the members, that there may be some reluctance to be "different" from other members in making these selections. The members can then be helped to define ways in which they can support differences within the group.

In the school group mentioned earlier, the worker used the example of the student who wanted to be a dancer to initiate a fuller discussion of the importance of guarding against pressures to conform. The reasons for these pressures, in terms of security as well as reaction to parental control, were amply explored.

Group Composition

In a previous paper, I suggested that task-centered groups be composed so that tasks of members will be similar. In a time-limited framework members will then be most helpful to each other in specifying and accomplishing such tasks (Garvin, 1974).

In settings such as schools and residential institutions, the youths are often familiar with each other's problems through the communication channels existing among them. Because youths who are already concerned about one another will be likely to give considerable mutual support for task accomplishment, an alternate compositional strategy is to involve the youths themselves in the process of choosing members. The worker can also place members in the group and can share this prerogative with members. Skillfully handled, this may have the twofold consequence of enhancing group cohesion and facilitating out-of-meeting support for task fulfillment. As members are also exposed to some of the same environmental stimuli, they may help each other in assessing the feasibility of choosing particular tasks, thus selecting them more appropriately. In the school group noted above, the members encouraged a student to drop a particular course of study and related tasks because of their awareness of the prerequisites for the course, knowledge which the student in question lacked.

One of the controversial issues in forming adolescent groups is whether to include both sexes. Unless the tasks of group members relate to resolving heterosexual relationship problems, it is our experience that groups of one sex begin to work on tasks earlier and devote more time to task accomplishment. Coed groups of adolescents stimulate their members to deal with heterosexual relationships. Energy is invested in maintaining postures consistent with whatever image the member wishes to maintain with the opposite sex. Thus, some boys project a "silent" image with girls; some girls appear unconcerned about problems with boys, and so forth. These facades may not be as strictly maintained in single sex groups so that task-centered processes will be facilitated.

Group Formation

In some adolescent groups, the members are relatively comfortable in identifying their problems and choosing specific tasks. These are likely to be groups in schools where admitting performance difficulties and improving academic performances are reinforced by both school personnel and some peers. The "pay-off" is also clear in terms of grades, diplomas, and the promise of jobs.

Acknowledgment of other types of adolescent problems may provoke more anxiety. These include relationship difficulties with the opposite sex, drug usage, and criminal acts. Family problems sometimes fall into this category. While the worker should begin a task-centered group without being defensive about asking members to relate problems, this direct approach may not work. The worker then should employ a strategy to overcome this. One approach is to ask each member to talk about the things in his or her life which led to the member seeking help—an abbreviated life story. The worker can then model for the members, at least at first, the identification of problems uncovered by this means. When this tends to be lengthy, after suitable instruction, the worker can use the "consulting pair" technique described by Rooney (chapter 12). In this technique, members pair off and help one another. The worker then functions as a consultant to each pair.

Because of the powerful effects of norms in adolescent groups, the worker must strive in the first meetings to establish norms which will facilitate task work. It is relatively simple for the group worker to state rules related to attendance, working on tasks, and helping others. The more difficult job is to identify and challenge subtle resistances to these expectations. These include "putting down" of other members, boasting as opposed to a more modest self-appreciation for accomplishments, strong competition which is experienced as defeating by some members, and withholding information relevant to charting progress on tasks. The worker can identify the existence of such resistances through the failure of some members to work on tasks, withdrawal of members from interactions in the group, emotional reactions indicative of anxiety or depression, reluctance to come to meetings, and frequent demands for the attention of the worker. Hopefully, the worker can identify member actions early which lead to these consequences and can model the kind of concern for the feelings of *all* members which is demonstrated in awareness of these behaviors.

Because adolescents seek role models among adults, the group worker with adolescent groups takes on a meaning different from workers with other age groups. The members will frequently take their cues from what the worker does as well as what he says. For this reason, as Rooney suggests, the worker can define his or her task as helping the group and can chart progress in achieving subtasks related to this. The worker can go even further, however, by asking members to suggest better ways of accomplishing these tasks. This association of strength with seeking help can be important to teenagers. This behavior from the worker will also help in short-term groups to maintain cohesiveness, because the members will be more likely to identify with a worker who is open and nonpatronizing toward them.

Task-Specification

A crucial part of this model is the selection of a task which the group member believes will help resolve the problem. The likelihood this will happen and that the task will be completed depends upon the care with which the task described is chosen. Detail is essential so that progress can be monitored, and so that the individual knows what he or she has undertaken to do.

Adolescents who enter task groups, particularly those without preconceptions as to what "treatment" is, are often creative in developing tasks. For example, a youth whose task was to complete course assignments was encouraged by other members of the group to fulfill the assignment in an innovative way, thus enhancing his motivation for task accomplishment. He prepared a report of a visit to the offices of a unit of government which was more interesting to him than a summary of a chapter in a book. Social workers can be very successful in stimulating adolescent to choose creative tasks and this can add to the potency of a task approach.

Instruments can be developed to help the adolescent plan the details of task accomplishment. One such is a "work sheet" which poses such questions as the sequence of task activities in one column and the conditions which other persons or institutions will have to meet in the other. Thus the adolescent whose task it is to fulfill the requirements for termination of probation will list the things for him to do in one column, and in the other column the responses needed from significant others who must evaluate these behaviors in order to make recommendations. On these worksheets, the adolescent can also list rewards which he grants himself or which are presented by others as subtasks. When these sheets are created with some artistry, this will also appeal to many adolescents.

Task Implementation

In addition to strategies for task implementation which may be useful with any task-centered group, some procedures must be selected in work with adolescents which take into consideration the characteristics of this age. These characteristics not only include such emotional responses as mood swings and regressive behavior, but also the social position which adolescents find themselves in within our society. This social position places them severely at the mercy of such institutions as schools and juvenile courts while limiting their opportunities for autonomy, such as that provided by meaningful employment.

In view of these characteristics of adolescents and their situations, several perspectives should guide any strategy. In terms of emotional considerations, the worker should be able to display a reasonable optimism, should be especially empathetic to mood and should not be easily discouraged by temporary violations of contracts. In terms of situational constraints, the worker both on behalf of and with the adolescent must be prepared to intervene in the various social systems of which the adolescent is a part. Frequently, fulfillment of tasks will rely upon teachers, parents, and other authority persons assuming tasks in relationship to the adolescent, and the worker must be prepared to secure these. Task-centered group workers with adolescents have advocated teacher recognition of task attainment, have helped parents provide conditions for performing tasks, and have secured institutional resources required for some tasks.

In addition, the tools used in meetings to help members with tasks can often include various types of simulations to enhance interest (Boocock and Schild, 1970). Simulations have been devised which illuminate ways of changing institutions; others on a "careers" model help to identify task sequences related to employment. While workers have used simple role playing to identify problems as well as practice tasks, more complex role playing in the form of scenarios can help adolescents to think about overcoming barriers to accomplish tasks. Adolescents also sometimes have difficulty fulfilling tasks because of value conflicts, and value clarification exercises may be helpful here (Simon, Howe, and Kirschenbaum, 1972).

As noted above, for some adolescents considerable support will have to be supplied to overcome discouragement. While this can be offered by teachers and parents who fulfill their related tasks, it is occasionally insufficient. The consulting pair idea can then be extended into a "buddy system" so that adolescents can call each other to secure empathy, encouragement, and problem-solving help. Some members may even take the assignment, when this is mutually agreeable, of initiating a call to the person experiencing a particularly difficult task attainment problem. The worker can also be used in this way and can recommend the most effective alternative for delivering such help.

Various activities are likely to be undertaken by members to facilitate task attainment, such as offering support, maintaining charts, and securing information needed by other members. The worker can use these assignments to bring fringe members closer to the group, to reinforce the learning of some members, and to regroup cliques whose presence is detrimental to task accomplishment.

Finally, the worker must seek to understand the effects of institutions upon the members of the task-centered group. The adolescent can learn that he or she is not only expected by adults to change to meet social requirements, but is fully entitled to seek to alter these requirements. The adolescent who seeks to create a more appropriate classroom situation not only can achieve that, but in the process, learns to plan rationally, to compromise when necessary, and to communicate more effectively. There are few clear-cut cases in life of problems solved only by personal *or* situational change and the adolescent will often see the hypocrisy of polarities here.

Conclusion

In this paper, a summary has been presented of some of the traits of adolescents which should be considered in work with task-centered groups. In reviewing this discussion, it appears that many of the tasks described for adolescents and the model for dealing with these may be relevant for all adolescents. For this reason, the idea of teaching the task concept as part of the educational program in secondary schools can be tested out as a mental health measure. Teachers can assist students in identifying and fulfilling tasks and can establish mutual aid systems. Under this arrangement, social workers will function as consultants and task-centered groups outside of the classroom will be reserved for adolescents not in the school system (e.g. residential treatment; training schools) or for those with problems related to confidential matters, such as severe difficulties in coping or other problems clearly beyond the purview of the school. In these cases, however, the youth will have been prepared by the school system for making use of a task-centered approach.

References

Boocock, Sarane S., and Schild, E. O., eds. 1970. *Simulation games in learning.* Beverly Hills, Cal.: Sage Publications.

Garvin, Charles. 1974. "Task centered group work." *Social Services Review* 48:494–507.

Garvin, Charles; Reid, William J.; and Epstein, Laura. 1976. "Task-centered group work." In *Theoretical approaches to social work with small groups.* Edited by H. Northen and R. W. Roberts. New York: Columbia University Press.

Reid, William J., and Epstein, Laura. 1972. *Task-centered casework.* New York: Columbia University Press.

Simon, Sidney B.; Howe, Leland W.; and Kirschenbaum, Howard. 1972. *Values clarification: A handbook of practical strategies for teachers and students.* New York: Hart.

Turner, Ralph H. 1964. *The social context of ambition.* San Francisco: Chandler Publishing Co.

Vorrath, Harry H., and Brendtro, Larry K. 1974. *Positive peer culture.* Chicago: Aldine Publishing Co.

Chapter 12

~~~~~~

Ronald Rooney, M.A.

Adolescent Groups
in Public Schools

This paper will describe clinical trials of the task-centered group work model (Garvin, Reid, and Epstein, 1976). Between January and June 1974 three groups were organized in an elementary school. Later, from October 1974 to June 1975, five groups were formed in a high school. In addition to the author, there were three other social workers as co-leaders.[1] Both schools were located in a south side Chicago neighborhood. The group members were similar to the general school population: a mixture of middle class, working class, and poor children. In both schools and in the groups, black children were in the majority. Seventeen boys and girls, from 12 to 14 years of age, participated in the elementary school groups. In the five high school groups there were 26 boys and girls.

---

[1] The author is indebted to the following collaborators in the task-centered group work project: Susan Annis, Ellen Washington, and Timothy Plant.

Target Problems

THE ELEMENTARY SCHOOL

The "Boys' Group" members were drawn from the sixth, seventh, and eighth grades: 3 black, 1 Mexican-American, 2 white children. Four boys identified target problems of academic underachievement. The fifth chose to work on difficulties in getting along with his teachers and peers; the sixth selected poor school attendance.

Two "Borderline Groups" were added in March 1974. The members were 11 eighth graders, identified by teachers as unlikely to graduate in June. "Borderline I" was composed of 3 white girls and 2 black boys. "Borderline II" was composed of 1 white girl, 1 black girl, and 4 black boys. All "Borderlines" were failing in two major subjects. All chose academic failure as their target problem.

THE HIGH SCHOOL

All the high school groups were composed of both boys and girls. The first two groups began in October 1974, recruited from a sophomore homeroom containing pupils who had failed three or more major subjects in freshman year. Sophomore Group I had 4 members and Sophomore Group II had 7. After these groups had made progress, the sophomores recommended that groups be formed to help freshmen known to be in trouble because of failing grades. A recruitment drive resulted in 15 freshman members, distributed into 3 groups who met for five weeks. Freshmen were admitted to the groups if they had failed one subject in the last marking period. All the students in all the groups chose "failing grades" as their target problem.

Group Formation

Social workers solicited referrals from teachers, explaining the objectives and procedures of the project. Four elementary pupils heard of the groups and referred themselves. Preliminary interviews in the elementary school were conducted with both children and their parents. In the high school, the preliminary interviews were only with the student. The project practitioners were of the opinion that involving parents of that age group might undermine the independence strivings of these older adolescents.

All preliminary interviews included the following:

1. Reason for referral
2. Reason for the student's becoming a member
3. Interpretation to the member by the staff of the four basic group rules (attending all sessions on time; working on tasks; helping others with their tasks; keeping confidential what went on in group sessions)
4. Explanation of the purpose of the group (to work on tasks to reduce the student's target problem)
5. Decision on whether or not to join the group
6. Tentative formulation of target problem
7. Agreement on the number of sessions for the group.

The usual number of sessions was 12. The two elementary school "Borderline" groups began late in the school year and were able to complete only 6 sessions. In forming the groups, it was considered that homogeneity of target problems was essential (Garvin, Reid, and Epstein, 1976). When a pupil wanted to work on a problem other than failing grades, or in addition to that problem, he was offered individual sessions only or individual sessions in addition to the group. Experience suggested that 5 to 8 members were the appropriate numbers for these task-centered groups.

Treatment Procedures

Class schedules determined the hours at which groups could meet and their length. The flow of school "breaks," such as Christmas, spring holiday, the grade marking times, and the school calendar provided natural closures for the groups' duration.

The treatment structure followed the task-centered casework model (Reid and Epstein, 1972). Special adaptations of that model were developed to take into account the conditions of the setting, the developmental stage of the group members, and the effects of group process. These techniques were: visual aids, pupil advocacy, practitioner task contracts, consulting pairs, and indigenous leaders.

VISUAL AIDS

Visual aids are well established in teaching methodology. The device used in these task-centered groups was large sheets of newsprint. Each student made out a sheet specifying his own academic problem. On the left side the member wrote his tasks. On the right side he wrote what he had been able to do or what difficulties he had encountered. At each session, task work was reviewed: the task was scratched if completed, or new tasks were written.

These "task sheets" were helpful in reducing vagueness, pinpointing obstacles, providing the basis for discussion and task alteration, and sharing information necessary for the group to work. They were also helpful in making it possible for each member to get attention to his situation within the brief time which was available.

ADVOCACY AND PRACTITIONER TASK CONTRACTS

Group members frequently attributed their problems to the behavior of others. Teachers and school attendance officers were held particularly responsible for the student's problems in the high school. Following the task-centered model, the member's ascription of responsibility to others was accepted, unless blatantly erroneous. As work was begun on the students' terms, most of them eventually were able to take personal responsibility where it was justified. This procedure avoided unnecessary confrontations. Adolescents are uniquely resentful of an adult practitioner who discredits their own perception of a situation.

There were, in fact, obstacles to task work in the school environment. The most frequent difficulty arose in the high school. Pressured teachers often did not take time to explain work in detail to failing students. When students doing poor work began to cut class to avoid difficulty, they could not return without a readmission paper secured from the attendance officer. Often students became locked into continuation of class cutting because of their stress when confronted with long lines waiting outside the attendance office. Students who could tolerate the wait might then face a well-intentioned officer who delivered a lecture on the evils of cutting and the values of an education. After getting himself through all that, the student often received a cold reception from the teacher when he presented his readmission paper.

To cut down these negative experiences, the social work staff often accompanied the student to see the teacher and attendance personnel, or, if warranted, the practitioner would confer with school staff alone. The students placed a high value on advocacy on their behalf. Usually, it took no more than one contact with a teacher to get the information needed to start the student on a corrective program. Teachers were exceptionally cooperative when they found a failing student doing something about his problem. Attendance officers were likely to dispense with the lecture when they saw that the "offender" was "in good hands."

Advocacy actions were planned in the group sessions. As a result, social work staff began to make task sheets for themselves, posted on the wall, to indicate what they were to do between sessions. This practice seemed fair to the members. It provided a means for the practitioner to model task work and see how to proceed when tasks were not done.

CONSULTING PAIRS

Consulting pairs consist of two members who agree to help one another identify problems, devise tasks, and get tasks done. Dividing into subgroups is a frequent practice in group work (Lieberman, 1972; Rose, 1972; Lawrence and Sundel, 1972). The purpose of subgrouping, in general, is to partialize problems in more detail than time allows in the whole group session, and to insure the participation of all members. Additional purposes of consulting pairs in task-centered groups are: achieving specificity of target problems and tasks, clear identification of obstacles, and monitoring task achievement. Originally it was expected that the same two members would remain together throughout the contract. However, considerable switching of pairs occurred because of absences, personal preferences, and members' interest in getting to know everyone. One advantageous result of this process was strong group cohesion. Task work did not appear to be impaired by switching.

The standard structure for sessions was as follows:
In the first part, all members were present. The practitioner set the focus. In early sessions attention would be centered on clarifying the

individual member's target problems. This strong lead prevented the consultant member of the pair from moving into irrelevant areas. When the group was at an early stage, the practitioner modeled the consultant role, followed by a role play in which members practiced the role. This process usually was repeated several times. Guidelines for consultation were written on sheets posted on the wall. Depending on the phase of the group, these consultant guidelines were: to find out what prevented the member from doing his tasks; to give a reward for accomplishments; to find out if tasks should be changed and how they should be changed; to evaluate the group and practitioner.

Practitioners would look in on the pairs during the middle period of a session to ascertain needs and to provide help. At the end of the session the group would again meet as a whole. A summary was made, and a general direction given for the time between sessions. The high school students adapted to the consulting pair technique readily. The younger children in the elementary school needed more "trouble shooting" from the practitioners.

INDIGENOUS LEADERS

In the high school, "junior leaders" were recruited from the entire school population. It was believed that a corps of junior leaders would both add manpower and peer influence to augment task achievement. A notice was put on the school bulletin board stating that the social work staff would train and provide experience to upper-grade students who were considering a career in a human service field. Thirty pupils applied. The 10 selected were those who could meet all the criteria: attend all sessions of a three-hour training course, secure parental permission for participating, attend all sessions of the task-centered group to which he would be assigned, agree to carry out all tasks assigned to help members of the freshman groups. The 10 junior leaders who accepted these conditions emerged as an enthusiastic, dependable group.

A curriculum was drawn up for the junior leader training which was part didactic and part experiential. Some members, who had completed a sequence of task-centered group work, attended the training sessions as resource persons. This part of the project achieved positive recognition throughout the school. The junior leaders became valued role models for the freshmen who sought them out continuously between group sessions. The following two group summaries, one from the elementary school and one from the high school, will illustrate how these groups carried out their work.

BORDERLINE GROUP II: ELEMENTARY SCHOOL

Teachers and administrators in the school were concerned about the high number of students in danger of failing the eighth grade. Failure would mean attending summer school or repeating the grade before moving to high school. The principal compiled a list of all "potential failures" and notified the children and their parents of the problem.

The social work staff saw the potential of forming a task-centered group to help students marshal their efforts toward passing. Administrators and teachers were also favorable to the idea. Social workers asked the teachers to refer students who had a possibility of graduating if they made a considerable effort in the final month of school. It was stressed that students should not be referred who had no or only a very small possibility of graduating no matter how much effort they expended. Fifteen students were referred. Eleven accepted interviews. As parents and students had just received official "warning," an invitation to join a task-centered group to improve chances of graduating was welcomed.

In the preliminary interview, practitioners stressed that membership in the group was no guarantee of graduation. However, they relayed the teachers' commitment to cooperate with the task efforts of those students who joined the group. All of the students were worried about failing and saw the group as a potential aid. Parents were enthusiastic.

In the first session, the common problem facing the students was discussed. Consulting pairs helped one another quickly identify the most prominent academic problem. Members were directed to a common task: to compile a list of what had to be completed successfully in order to pass each subject in which they were failing. Teachers agreed to help students make the list. Members were given weekly assignment cards on which they were to keep a record of each assignment turned in. They gave the card to the teacher who checked off the work that she received.

In subsequent sessions, assignment cards and member reports on tasks completed were reviewed in consulting pairs. The common prob-

lem was academic failure. Each member had his own individually specified subjects and unique problems with the subjects. Some students
were failing math but passing English, and vice versa. The pair partner
was often able to identify the next steps required to complete the work
and to give helpful tips. Task sheets were posted on the walls of the
meeting room. At the beginning of each session, members would
record what they had completed of their tasks from the previous week.
By the end of the session, the members would record their new tasks
on the sheet. By the third session, consulting pair work was being completed in about twenty minutes, leaving greater time for group discussion. Discussions were lively but stayed close to the common theme of
graduation.

Frank was a star basketball player. He played basketball after school
until supper time (around 7:30 P.M.). After supper, he was often so
tired that he would sleep for a few hours and get up to study later. His
partner in the consulting pair tried to help him deal with the obstacle
of needing more time to spend on his homework in order to graduate,
but no solution was found. When the pair reported to the group, the
practitioners invited the other members to help Frank. One of the
members suggested that Frank would be playing basketball in the
eighth grade next year if he did not "get his act together." Frank re-
torted that no one could make him stop playing basketball, that he
could do with his life whatever he wanted. Katey chimed in, agreeing
with Frank that it was his life and his choice. She added that he was
choosing to fail the eighth grade if he did not find more time to study.
Frank agreed to try to cut down his afternoon playing to two afternoons
a week.

In the next session, the group worked with Katey who found her
schoolwork boring and much preferred to read novels. Frank asked if
she could do any book reports on novels she had read. No, she replied,
it was too late in the year to get credit for them. Darryl asked if it
might be better if she studied for an hour or two *before* she read her
novels. The group convinced her to give Darryl's idea a try. Katey
tried out her task and began to get her required work done.

Johnny was a problem in the group. Though a good consultant, quick
to suggest subtasks for himself and others, he procrastinated in carrying
out his own. The group thought he could do his work. In the next to

last session (the fifth), Johnny came in triumphantly. He marched purposefully to his task sheet to record that he had turned in his autobiography (due a month earlier), completed his science experiments, and studied for the required American History exam.

Members responded to the task format at different rates. Myron and Roselle completed most of their tasks regularly, from the first session. Frank and Katey did much better after the group prodded them. Johnny roused himself near the end. Jerry did not make the last minute push. The obstacles blocking him were identified and dealt with one by one. He had to baby-sit for his sister after school while his older brothers were allowed to go outside. His mother's cooperation was enlisted and she arranged for his brothers' help while Jerry was given more time to study. He started too late and did not complete all that was required.

The practitioners were notified of the graduation results on the day of the last session. Neither the students nor the parents had yet been told. The practitioners reviewed with the group that there had been no guarantee of graduation. Everyone could be pleased with their efforts and the benefits could be taken from no one. The practitioners gave each member a card showing his results. Next, the consulting pairs met to share whatever they wished about the results. Only Jerry had not passed. Jerry's partner was supportive and Jerry did not reveal any overt upset. Johnny was overcome with relief and cried. Katey and Myron passed both of their problem subjects. Frank passed math, was reported greatly improved in social studies, but still failing English. Roselle passed math and social studies while continuing to fail science. Johnny barely passed history, failed English. Jerry failed both his target subjects.

Sophomore Group II

The school had three special homerooms composed of students who failed three or more major subjects the previous year. Homeroom teachers were to give special help and encouragement to these students in the "demoted" division, as it was called. The students were entitled to priorities in access to services from the counselors and social workers. Such a congregation of "problem" students provided few role models. It may have solidified a "failure" identity. Many members mentioned the stigma involved in being members of the "dumbell" division.

The author suggested to the division teacher that the students might benefit from a task-centered group to help them cope better with the academic environment. The teacher was skeptical. She had previous experience with groups and had not found them beneficial. Nevertheless, she consented to my speaking to the class. Students were also skeptical. One said, "Just because we messed up in school doesn't mean that there is something wrong with us!" Several students indicated some interest, but few actually came for a preliminary interview. Sophomore Group I was formed with four members. One dropped out and one was added. Members of Sophomore Group I passed the word that the group was "alright." Recruitment for a second group was more enthusiastically received.

Seven students came for preliminary interviews and joined Sophomore Group II. The two white members, Larry and Becky, left the group. Larry had not attended classes for several months. He reached his sixteenth birthday and was dropped from school. Becky was eighteen and decided that she would rather drop out of school and study for a high school equivalency degree than remain a sophomore. "Popeye" joined but came only one time after the group had been reduced to three girls.

The three remaining girls (Barbara, Veronica, and Toni) were already friends. They cut classes frequently and were not passing any subjects. Advocacy interventions helped Barbara and Veronica to be readmitted to classes. Alice, Veronica's sister, attended the next session and declared her intention of joining. She had problems similar to those of the other three, though not in the "demoted" division. She had been impressed by the help given Veronica to have her readmitted to class.

These four became the group. The four, or pairs of them, often cut classes together. An early task, suggested by Toni, was to walk Alice to the door of her history class until she became courageous enough to go alone. Barbara was always late for school. Veronica offered to telephone her to wake her up. Alice had been missing one class for three months and another for six weeks. The group wanted her to try to get back into both, but I advised her that she try to go to the more recently cut class first. All of these tasks were completed.

The members did not like school and saw little hope of much academic improvement. In the consulting pairs, they were asked to talk about their plans after high school. Next they discussed what they might do while in school to further those plans. Finally, they specified what they might be able to do during this school year and the last six weeks of the group to aid them in their quest. Veronica wanted to become a switchboard operator. Toni wanted to become a nurse. Barbara and Alice wanted to become secretaries.

Alice told the group that she had a stenography test book which she was studying on her own. The group helped relate her occupational plans to her current lack of attendance and failure in English. A stenographer would need to know grammar to be able to transcribe business letters. As Alice saw the connection, she became more motivated to start back in English. She went with the practitioner to see her English teacher about being readmitted to class. The teacher said that Alice had no chance of passing for the year, and would not be able to understand what the class was doing after having been absent six weeks. The teacher recommended that Alice forget about English for this year. Alice had role-played, in the group, the possibility of her teacher taking this position. She had already decided that she wanted to be readmitted even if she could not pass. Her persistence seemed to surprise the teacher, who agreed to allow Alice back, with the specific understanding that she would fail, nevertheless. Alice attended the class regularly thereafter and made plans for taking English during the summer.

All four members were readmitted to classes and reduced cutting. Only Veronica, however, raised grades significantly.

Outcomes

Information was secured about the results of the task-centered groups from members, teachers, and observations made by the practitioners. Teachers were always interviewed at the end of each group. All the groups were visible to a good many persons in the schools. Principals and teachers participated in discussions about the purposes and procedures of the task-centered groups. All of the important school personnel had consented to trying out these types of groups and observed the pupils continuously. Teachers knew what the members' tasks were, and they had made agreements with the staff and the pupils to take certain actions to support task achievement. Without giving it the name, teachers made contracts, as had the practitioners, to do specified task work on behalf of the group members in their class. Principals and teachers wanted the groups to get results. They were kept informed periodically about task progress, or its absence. Many informal contacts maintained their interest.

In general, not all tasks were accomplished nor did all group members improve. There was enough improvement, however, to be impressive to teachers who had labored with these students with little tangible reward. In the high school, the teachers and principals were moved to hold an awards ceremony for students who had been in the task-centered groups. Since the school year ends in June, it is customary to give prizes or certificates to recognize student achievement at that time. A ceremony was held in the assembly room to honor the task-centered group members. Parents, teachers, and guests came. Group members spoke to describe their experiences. The students posted their task sheets on the wall for all to see. A videotape of a group session was played for the teachers and parents. The principal made a brief address giving recognition to the efforts of the group members. There could be little question that the consumers had judged the task-centered groups and found them good.

Some of the individual results give a more complete picture of the outcomes. In the Boys' Group at the elementary school, one pupil whose target problem was poor grades in English did, in fact, improve his performance. The student who was having difficulties in relationships with his teacher and peers was getting along slightly better. A student doing poor academic work was successful in accomplishing his main tasks—to turn in his homework—but his grades did not improve. The remaining three members did not complete their tasks or raise their grades.

The two Borderline groups, the six-week effort in the elementary school to graduate 11 failing students, was spectacularly successful. Nine graduated. Five members brought failing grades in two subjects up to a passing level. Four members brought grades in one subject up to passing. Two failed, even though they had completed many of their tasks. Responding to an evaluation questionnaire, the teachers stated their belief that substantial change had occurred in most members.

A year later, 8 of the 11 students were located and answered a follow-up questionnaire. Four responded that they "could not have graduated" without the groups. The remaining 4 thought they had been "considerably helped." All 8 were concluding their freshman year in high school when they answered the questionnaire, and all reported doing satisfactory or better work in school. One of these former Borderline members became a junior leader of a task-centered group in the high school.

In the high school, the Sophomore groups drawn from the "demoted division" lost 3 members. One dropped out of the group; 1 was dropped by the school when he reached 16 years of age; 1 girl, 18 years old, dropped out of school altogether. Of the remaining 8, 3 made grade improvements of one letter in their target subjects. Seven increased their attendance in classes. Of the 30 students assigned by the school to the special homeroom for failing students, only 15 survived the term. In other words, half the students in the special homeroom had dropped out of school, transferred elsewhere, or been dropped by the school at 16 years of age. All 11 of the task-centered group members who completed the twelve-week contract were in school at the end of the term. That fact was impressive to the school personnel who were watching the program. Although this result should not be ignored, one must be cautious about attributing school continuance to the groups. Other factors undoubtedly played a role.

The evaluation questionnaire given to the sophomores revealed that Sophomore Group I liked the group moderately. They liked the total group discussions but disliked the consulting pairs technique. Sophomore Group II was a natural group of four girls who were already friends. They liked the group very much and were satisfied with all the techniques used. Twelve of the original 15 members of the three freshman groups completed the five-week contract. Outcome information for these groups is incomplete. The groups ended with the close of the school year, before the information was obtained. What is known is that at least 3 students raised their letter grades one increment in the subject in which they had been failing. Increased effort was observed in most of the members. All 11 group members completed evaluation questionnaires at the last session. These students were enthusiastic about the groups and felt they had been substantially helped. The favorite techniques were working with the junior leaders in consulting pairs and whole group discussions.

Conclusion

This review of the structure, processes, and outcomes of eight task-centered groups with adolescent members suggests that the model is feasible with this age group in school settings. The adaptations developed during this project were intended to make the most of the limited time. They concentrated on problems of great significance to the students. The adaptations used peer influence, which is exceedingly important to adolescents. It is likely that the inclusion of teachers, officials, and parents of the elementary school children strengthened the ability of the students to concentrate on task achievement. The high visibility of the project and the interest of the teachers and principals seemed to have given the group members the sense that they were doing something important. They were recognized and rewarded appropriately.

Task-centered groups or any variety of counseling are no panacea for pupils with educational and behavior problems or for school systems with enormous social, educational, and administrative problems. The students in these groups were not "creamed." They were students considered in the system to have difficult problems, although not the most difficult. Gains were modest but real. It is hoped that future work can be accompanied by a systematic research program directed toward technical specification and understanding of what practices work best under what conditions.

Ronald Rooney

References

Garvin, Charles D.; Reid, William J.; and Epstein, Laura. 1976. "Task-centered group work." In *Theoretical approaches to social work with small groups.* Edited by Helen Northen and Robert W. Roberts. New York: Columbia University Press.

Lawrence, Harry, and Sundel, Martin. 1972. "Behavior modification in adult groups." *Social Work* 17(2):34–43.

Lieberman, Morton A. 1972. "Behavior and impact of leaders." In *New perspectives on encounter groups.* Edited by Lawrence N. Solomon and Betty Berzon. San Francisco: Jossey-Bass, Inc.

Reid, William J., and Epstein, Laura. 1972. *Task-centered casework.* New York: Columbia University Press.

Rose, Sheldon. 1972. *Treating children in groups.* San Francisco: Jossey-Bass, Inc.

Chapter 13

~~~~~~

Michael Bass, M.A.

Toward a Model of Treatment
for Runaway Girls in Detention

While working at the Juvenile Court of Cook County, Illinois, as a Probation Officer and handling a normal caseload of 25 to 30 cases, I attempted to identify specific client populations that might especially benefit from task-centered casework, which seemed to offer promise in the treatment of troubled youth. Certain features of the model—particularly its planned brevity and its focus on client tasks (Reid and Epstein, 1972)—seemed particularly well suited for one client group at the Court, runaways in detention and their parents.

The pilot project, which I developed and worked on from April 1974 through March 1975, evolved as follows: (1) I selected runaway girls in detention as a target population. (2) I devised a service strategy for this population based on task-centered casework and congruent approaches. (3) A step-by-step plan for treating cases was integrated with the procedural complexities and institutional realities of the Court (4) Data collection instruments were developed to record and guide interventions and to measure their results. (Selected tape-recordings ensured there was correspondence between the written material and what had actually occurred.) (5) At my request, cases involving female runaways in detention were assigned to me. During the year I worked with (and collected data on) 10 cases which comprised the pilot project sample.[1]

Selection of the Target Population

After using the task-centered model for several months with all my clients at the Court, I decided that runaway girls in our detention facility (Audy Home) were the most appropriate target population for my pilot project. I focused on runaways rather than delinquents because the parents of runaways were coming to the Court asking for help and the runaway himself was often tired of an intolerable situation. Delinquent youths, on the other hand, are not referred to the Court for a problem they have but for one they have created for police, a teacher, or a victim.

It is essential to the task-centered model that the client agrees that he has a problem that he wishes to work on. I had used the model with delinquent youngsters who had difficulty with formal organization (including the Court itself) and for problems of inadequate resources, but often the delinquent youths did not want to work on any problem nor did they or their parents think they had any. When the parent of a runaway brings his child into court by swearing out a complaint, he has admitted to having a problem. Runaways and their parents consistently admit to having problems, but their admission does not always mean they are willing to do something about them.

I chose detained runaways rather than runaways out of custody because of a procedural situation. Runaway cases in which the child was returned to his parents' custody took between two and four weeks to be assigned to me as a Probation Officer. By that time, in most cases, the family no longer thought they had a problem, or the problem was so exacerbated that the only alternative was removal from the home.

[1] For their assistance and support on this project, the author is indebted to his supervisor, Mr. Robert Schwartz, and to Mr. James Jordan, Administrator of the Cook County Juvenile Detention Center.

Often, by the time I made my first home visit, the youngster had already run away again. Runaways in detention were assigned more quickly. Because detention itself was a crisis for both the child and the parents, I was more likely to be able to meet the girl and her parents without delay, and they were more likely to focus and work on the issues which were really bothering them.

The reason for choosing girls rather than boys for my sample was that there were more runaways girls (658) than boys (364) placed in detention in 1974. Also, the proportion of runaway girls to the total female population of the detention center was much greater (56 percent) than the proportion of runaway boys to the total male population of the institution (11 percent). Consequently, I thought that a greater institutional impact could be made by working with the female population if this treatment procedure could reduce the number of days or the number of times a child was held in detention.

The number of days runaways spent in detention had already been substantially reduced by an order from the Chief Judge of Cook County Juvenile Court, William Sylvester White. Effective January 1, 1974, this order limited the number of days a runaway could spend in detention to ten judicial days (actually fourteen days) and fifteen judicial days if placement outside of the home was necessitated. Prior to this order it was not uncommon for status offenders to remain in detention for over thirty days. This commitment by the Court toward setting definite limits on the incarceration of minors in need of supervision made this target population compatible with task-centered casework's own time constraints.

The Treatment Plan

The treatment provided, although very individualized and flexible, followed a definite pattern and time table. In its final form (presented below) it emerged as a step-by-step plan with several theoretical bases, task-centered among them:

1. *Assignment of case.* Ideally this step was to take place within twenty-four hours of the time when the girl was detained.

2. *Telephoning the parents.* I contacted the parents the same day

the case was assigned to let them know that someone was working with them. This put many parents at ease and let them know I was concerned about their child. During this phone call, I would obtain a preliminary description of the presenting problems from such answers as, "She just keeps running away." It did little good to focus on the runaway behavior per se. In fact, encouraging parents to dwell on such behavior only adds to parental tendencies to reinforce it by giving it attention. De Risi and Butz (1975) suggest that "by finding out what behaviors have *previously* gone unrewarded or punished and by seeking to alter these, the rate of running may be reduced" (p. 9, italics added). Presenting problems such as "She won't listen, talks back, and if she continues I will hurt her," or "She won't go to school and has been away for three months with her boyfriend," were far more helpful for the formulation of tasks which would soon be developed.

I would then ask the parent to meet with the daughter and me in the detention facility at the earliest convenience. If parents refused to come, I requested their suggestions as to what should be done. When parents did not take an interest in their child, it was sometimes necessary to inform them that their child would be placed with a state agency. Most parents were eager to come, however. One parent had refused to come to this joint meeting because she thought, at first, that I wanted to see her alone. When she found out the meeting was to be with her daughter as well, she impatiently asked, "When can I come?"

3. *Visiting the girl in detention.* Following the phone call to the parents, I would visit the girl in the detention facility, usually later that day. After introducing myself, I would explain my role as a probation officer, a person who reports facts and makes recommendations to the judge, and one who attempts to help young people and their parents get what they want, within the law. Most of the girls wanted to leave detention as soon as possible. If so, I told the girl that I would help her figure out some way to achieve this goal. Most girls were very upset and angry at their parents. After they had expressed these feelings, I would then present the parents' statement, for example, "Your mother says that you never come home on time." If the girl agreed with the statement, we explored further to see what could be done by the girl to meet the expectation. When she disagreed, I pointed out that her parent was coming to see her, and they could discuss it.

Letting the girls know that a conjoint interview would be taking place and that it would be an opportunity for them to "put their cards on the table" made it possible for the girls to talk to me about what they felt needed to be different in their home situations. I also explained that no changes would occur at home unless her parents knew what changes needed to take place. I then wrote down these complaints in the girl's own language and had the girl place them in the order of importance. (For some girls I called this a "Christmas list"— some things they would get, others they would not.) One such list contained the following: (1) "Mother does not tell me what she wants, she has others tell me"; (2) "My brother bugs me"; (3) "After I clean the kitchen, everyone leaves dishes all around for me to pick up."

I attempted to meet with the girl as soon as possible after she was detained so that rather than focusing on her life in the institution, she would concentrate on what needed to be done so that she could reenter her home and community. For those girls who did not want to go home, I explained that state placements were not necessarily less problematic than their own home and that they might have to wait three weeks in detention for placement. If after this warning the girl still requested placement, I immediately began the complex procedure necessary to procure it.

4. *Meeting with parents prior to conjoint interview.* At this meeting (usually at my office the day following) I would elicit and write down the changes their daughter would be expected to make in order to remain at home. In the case above, the mother's list was as follows: (1) "She must do her chores in the house"; (2) "She should stop mumbling under her breath"; (3) "Communication between her and her brother needs to be improved." I tried to help parents by pointing out expectations that their child could not meet. However, when a parent insisted, I even included unreasonable expectations. I also explained that their daughter could not be expected to be the only person in the family who makes changes and that their daughter had expectations (she would reveal to them) of what she needed so that she could stay at home.

5. *Conjoint interview with parents and girl in detention.* In this interview, which took place immediately after the session with the parents, I tried my best not to side with either the parents or the girl.

In these negotiations my primary role was to remind each party of what they really wanted. The girl often just wanted to leave detention and the parents often just wanted their child to stay at home. Some parents were very rigid about changing and I would warn them that the same problems might continue to occur if they did not, but most parents, to my surprise, were willing to listen to what their children had to say. Perhaps they felt guilty when they saw their child in detention, dressed in a uniform, which could have made them more conciliatory than they would have been ordinarily. The girls were often in a much better bargaining position than I had expected. Because she was in a protected environment, the girl could even tell her parent that she would not come home. Two girls I worked with did just that.

After the parent and child had talked for a while and seemed to be comfortable, I read and compared the parent's and child's list. First, I found problems that both parent and child mentioned, as in the example: "brother bugs me" and "communication between her and brother needs to be improved." Second, I would explore those problems which they felt they could solve themselves and then find out what their solution was. The mother in the example decided that what she needed to do was reduce the amount of favoritism she was showing her son and her solution was "to crack down on both children equally." Last, I focused on those problems which the family might want to work on with me. We then worked together on figuring out tasks. In the present example, the mother, who was having difficulty disciplining her daughter, agreed to try to speak to her daughter herself about her daughter's behavior, rather than having friends and neighbors do it. Her daughter, who had difficulty controlling her temper, agreed to go into her room and close the door when she got angry.

A list of all the reciprocal agreements, including those which I would work on with the family, was signed by the parent and the girl. De Risi and Butz (1975) give the following advice, "When a contract is put on paper, it should not contain legal jargon that might be confusing. The contracts you write will seldom have any legal status; they are simply agreements between people and clear statements of how those people will behave towards one another" (p. 44). This advice was followed. The reciprocal agreements were not as precise as Homme (1969) or Stuart (1971) suggest but they were easily understood by the clients because they were not complex and were in their own language. Thus, in one case the reciprocal tasks were "Daughter is to stop arguing with mother after she has said 'no' "; "Mother is to allow daughter to do more things." The contract was not precisely worded but both mother and daughter understood quite well what was expected. Writing down expectations seemed to help clients make their ideas more precise. The importance of the agreements was underscored by reading them out loud after they were signed.

The next step was to offer to meet the parent and child at home within one week or so of the girl's release. This offer tended to reassure parents who had been hesitant about taking their daughters home. Knowing that they had already done something about their problem helped the family to feel more confident about being reunited. I then asked the family how many sessions they thought that they would need to work on the problems they had chosen. The families usually, in return, asked me how many I thought were necessary. About three interviews were settled on in most cases. It would have been difficult to contract for a much longer period of service, given the limited motivation of most families.

6. *Using the* "instanter" *procedure. Instanter* is a procedure by which a petition can be heard by the Court immediately rather than on the day it had been scheduled. A form must be signed by the parent and the Judge. The parents of these runaway girls in detention were, in effect, signing a document requesting the return of their child. The judge who heard all runaway cases readily signed the form and released these youngsters when they and their parents had reached some accommodation. There were some problems, however. For example, a court psychiatrist had spoken to a mother telling her to leave the girl in detention the full amount of time to teach her a lesson. I explained to the mother that the extra time her daughter would spend in detention would merely be "angry time" for her daughter and would not make either of them feel better toward the other. The mother then requested her daughter's release.

7. *Home visit.* I met with parents and child after a period long enough for the family to reacclimate and work on tasks, yet not so long that they had forgotten the Court or me. The visit was made at home so that I could fulfill the administrative requirement of the social inves-

tigation report. During this session I found out what progress had been made and whether there were any problems with the set of agreements. Exploration, problem identification, task formulation and some use of the support I provided was as far into the treatment process as these clients were willing to go. However, for clients of a coercive agency such as the Court, this degree of involvement is not to be minimized.

Subsequent interviews were scheduled for my office, if the clients felt the need for them. Meeting in my office rather than in the home contributed to making the treatment a more voluntary matter. I visited all my cases once a month because it was administratively required. This gave me an opportunity to check on the progress that was made. A client who went through this entire intervention procedure smoothly was Margie.

I received the case on Thursday, three days after the girl was detained. I called the mother, who said that the girl (fifteen and a half years old) had not been attending school and had run off with her boyfriend several months ago. I visited Margie in Audy Home that day. She said that when she had returned after several months with her boyfriend, she joked with her mother that she would run away again. She mainly wanted (1) to get married when she turned 16 and (2) to get out of Audy Home.

The mother came in the next day. She was upset at seeing her daughter in the Audy Home. She spelled out rules that she wanted Margie to follow: (1) go to school, (2) tell mother where she was, and (3) not be with boyfriend constantly. She accepted Margie's plans. It was too late to go to court on Friday, so Margie had to stay in Audy Home until Monday, when her mother came down again, signed the *instanter* to go into court early, and took Margie home. That Wednesday I visited the home. There were no problems that they were interested in working on. So far they had kept all agreements, were getting along well, and requested no further assistance. I offered to call them in two weeks. They agreed.

The treatment plan presented here could be seen as a form of crisis intervention. Reid and Epstein (1972) readily acknowledge congruencies between task-centered casework and crisis theory. In writing about crisis intervention in probation, Cunningham (1973) cites points of intervention such as the initial referral, violation of probation, and return to the community as times when the probationer is more willing to work on problems with his probation officer. "Because of his acute feelings of discomfort and helplessness and the heightened motivation to do something about it, the individual in crisis is more likely to respond positively to anyone who can provide direction and hope in restoring a degree of emotional equilibrium" (p. 18). The only exception task-centered casework would make is that tasks should not be "confined to points of transition of crisis but is rather applied to the individual's efforts to resolve any problem of living" (Reid and Epstein, 1972, p. 95).

One girl in detention, whose mother refused to make any changes, decided to try improving her appearance after her release to mother. The following tasks were formulated: (1) wear clean clothes, (2) comb hair, (3) bathe everyday. In two weeks her appearance had improved remarkably and no further intervention was requested. The problem of appearance had nothing to do with her crisis or restoring her "emotional equilibrium," yet it was important to her.

Data Collection

A recording form was developed to obtain data relating to steps of the treatment plan. It called for recording of *when* the steps were carried out, which proved useful in identifying delays and working out time-tables in particular cases. The headings of the form followed the steps of the treatment plan outlined above. Thus, under *Meeting with Parents* and *Girl in Detention*, I recorded the problems and tasks that were formulated and the number of future sessions agreed upon.

This instrument served as a useful tool to guide me in knowing what to do next in a very complex situation. It also served to remind my clients and myself of what they had said. Through the structure it offered, I gained control over the kind of treatment I was offering clients. When the cases were completed, I knew that I had given a very specific and definable treatment to a very specific population. I believe that this structure also helped my clients feel comfortable.

I developed two other questionnaires: a face sheet for information required for the social investigation, which was filled out at the first home interview, and a case closing questionnaire (adapted from instruments in the Appendix, which assessed mainly problem reduction and task completion).

Results

The sample group of 10 girls I treated was fairly diverse; 4 Afro-Americans, 3 Caucasians, and 3 Spanish speaking. All were residents of the inner-city. The girls were fairly representative of the ages of the larger population of runaway girls in detention during the time of the project. The ages of the girls in the sample ranged from 13 to 16 years; median age was 14.5 years. Seven of the girls came from homes where the parents were divorced or separated. The girls were missing anywhere from one day to six months before their apprehension. Four girls had never previously been reported to the police for running; an equal number had been reported 1 or 2 times previously. One girl had run 4 times and one 6 times.

Six girls and their parents agreed to work with me on some problem or task. Five of the six problems I helped families to work on were developed in the Detention facility. In all these cases the major problem showed at least some alleviation; in most it was considerably alleviated. Some progress was made on at least one task in all cases (there were usually 2 to 3 tasks per case). Three-quarters of the tasks were substantially achieved.

The four remaining cases had the following outcomes: 2 girls went into foster placement after I received both parent and child's agreement. In the third case, the mother and daughter left the state without the Court's permission. In the last case (the most difficult in the project) the only problem the parents could focus on was their child's runaway behavior. The parents requested that the case be dismissed because they were not pleased with me. (I had protected their daughter's confidentiality when she had run away.) One week later they returned because their daughter ran again, and this time another officer was assigned.

The majority of cases were seen within a day or two of the optimal timetable set forth in the treatment plan. It was alarming, however, to find out that it had taken seven full days between the time two of the girls were detained to the day the case was assigned to me. One case took five days. None of these three cases ever contracted with me. Seven of the 10 youngsters had their cases brought into court earlier than had been scheduled. These cases were supposed to be in detention approximately two weeks but their parents requested their release in one week.

For these 7 families, there was some factor which allowed both parents and child to return to a situation which had previously been intolerable. In the cases of the families with whom I had contracted to work on problems and tasks, I was able to terminate their supervision satisfactorily. This does not mean that these families exhibited no further problems or that their children never ran away again. My criterion for closing a case was that the parents and daughter felt that they no longer needed service. The case was closed if the parents and child felt that things had improved to the point where they believed that they were more comfortable.

Conclusions

One of the conclusions, from a study by O'Connor (1970), is that, "Detention is a period of influence . . . yet most juvenile halls operate under a 'detain, don't treat' policy" (p. 199). Detention facilities should provide humane environments, but at Juvenile Court, the actual agents of change are the probation officers. The probation officer is the youth's connection between the institution and the community (Studt, 1967). Detention often is not appropriate for runaway youngsters. The development and implementation of a task-oriented approach at intake could divert many youngsters from detention. The development of some short-term placement facilities in the community would be an advisable alternative to locking them up and treating them like criminals. With some modifications, task-centered casework could be designed for these situations as well.

Task-centered treatment made it possible to develop a treatment plan which met the following criteria:

1. Treatment and data collection should be completed on cases by a probation officer carrying a typical caseload.

2. Staff should be trained to use the treatment method in a short period of time.
3. Treatment should be controlled and monitored by use of questionnaires and by tape-recording the interventions.
4. Treatment should be empirically tested.

Task-centered casework lends itself to these goals because it is short-term treatment whose methodology is explicit and not overly complex and, most importantly, because it has been empirically developed. It is hoped that public agencies have become tired of using treatment models that cannot be defined, cannot be taught, and cannot be tested.

References

Cunningham, Gloria. 1973. "Crisis intervention in a probation setting." *Federal Probation* 36(4):16–25.

DeRisi, William J., and Butz, George. 1975. *Writing behavioral contracts: A case simulation practice manual.* Champaign, Ill.: Research Press.

Homme, Lloyd; Csanyi, Attila P.; Gonzales, Mary Ann; and Rechs, James R. 1969. *How to use contingency contracting in the classroom.* Champaign, Ill.: Research Press.

O'Connor, Gerald G. 1970. "The impact of initial detention upon male delinquents." *Social Problems* 18(2):194–200.

Reid, William J., and Epstein, Laura. 1972. *Task-centered casework.* New York: Columbia University Press.

Stuart, Richard B. 1971. "Behavioral contracting within the families of delinquents." *Journal of Behavior Therapy and Experimental Psychiatry* 2(1):1–11.

Studt, Elliot. 1967. *Studies in delinquency: Reentry of the offender into the community.* JD Pub. 9002. Washington, D.C.: U.S. Department of Health, Education, and Welfare, Office of Juvenile Delinquency and Youth Department.

Chapter 14

~~~~~~

Milton O. Hofstad, A.C.S.W.

Treatment in a
Juvenile Court Setting

The project described in this paper was conducted in the Lancaster County Separate Juvenile Court, Lincoln, Nebraska, between November 1, 1974, and May 1, 1975. The objective was to study the feasibility of the task-centered approach in this juvenile court setting. The youths who received service from the project were on probation because of violations of law, or they were receiving "special supervision" because of serious misbehavior. These are two types of mandatory counseling found, at present, throughout the juvenile court system in the United States. Judge W. W. Nuernberger gave the project strong administrative support, in keeping with his leading role as a progressive innovator in juvenile court programs. The practitioners were students in the Graduate School of Social Work, University of Nebraska. Five were seniors in the undergraduate program, and one was a first-year graduate student. Supervision was provided by the author, their field instructor.

Adapting Task-Centered Treatment to the Court

One of the first issues considered was adapting the emphasis in the task-centered model on voluntary client participation to the mandatory constraints of probation and "special supervision." Juvenile court procedures usually are as follows: first, there is an adjudication hearing in which a decision is made about guilt or innocence of the charge of violating a law, or finding that the youth is a "minor in need of supervision" (MINS); second, there is a period to permit a "social investigation"; and third, there is a disposition hearing. In this third step the judge decides if the youth is to remain in his own home and what the outlines of the plan for him should be; or if he is to be placed in foster care, a residential institution, or a correctional facility (Revised Statutes of Nebraska, 1943, Section 43-210).

The project's plan was to use the time between the adjudication and disposition hearings to collect the social history information wanted by the court, and to assess the appropriateness of the task-centered approach to each individual case. In the particular conditions of this project, it was the court which was to decide finally on the appropriateness of the approach, based upon its own judgment and information supplied by the social workers. If the court adopted the task-centered approach as part of the disposition plan, treatment could begin immediately following the disposition hearing. In practice, cases judged inappropriate were those in which long probation was ordered because the duration of probation exceeded the time limits of a single task-centered sequence. One other group judged inappropriate was that in which the court was considering commitment to a correctional institution. The criteria for selection centered on judicial decisions about length of probation and on removal of the youth from the community.

There were occasions when the court would independently set conditions of probation, in addition to including in the court order the tasks agreed upon between practitioner and client. These court ordered conditions were necessary because of requirements in the statutes and expectations of the legal profession. Working in an interdisciplinary relationship and being governed by statutes, it seemed proper that such conditions be respected by the social workers and taken into account as part of the client's social context. Furthermore, it was not considered advisable, nor would it have been possible, to separate the role of the probation officer from the authoritative role he possessed as a court official.

Sometimes the practitioners lacked sufficient skill to make plans clearly enough to satisfy the expectations of the court. In such instances there was a higher likelihood that the court itself would assign tasks to the youth on its own initiative. The clearer the social worker's task planning, the less was the likelihood that the court would take initiative in assigning tasks and would restrict its orders to legal matters. The most important technical weakness of the project's work was difficulty in formulating tasks specifically and in behavioral terms, leading to shortcomings in measuring progress. To correct this situation, student practitioners began to obtain baseline information regularly so that they could assess change. Use of a schedule to monitor task implementation was valuable. Also helpful was structured case recording which followed the steps of the task-centered model—from target problems, to tasks, task changes, obstacles, and achievements.

The Clients' Problems, Tasks, and Outcomes

A total of sixteen male youths were referred to the project. Following the "social investigation," seven youths were judged inappropriate for application of the task-centered model because of court-ordered, long-term probation and the possibility of commitment to a correctional facility. Of the nine remaining cases, five completed task-centered probation or supervision successfully and on schedule with an acceptable degree of task achievement and were released by the court. A sixth youth also completed the tasks agreed upon; but he was thereafter placed on "administrative probation" to complete the balance of his one-year probation order. This meant that although still under court order, this youth's probation was considered "inactive" while he awaited release from the court's order. Presumably, if he were again to become troublesome, his probation would be reactivated. The remaining three youths were not able to complete the tasks necessary to obtain release from the court's jurisdiction. They were not sufficiently interested, it appeared; and they repeatedly did not follow through on tasks. We do not have, at this point, the explanations for these failures.

Of the nine boys, the major target problem for seven was school underachievement. At least four were in conflict with school authorities because of disruptive or hostile behavior. Two of the youths had, in addition, problems of conflict with parents and siblings. Two older adolescents had target problems concerning lack of skills for employment. For the seven boys in school, the initial general tasks included: improving school grades, doing assigned school work, making restitution for the cost of damage to property, reducing fighting with siblings. The older adolescents agreed to the general task: attending vocational training classes. Some general tasks which lacked sufficient specificity called for refraining from running away from home, from taking drugs, and disrupting classrooms. During the course of treatment, many of these tasks became more specific.

It was possible to conduct interviews with seven of the youths after their cases were closed. These interviews revealed considerable agreement between the practitioner's recording of problems and tasks and the client's perception of the areas worked on during the service. Most of the youths were favorable to the length, content, and quality of the social service they had received. All the responses were positive to the time limits which helped them to be released from probation. Of the seven interviewees, one thought he had partially achieved the agreed upon tasks; five judged they had substantially achieved tasks; and one thought he had complete achievement. Six of the seven believed they had been considerably benefitted by the service, and one thought he had been neither helped nor harmed.

The average length of probation for the five youths who were released from probation was 3.3 months. The average number of interviews was 9.4.

Case Illustration

Larry, age 17, was brought before the juvenile court late in September for a law violation. At the disposition hearing, the recommendation for task-entered probation was approved by the court. The target problem identified was school malperformance. The tasks were: (1) to improve school grades; (2) to improve his role performance in school; (3) to improve his attitude towards school; (4) to avoid disruptive acts in school; and (5) to make restitution for damages. Tasks 2 and 4 are similar and lack specificity; however, they were accepted by the court. A time limit of two months was approved by the court. Intervention consisted of eight interviews between the worker and Larry, and two interviews with Larry's parents. The worker held two meetings with Larry's teachers and the school principal, one during the first week of intervention and another the week prior to termination. At the first meeting with the school personnel, they expressed the wish to "support and reinforce" Larry whenever possible and to follow suggestions the probation department might make about changes in the school situation which might help Larry.

Larry elicited negative responses from his teachers through set patterns of interactions with them. Larry began to change first by taking initiative to become better acquainted with his teachers. They, in turn, began reinforcing this behavior by reacting more positively towards him. Larry had relatively low self-esteem. He started feeling better as the teachers showed interest in him. Larry established a friendship with one of his teachers which may help him sustain the changes he has made. Larry began to learn that he could disagree with teachers without giving them a "mouthy" response. The practitioner taught him how to talk about disagreements without getting angry and provoking teachers, and how to avoid disruptive incidents at school. He learned to get approval from others. Larry began working on raising his grades immediately. He was shown new study methods and how to use reference material. In the past he had a tendency to forget about assignments. He learned to write them down or use other means for remembering.

Larry responded positively to his teachers' interest. He stated several times he "felt good" after talking with them. The worker discussed with Larry ways he could initiate interaction with the teachers by discussing his progress and grade achievement. Larry initially expressed fear of what the other kids "would think" and how his teachers would respond to his new behavior. However, experience showed he had nothing to fear. At the end of the school semester he received C's in all of his courses. In mechanical drawing he raised his grade from a failing grade at mid-semester to a C. In home economics he received a grade of C, which was a considerable improvement from his nine-week grade of D–. The principal stated in his report at the time of termination that "Larry and I have never communicated very well, but I do feel that we communicated better in our last conference than in the past." One teacher summed it up: "In general, Larry has shown a real effort to improve behavior and grades. He has not succeeded 100 percent of the time but has about 75–80 percent of the time." Larry was released by the court after a two-month probation.

Two months after termination, Larry said he was "considerably benefitted" by the service, that the most important problems worked on were improving school grades and learning to talk with school teachers. He was excited about joining a boxing club. He was getting along well in school and had only one troublesome incident since his release from probation: skipping school one day. Larry reported that he was getting along with his teachers. He thought he would pass all his courses, but might not get all C's. Larry reported that he was getting along quite well with the principal and that the principal had changed. Larry said that he heard a lot of kids say the principal had changed. Larry would be attending summer school to pick up some credits.

Conclusion

This small-scale project suggests that the task-centered approach can be adapted to a juvenile court. The results warrant further clinical trials and more complete evaluation. There are issues needing analysis in order to develop adaptations of the model to the juvenile court. One issue is determining which youth might benefit from the task-centered approach. Another is developing techniques for specifying tasks which can be achieved within the estimated period of probation. The quality of agency support can be expected to influence the effectiveness of clinical trials. In this project strong agency support facilitated its purposes. The suggestions received from the agency aided in developing the methodology.

The potential values for continued use of the task-centered approach in a juvenile court might be: more purposeful probation, supervision, and economy. In our opinion, the task-centered approach reduces the likelihood of purposeless probation. It also draws on the adolescents' need for independence. The process of mutual goal-setting found in the model gives considerable responsibility to the youth for determining the problem area and formulating tasks. The task-centered approach has potential for financial savings. For example, short-term probation services that are task-centered might lessen the probability of youths remaining on probation unnecessarily. Termination could be recommended when identified tasks are completed. Because termination is planned initially, the probability of short-term probation is increased. Projects of this type in other juvenile courts would clarify the feasibility of the model. The limited number of juveniles in this project precludes drawing conclusions. However, the writer recommends experimentation in other court settings.

Part III: Adults

∿∿∿∿∿∿∿∿∿∿∿∿∿∿∿∿∿∿∿∿

Introduction

Papers in this section emphasize task-centered treatment with individual adults. The settings are diverse: an outpatient psychiatric clinic in an inner-city medical center; two industrial social service departments, one serving white-collar and professional employees and the other blue-collar workers in the steel industry; an area social service office in a mixed urban and rural section of Great Britain, 50 miles distant from London; and a varied group of clients selected from a range of social agencies in the Haifa area in Israel.

Application of the task-centered model to psychiatric outpatients is described and analyzed in Brown's paper. Experience with 109 cases provides support for using the task-centered approach in such a setting. Patients were primarily young black adults, 70 percent of whom were women. Treatment was accomplished usually with eight interviews, although there was variation in numbers. Clinical diagnoses included a typical representation of clinic practice. Highest amounts of problem change were found among those diagnosed "neurotic" and those experiencing an acute psychosis. Problems of reactive emotional distress and social transition had the best alleviation rates. The majority of all problems were changed in the desired direction. These results are similar to Ewalt's findings in the Youth Guidance Center and Reid's findings in two family service agencies, both reported in the first section of this volume.

Brown illustrates straightforward, adroit formulation of target problems. Involvement in the unpredictable and intractable manifestations of old, ingrained character traits, habits, and attitudes is avoided.

In this outpatient clinic, procedures for planned extension of treatment were developed. Two or more sequences of task-centered treatment were provided to clients who stated problems too numerous for one sequence and who requested additional assistance. This development has useful possibilities. Guidelines for extensions should follow the basic steps: specific target problems, clear tasks, and strong focus on problem reduction. In Brown's situation, practitioners had firm practice skills which allowed freedom to extend the time. In other settings where task-centered skills are being learned and where accommodations must be made to existing practice repertoires, loose management of extensions would undermine the structure and objectives of the model and encourage diffuse, inefficient practice.

Taylor and Weissman, in two separate papers, describe similar applications of task-centered treatment to a range of problems occurring among employed persons, many of whom ordinarily do not use social services at all, or who become clients at a late period, after their problems have worsened. Between the two services described in both papers, approximately 500 cases have been handled through task-centered treatment of a wide range of problems concerning work, personal adjustment, and family life. Outcome information included in these papers is derived from studies of client satisfaction. This information suggests that, from the client's standpoint, treatment was considered successful in the great majority of instances. This type of information, in itself, does not permit making firm conclusions about outcomes since client reports may be influenced by tendencies to provide socially acceptable evaluations. On the other hand, both these services can exist only if the company managements judge their results to be worth the expenditures made from company funds. It seems reasonable to assume that the high client satisfaction reported by Taylor and Weissman's inquiries does in fact reflect that clients were receiving valued services which had impact on their problems. As in Brown's report, the important technical themes in these papers are concreteness and specificity of target problems, tasks adjusted to maintaining a concentration on problem reduction, and the avoidance of protracted attention to problems not congruent with the client's present interests.

Goldberg and Robinson's paper describes a study of the feasibility of task-centered treatment in an English social service office. Nearly every issue which has been referred to in the American reports arose in the British context. Although no broad conclusions can be made from this pilot study, their observations are enlightening. The British public social services are based upon a firm policy stated in legislation. Social services in Britain are expected to provide comprehensive coverage to the entire population. Goldberg and Robinson raise the question of "paternalism" in the English system. There is a suggestion that the expectation that these services regulate conduct and supply needs inclusively may not be practical and may have undesirable effects as well. Handler, an American observer, has in fact characterized the British system as "coercive." He has stated strong cautions about American tendencies to go this route (1973). American public social services at present are tending to move toward comprehensive coverage policies but in an ambiguous and incomplete manner.

It could be expected that a sharp contrast would occur between long-term surveillance of clients (being a "general aunt," as Goldberg and Robinson call it), and the demand of the task-centered approach to be concrete and limited. In Britain, public demand to achieve complex and far-reaching change in behavior of troublesome people is perhaps stronger than in America. Nevertheless, in the United States powerful influence is exerted on the direction, content, and goals of treatment by attitudes expressed in the press, by referral sources, and by legal and administrative authorities. This problem has been explored in this volume by several contributors: Bass and Hofstad commenting upon task-centered efforts in juvenile courts; Epstein describing referral sources' expectations in the public schools; and Salmon's observations about public expectations for families of children in placement. The practice of involving referral sources in problem definition, clarification of the realism and advisability of their expectations, and negotiating contracts with them seems to be developing in America as part of a solution to these pressures.

It is interesting that despite the broad caretaking function of the British social services, many cases seemed to be handled quite satisfactorily through planned short-term interventions. Experience with the task-centered model made it clear that inconclusive drifting of cases can and should be controlled. In fact, Goldberg and Robinson's appraisal of the use of the task-centered model to emphasize economy of intervention and client participation are virtually identical to Salmon's analysis of the same issues in Louisiana. In this initial effort to apply task-centered treatment, there are questions about the skill of the practitioners in performing the activities called for by the model. Probably of more importance, however, is a set of difficulties encountered also in America: deficiencies in the task-centered model's guidelines for practice in marital conflict and in families with a large number of problems. It is anticipated that future work in the projects at the School of Social Service Administration and experience with American practice in public child welfare will develop a more robust framework for specifying guidelines with such cases. It is of interest, however, that in some settings scarcity of specific guidelines has not been an obstinate problem. Taylor and Weissman, as well as Brown, were able to construct treatment plans in marital and multiproblem families when it appeared useful to involve spouses and family members in treatment of an individual. However, there may be unspecified differences among the types of problems encountered in various settings.

Golan's paper is a report on a series of clinical trails in Haifa, undertaken under special circumstances. The practitioners were highly experienced. Although many were currently employed as administrators, supervisors, and field instructors, their backgrounds indicate considerable sophistication in treatment theory and practice. The Israeli project was supported by excellent training arrangements, thorough study and discussion, and productive peer supervision. The practitioners selected from a variety of cooperating agencies a small number of clients who they inferred were good treatment candidates. However, it is clear from the report that difficult situations were included: severe grief reactions, multiproblem family situations, stressful reactions of adolescents to critical threats and dislocations in their families and living conditions, and the like. In Golan's report, as in all of the others, one of the most obdurate technical problems was developing specific tasks. Golan's experiences are similar to those of many others. It appeared that skills needed to identify, construct, limit, and alter tasks took time to learn. Golan's suggestion about another difficult area, multiproblem families, calls for concentration upon a limited segment of a chaotic situation. Golan suggests that such a focus is particularly useful if the target problem involves some new development. We do not know of any other writer who pinpointed "newness" as especially useful in identifying a problem segment. Perhaps Taylor's use of "critical incidents" to direct problem exploration is similar.

What is striking about this set of papers, when considered together with those discussed in earlier sections, is that unresolved issues in developing technology appear repeatedly, regardless of setting and location. Yet one also finds evidence that the task-centered model is useful, adaptable, and can be taught and learned. These kinds of experiences provide encouragement to improve and expand the task-centered approach.

Chapter 15

~~~~~~

Lester B. Brown, A.C.S.W.

Treating Problems of Psychiatric Outpatients

Since 1973, task-centered treatment has been used by graduate social workers and social work students with psychiatric outpatients at Jackson Park Hospital. In this chapter I will report on our experience with the model, giving particular emphasis to its application in a psychiatric setting.

The Setting

The Outpatient Clinic at the Hospital provides psychiatric services to an inner-city catchment area of 200,000 people on the south side of Chicago. The services include after-care for ex-mental hospital patients, counseling for adults and families, and emergency psychiatric care. The staff consists of psychiatrists, social workers, psychologists, and nurse-clinicians.

Use of the task-centered approach has been confined to the social workers (three at present) and the students. Other staff use a variety of treatment modalities, primarily psychodynamic in nature, although behavioral methods are also employed. There is no opposition to the more structured approaches, such as task-centered treatment or behavior modification. In fact, a psychodynamic practitioner and a behaviorist will often work together on the same case as cotherapists.

An Example from Professional Practice

Although students, because of their greater numbers, have carried more of the task-centered cases than professional staff, applications of the approach by trained and experienced social workers may be of particular interest. The following case is typical of my own use of the model.

Miss Green is a 51-year-old woman, unmarried, who lives with her 79-year-old mother. She came to the clinic accompanied by her landlady. For six months she had been terrified of leaving her house alone. If she tried, she would break into a cold sweat, shake so violently she could not move, would have rapid heart beat and difficulty in breathing. In addition, she was concerned that twenty years of heavy drinking might have damaged her physiologically. The alcoholism and phobia were confirmed by her mother, on the telephone, and her landlady, in person, during the interview.

The duration of treatment was set at eight interviews by the worker; the client agreed to this without overt reaction. She did not say it was either too brief or too lengthy. In this same interview the target problems were agreed to. I reiterated what I had garnered from the interview as possible problems—excessive drinking, her fears about going out alone, and her worry about physical damage due to alcohol consumption. Miss Green quietly insisted on the second and third as the target problems and reacted positively to my agreement to work on the problems she emphasized. This process not only seemed to increase her motivation for treatment but reflected the ethical stance of task-centered, open and aboveboard treatment contracts and no hidden agendas.

Although I thought the somatic symptoms (rapid heart beat, etc.) associated with her phobia had no organic base, I felt that it was important that her concerns over her health be dealt with immediately. This was explained to the client, and she agreed to undergo a thorough physical examination as soon as an internist was obtained. I further explained that once this problem was clarified we would begin work on the second targeted problem.

The general task (or goal) for the first problem, therefore, became for her "to find out the state of her physical health." The first operational tasks for this problem were as follows:

1) Miss Green would see an internist that I would find for her at Jackson Park to obtain the desired physical examination.

2) If required by the physician, she would enter the hospital for medical tests or treatment.

Miss Green was admitted to our facility onto a medical floor where she remained for eight days. She complied with all tests and was found to be in good health. The physician commented that she looked older than her years but that there was no damage (not even to the liver) that one would expect after such a long history of alcoholism. During the hospitalization, I visited her on several occasions and praised her for following through on the tasks and tests.

The second treatment interview occurred ten days after the first. With her first problem resolved for her, Miss Green was even more committed to working on the second—her fear of going outside alone. She had functioned well before the onset of her phobia. She had worked in catalog sales for a national chain and had gone here and there with no difficulty. The only major adverse event within the previous year had been a large lay-off of employees at the business. She was one of the casualties. She had been unable to find another job (her age and limited experience were factors here). The beginning impetus to find work gradually wore off after repeated failures. The fear of going outside alone began. I would posit that it began as an avoidance of applying for jobs that she would not get and became an habituated avoidance behavior, intensified, perhaps, by feelings of worthlessness. Although she needed to work to supplement her meager general assistance grants, she may not have been able to face any more defeat. What Miss Green stated she missed was visiting friends, going shopping, and the many trips individuals do alone. Although I had my speculations about the causes of her fears, I concentrated on helping the client achieve directly the tasks she saw as goals.

In the second interview I explained the plan I had in mind for working on the general task for the second target problem: "To be able to come and go from her home without hesitation." I proposed that together we would plan out for her small steps she could take to achieve this goal. The client agreed. Because she had no ideas about how to begin, I suggested that she begin by just looking out her front entrance. I explained that I knew she would be able to do this but that to avoid undue hardships she would only be asked to take small but important steps to begin with. Since Miss Green thought she would be able to do more, the following operational tasks were devised, all to be carried out prior to the next interview:

3) to go to the front door of the building she lived in three times a day: at 9 A.M., 12 noon, and 3 P.M.;

4) to open the door completely at these times; and then, to stand in the open doorway for ten minutes.

It was thought that these repetitive tasks, if successfully completed, would increase the client's motivation to continue and give her a sense of being in control of her body.

In the following week's interview (the third) she told me that she had successfully completed all the assigned tasks. Although I had the impression that she had become bored doing them so many times, she expressed pleasure with her accomplishment. She revealed her hope that she would successfully overcome her phobia. I assured her again that she would not need to go any faster than she felt comfortable in doing. Her progress to date was praised; she was reassured that her reluctance and fear were not unusual under the circumstances and that with continued perseverance she could overcome her fear.

Due to the severity of her physical and emotional reactions to going out alone, the worker purposively planned the next tasks as small but significant increments to the first ones. For the next week, client would do the following:

5) Step across the threshold of the house, walk down the front steps, and stand there for ten minutes. This was to be done three times a day.

At this point I added an injunction. Hypothesizing that, if successful, Miss Green might be tempted to do more, I stated that under no circumstances was she to go any farther than the foot of the steps. Thus, she was essentially enjoined from walking around outside alone which, I hoped, would prevent her experiencing excessive anxiety. During the next (fourth) interview she told me, with some glee, that she had successfully "gone outside alone," which, in fact, she had although the task had not been phrased that way. She had not experienced any anxiety. Again, I praised her efforts enthusiastically but also emphasized that she should do no more than the tasks assigned. For the next week the following task was agreed on:

6) Three times daily she would walk to the corner (about 25 feet) after having stood in front of the house for ten minutes. If necessary, she could run back from the corner. However, even if she did, I asked her to continue the regimen three times daily.

During the next (fifth) interview, she reported that she had accomplished these tasks. She had done so without distress, although she still seemed to lack confidence that she was over her fears. In addition to my approval, she received daily praise and encouragement from her landlady and her mother. The landlady, who continued to accompany the client to the clinic, had confirmed that she had done her tasks.

As all tasks had been completed successfully up to this point, I asked her if she felt comfortable with the idea of walking alone outside for a limited distance. The client, somewhat hesitantly, said that she thought she could if it were not too far. We then formulated the following tasks:

7) She was to go out of the house and walk halfway around the block. She was to walk slowly to that point and stop. At that time, she was to make a choice: either continue around the block or turn around and return home. In either case she was to walk; walk not run.

Although in the preceding task the client had the option to "run back," this time she was asked only to walk. She could choose, however, to continue around the block or return home. I did not want fear to cause her to return (by running) but, rather, hoped that she would make a deliberate decision to return home, if necessary.

In the sixth interview Miss Green, again accompanied to the clinic by her landlady, reported happily that she had been able to complete the task and she had not turned back even once. The client was obviously in good spirits, judging by her changed facial expression. She asked what she could do next. The focus of discussion at this point began to shift: more time was now being spent on positive behaviors by the client than on her fears. We decided on the following tasks to be carried out during the week:

8) At 12 noon and 3 P.M. she was to continue to walk around the block.

9) At 9 A.M. each day she was to go to the nearest grocery store (one and one-half blocks away), make a small purchase needed at home, and then return to her apartment.

The walks, though short, were designed to strengthen her belief that she could go out alone. The last task was designed to restore going out alone as instrumental behavior, that is, as behavior that would enable her to do the things she wanted to do. I assumed that, if she could accomplish these tasks, she would have little further difficulty with the target problem. This supposition was confirmed in the next interview.

Miss Green's mother, a semi-invalid, came to the seventh interview. Up to this time I had spoken with her only by telephone. Although she needed help to walk, she had wanted to come and thank me for what had been accomplished. Miss Green reported (and her mother confirmed) that she had gone downtown by bus and subway alone to do some shopping. Although it was not part of the program, needless to say I did not object. On the contrary, I praised her initiative and her success. It was mutually decided that the eighth interview was unnecessary.

In this case, major use was made of task-centered activities described elsewhere (Reid and Epstein, 1972; Reid, 1975; Reid, chapter 1). These included problem specification, task formulation, planning task implementation, establishing rationale, and commitment for work on the task and use of others to facilitate task achievement. In respect to communication techniques (Reid and Epstein, 1972; Reid, chapter 1), stress was placed on structuring, encouragement, and direction. The practitioner assumed greater responsibility for task formulation than is perhaps typical in applications of the model. Like Rossi (chapter 10), I attempted to incorporate behavioral methods, notably the use of forms of in vivo desensitization and successive approximations, within a task-centered framework. The case illustrates well how the task-centered model can be employed to deal with rather disparate problems in the same case: in the present example realistic concern over physical health, on the one hand, and irrational fears of leaving the house, on the other. Thus, the first type of problem lent itself to a more conventional social work approach; the second, a behavioral approach. Both could be fitted within the task-centered framework.

The Student Program

The bulk of our experience with the task-centered model has been gained through the work of first-year social work students from the task-centered sequence at the School of Social Service Administration. During the past two years, approximately 20 of these students have been placed at the Clinic. Supervision is conducted through group seminars supplemented by individual conferences with the social work staff. In addition, staff members from other disciplines are used for consultation or medical evaluation.

In choosing cases for students, there is no preselection in terms of "appropriateness" for first-year students or for the task-centered model. In this way students carry a wide variety of cases with a range of problems. In addition, it becomes possible to test out the model across the spectrum of psychiatric categories.

The clients seen by the students have an array of behavioral and emotional difficulties, ranging from the bizarre to the more commonplace. Some typical examples are auditory and visual hallucinations, paranoid delusional systems, suicidal and homicidal ideation, depression (neurotic or psychotic), obsessive-compulsive behaviors, drug dependence, occupational difficulty, marital and family strife, and problems with children. Barring the need for emergency hospitalizations, clients with all of these difficulties have been seen by students using the task-centered approach. On a few occasions when hospitalization was necessary, a student has continued to use a task-centered approach during the in-patient period at Jackson Park and for aftercare. Many of the clients, at least half, have previously been hospitalized for psychiatric reasons. Students have seen clients recently discharged from Jackson Park, other private facilities, or state mental hospitals. The kinds of clients receiving task-centered help covers the gamut of problems-in-living (or "disease" categories, if you will).

The model has proved quite useful as a vehicle for student field training. When conventional long-term modalities are used, students often leave the placement before their cases are completed. In such instances they do not get much experience with the ending of treatment. Students in the task-centered sequence, by contrast, are able to begin and complete anywhere from five to ten cases during the academic year. Also they can see clients achieve success with target problems. In addition, they learn a variety of interventions used by psychodynamicists and behaviorists, since the task-centered model allows for the use of a wide range of different methods. The use of task-centered rather than conventional approaches yields several advantages for the agency: more clients can be served, transfers to regular staff are reduced, and it is easier to monitor the students' work and to obtain evidence on case outcome.

Diagnoses, Problems, and Outcomes

Data obtained from 109 student cases will be used to present a picture of the range of applications of the task-centered approach in the clinic.

The patients in this sample were generally young adults; 80 percent were under 40 years of age, the median age was 28. Almost all were black. About 70 percent were women. This demographic profile is quite similar to that for the clinic population as a whole. The cases (individual patients or family groups) received a median of 8 interviews; two-thirds received between 5 and 10 sessions. Only 2 cases exceeded the upper limit of 12 interviews suggested by the model.

The task-centered model does not treat psychiatric conditions per se but rather problems in living that may be possessed by patients with such conditions. Two patients with the same psychiatric diagnosis may have completely different problems in the task-centered problem classification system (chapter 1). For example, a patient diagnosed as having a depressive neurosis may want help with a family problem, or a patient's delusions may be seen as an obstacle to carrying out tasks relating to his job. The independence of the psychiatric and task-centered systems of assessment were revealed when the patients' primary psychiatric diagnoses (made largely by professional staff) were compared with practitioner classifications of their major target problems.

The type of psychiatric diagnosis given patients proved to be a poor predictor of their major target problem (and vice-versa). For example, the 30 patients diagnosed primarily as "depressive neurosis" (the most common diagnosis), were treated for a broad range of target problems: for 13 the primary target problem was *interpersonal conflict* (usually marital); for 7, *role performance* (mostly in family and occupational roles); for only 5 patients was the primary problem one of *reactive emotional distress*. Similarly for the next largest group, 18 patients diagnosed as schizophrenic (chronic undifferentiated type) were spread across 6 of the 7 categories of the problem classification system; problems of role performance and reactive emotional distress were the most common.

Although one cannot say that a patient with a particular diagnosis is more likely to have one kind of problem over another, the kind of problem a patient may have may make a difference in respect to case outcome. Ratings of problem change were made by practitioners for each target problem on a 7-point scale ("problem worse" to "completely resolved"). Although practitioner ratings have obvious drawbacks, samples of such ratings, collected as part of another study (Reid, 1975), did prove to agree reasonably well with independent ratings of change based on an analysis of taped interviews in which students reviewed problem change with clients.[1]

Tables 15.1 and 15.2 show how problem change relates to psychiatric diagnosis and to target problem. As can be seen, both types of classification appear to show some relation to outcome. Patients diagnosed as having neurotic and more acute psychotic reactions seem to do better with their problems than patients in the remaining categories. Problems of reactive emotional distress and role performance have the

[1] On 17 of 20 cases sampled, students' ratings of over-all problem change were within one-half point of the independent judges' ratings on a 5-point scale (r = .59). The students' ratings tended, however, to be *slightly* more favorable than were the judges'. These data were collected as part of a project on task-centered treatment to which the clinic is contributing a sample of cases (Reid and Epstein, 1974).

best alleviation rates. These findings might suggest that certain combinations of psychiatric disorders and problems might be expected to do particularly well, such as a neurotic with a problem of reactive emotional distress, and other combinations (e.g., an alcoholic with a problem of dissatisfaction in social relations) might be expected to do poorly.

Table 15.1
Diagnoses by Change in Target Problems

	CHANGE CATEGORIES						
	COMPLETE & CONSIDERABLE		SUBSTANTIAL & MODERATE		SLIGHT, NO CHANGE & WORSE		TOTAL	
DIAGNOSES	NO.	%	NO.	%	NO.	%	NO.	%
Depressive Neurosis	23	53.5	13	30.2	7	16.3	43	28.1
Transient Situational Disturbance	12	44.4	11	40.7	4	14.8	27	17.6
Schizophrenia—Chronic Undifferentiated	10	33.3	8	26.7	12	40.0	30	19.6
Alcoholism & Drug Dependence	3	33.3	1	11.1	5	55.6	9	5.9
Neuroses—Other Types	14	82.4	1	5.9	2	11.8	17	11.1
Acute Psychoses— Other Types	12	63.2	3	15.8	4	21.1	19	12.4
Other	3	37.5	2	25.0	3	37.5	8	5.2
Total *	77		39		37		153	

Table 15.2
Type of Target Problem by Amount of Change

	CHANGE CATEGORIES						
	COMPLETE & CONSIDERABLE		SUBSTANTIAL & MODERATE		SLIGHT, NO CHANGE & WORSE		TOTAL	
PROBLEM CATEGORIES	NO.	%	NO.	%	NO.	%	NO.	%
Social Transition	6	46.2	4	30.8	3	23.0	13	9.0
Role Performance	22	52.4	11	26.2	9	21.4	42	29.0
Interpersonal Conflict	16	53.3	6	20.0	8	26.7	30	20.7
Reactive Emotional Distress	23	67.6	9	26.5	2	5.9	34	23.4
Dissatisfaction with Social Relations	7	33.3	5	23.8	9	42.9	21	14.5
Other	1	20.0	4	80.0	0	—	5	3.4
Total *	75		39		31		145	

* N = 109. Totals exceed number of cases due to multiple diagnoses / target problems.

On the whole, patients with diagnoses of psychosis showed more positive problem change in a short period of time than many mental health workers might expect. The more acute psychotic reactions had, in fact, one of the best problem change rates of any group and the majority of patients with diagnoses of chronic undifferentiated schizophrenia showed at least a modest degree of alleviation of target problems. The relatively poor showing of patients with transient situational disturbances is puzzling at first glance but perhaps may be explained by the fact that this category tended to be used when the diagnostic picture was not clear. Thus it possibly collected more complex, and hence more difficult, cases.

As can be discerned from Table 15.2, three categories (role performance, interpersonal conflict, and reactive emotional distress) accounted for most (73 percent) of the target problems. Problems in these categories had a higher than average rate of alleviation. On the whole the majority of problems in each category were at least moderately alleviated during the period of service. The alleviation rate by this standard is 78 percent over all problems; 65 percent if substantial alleviation is used as the criterion; or 92 percent if at least slight change is employed as the cutting point. These outcomes are similar to those reported by Ewalt (chapter 2) for a population of presumably less disturbed clients in a child guidance setting. When problem change for each case is averaged, one finds that 72 percent of the clients showed at least a moderate amount of problem change. This outcome is similar for those reported by Reid (chapter 4) for family agency clients treated largely for family problems.

How durable are these gains? A representative sample of 22 patients were followed up an average of two months after treatment, as a part of another study (Reid and Epstein, 1974). Of the 17 patients located and interviewed in this study, all but one indicated that his overall problem situation was better than when service began. Even if one assumes that the five who were not interviewed had not improved, one still finds that 73 percent of the total follow-up sample reported favorable outcomes, about the same percentage judged to be improved on the basis of data obtained at closing.

I am sometimes asked if task-centered treatment is appropriate for mental patients. The data just presented strongly suggest that it is. The emotionally ill, like other groups, can be treated for problems in living that may be influenced by, but are by no means equivalent to, their psychiatric disorders.

Some case examples from student practice [2] will briefly be given to illustrate the use of task-centered treatment with three of the major diagnostic categories: depressive neurosis, chronic undifferentiated schizophrenia, and transient situational disturbance. In each example, the various task-centered components will be illustrated.

The Case of Ms. B: Depressive Neurosis

Ms. B is a 24-year-old woman, unmarried, with two children. From 1967 to 1972 she lived with a male friend, the father of the two children. During the past two years he has lived with other women. Ms. B's male friend came with her to the clinic. She was distraught; he had approached her and asked to live with her again. The problem, as stated by the client, was her uncertainty about reestablishing her relationship with her friend and their living together. This formulation agreed with the practitioner's and friend's assessment and was accepted by both clients and worker as the target problem, one best classified as a problem of social transition. The friend decided not to participate in any sessions after the first. A general task (treatment objective) was agreed on: to find ways to reestablish the relationship. Duration was set for eight interviews.

Operational tasks were established in interviews two and three. These were to limit the number and kinds of interactions between Ms. B and her friend. This was done to allow them to examine their present relationship. If it was as good as the first four years, Ms. B could seriously consider their living together again. The last two years of contacts had been mixed—good times but many fights, usually verbal arguments. The tasks were:

1) they were to see each other a maximum of three times a week, have only fun, and, if it involved his staying overnight, he would leave by 11:00 A.M.;
2) Ms. B was to seduce him if she so chose; and,

_____

[2] The practitioners for these cases were Timothy Plant and Holly Kushman Wellington.

3) Ms. B was free to go out and see anyone she chose the other four nights.

In interviews four and five, new tasks were established. These were designed to get at the pros and cons of her relationship with her friend at this time. Ms. B was to make a list of the positive and negative aspects of their relationship. Separately, she was to list what she wanted from a love relationship. The two lists would be discussed in the session and from the discussion, perhaps she could make a decision.

During the sixth week, Ms. B dated another male friend. They were seen and her former friend, who became enraged, made threats and began harassing her constantly. Up until that time all operational tasks had been completed successfully. However, the new development disrupted progress and required a rethinking of the objectives. Due to his untoward behavior, Ms. B decided not to consider reestablishing the old relationship. She decided that even though the first four years had been good, she could not, and would not, countenance such cruel treatment. The target problem was changed to her concern about being harassed by her former friend. She wanted to find ways to completely sever contact with her former lover. As he had a key to her apartment, her next task was to get the locks changed. In addition, she would see a legal aid counselor to obtain a peace bond and sign a statement at her job that she was being threatened. The last two tasks were to enable her to have her friend arrested by police, if necessary, and to prevent the loss of her job. Her former friend had come to her place of work and had threatened her and her children's lives. The duration was extended to ten weeks due to problem change.

In spite of the horror of the sixth, seventh, and eighth weeks, Ms. B continued evaluating the positives and negatives of the relationship, even as she took the necessary precautions to protect herself and her family. In the ninth interview she made her decision: she chose to discontinue all contacts with him. Additional tasks were to pack his clothes and have them sent to him. Also, she made arrangements for him to see his children under controlled conditions. This was done although he seemed reconciled to the situation, had stopped harassment, and only wanted visitation rights. The final treatment session consisted of a review of the decision-making process used and how she might use it in the future. Ms. B related that she felt good about her decision and looked forward to starting a new life.

The Case of Mr. L: Schizophrenia, Chronic Undifferentiated Type

Mr. L is a 22-year-old, unmarried man who has been in various types of institutional placement since he was five years of age. Most of his childhood and adolescent years were spent in a group setting in an institution housing 75 to 100 other boys. Since the age of sixteen or seventeen, he had been in psychiatric hospitals innumerable times. Our clinic space was shared by a state outreach program which originally worked with Mr. L before task-centered treatment was used. Mr. L came almost daily because he had nowhere else to go. As an entrée, he would usually say he was scared and needed to be hospitalized. No one had been able to focus with him on any problems in functioning, although numerous attempts were made. He lived in a substandard boarding house, had no friends, usually didn't bathe, panhandled frequently, but was charming. He had been diagnosed at an early age as schizophrenic.

Attempts at interviewing were thwarted by Mr. L's becoming very agitated and wanting to stop after five to ten minutes. He walked (or begged rides) halfway across the city in order to get himself admitted to a state hospital where he was unknown. Mr. L was, understandably, comfortable in an institution—it was all he knew.

Mr. L then was referred to the clinic for aftercare; a student worker volunteered to work with him. In a brief initial interview, Mr. L gave the following as his major problems: no planned activities, no apartment of his own, doesn't know himself (especially what women think of him), hasn't finished high school, doesn't sleep well, has to panhandle to get around, medication doesn't work well. The practitioner recorded that he had not been taking his medication properly, his hyperactivity interfered with social relationships, and that he had few activities—purposive or for fun. The following target problems were agreed to by client and worker: no activities during day, doesn't know how to spend his time, and lacks confidence in himself around others and does not feel he has much going for him. The problem classifications were inadequate resources and dissatisfaction with social relations. The first general task was to enroll in a day activity program as soon as possible. This would serve a twofold purpose. It would provide daily activities and a chance to socialize. This goal was selected by the client. Duration was set at 10 interviews, at a twice a week frequency.

It took two interviews to establish this contract with Mr. L. During the first interview, he left the room four times in 20 minutes. The practitioner expressed an interest in him each time he came back in. At the end of the first interview, Mr. L was told by the practitioner that he was glad he could stay 20 minutes and that he hoped Mr. L could stay 30 for the next interview. By the end of the treatment sequence, Mr. L would stay for 45 to 60 minutes in the interview without leaving.

With client's permission, contact was made with a hospital to initiate the process of obtaining an activity program. An appointment was made. In addition, Mr. L's medication was adjusted by a psychiatrist on the staff. Tasks set at the third interview involved the following: each morning for five minutes Mr. L would think about positives he had going for him, an example of what Ewalt (chapter 2) has described as a "mental" task. (A list of positives was compiled jointly by the worker and client during the third interview.) Finally, Mr. L would keep the appointment for the admission interview for the activity program.

Mr. L arrived for the fourth interview with clothes, asking to go to state hospital. He reported that a dog had talked to him. The practitioner asked that they again go over his list of positives. Mr. L agreed, but reiterated that he could not make it on his own. Again he was asked what he most wanted to change and he said his lack of activities. It was explained that he could have activities outside the hospital if he wanted them, that a staff member at the day hospital program was willing to talk with him about their program. By the end of the interview, he stated that he really had not tried other things (besides hospitalization) and then began to ask questions about the program. Another worker, one more familiar with the program, was called in to explain it in more detail. The interview ended with a discussion of ways for Mr. L to spend his weekend. He also agreed to read his list of positives each time he had "bad" thoughts about himself.

By the fifth interview, Mr. L began the day treatment program. Another target problem was added: dissatisfaction with his living situation because of distance from day hospital and lack of privacy. This problem was worked on, as practitioner and client attempted to maintain his going to the day-hospital regularly. He would miss days and it was determined that either his landlady would forget his busfare (She managed his public assistance funds) or he would forget his medicaid card which he needed for admission. With his permission, the practitioner spoke to the landlady and elicited her firm cooperation with regard to the busfare and medicaid card. Additionally, the day hospital made suggestions about housing nearby. In the interview, Mr. L called and made appointments to look at housing. Previously, when given a choice, he preferred that the worker make arrangements, although he did request he be accompanied to see the available rooms. Although he refused to role play his initial interview at the day hospital, he asked to do so about the housing appointments. Mr. L missed the first appointment, but he kept the second. He chose to move to the new boarding house where he would have his own room.

As his attendance at the day program was sporadic, Mr. L agreed that regular attendance and participation would be a repetitive task. By the ninth interview he was going regularly and participating somewhat, although he seemed at a loss around people. He had also moved to his new housing. In addition, he had seen his public aid worker and obtained regular transportation funds. He had helped the practitioner draft a letter to the Social Security Administration to change his address and insure the forwarding of his Supplemental Security Income checks. A surprising comment came from Mr. L during this interview. He reminded the worker that this was "the ninth session out of ten." The worker commented on his good memory.

The last interview was a summation of all Mr. L's accomplishments and ideas for future directions. Mr. L had begun individual treatment two weeks earlier at the day hospital so he would no longer be coming to the clinic for this purpose. The overlap was planned by Mr. L, the worker, and the staff at the hospital. He seemed eager to finish the sequence and during the interview pointed out plans he had: to learn budgeting, part-time employment. These things and others he would be discussing further in the day treatment program.

The Case of Mrs. K: Transient
Situational Disturbance

Mrs. K, a 39-year-old woman who had been married for 18 years and was living with her husband and her one child, came to the clinic expressing acute dissatisfaction with her marriage. There was no history of previous psychiatric treatment. She definitely expressed a wish to maintain the marriage and not divorce her husband. Mrs. K was self-referred; she got the name of the clinic from the telephone directory.

The client's perception of the problem was her inability to communicate with her husband. The practitioner stated, in her recording, that the client was having difficulty maintaining the marriage because her husband was hard to talk to about their problems. The target problems, as follows, were agreed to by the client and the practitioner:

1) Mrs. K isn't able to talk to her husband enough during the week;
2) Mrs. K's husband does not help her around the house, neither taking out the garbage nor occasionally doing the dishes;
3) Mrs. K is unable to get her husband to take her grocery shopping.

The problems were classified as interpersonal conflict, and duration, as agreed, was set for eight interviews held weekly. Although her husband would not come for interviews when the practitioner asked, he did agree to cooperate in fulfilling the tasks agreed on for the client. (As evidence of his cooperation, it turned out that Mr. K, three days later, washed and ironed his shirts and cleaned the house some, on his own initiative.) The client and worker agreed that achieving the general task of husband and wife spending more time together was the primary goal. In order to accomplish this, acceptable activities and times would be set aside for pleasurable encounters at home. The following operational task was agreed on in the second interview: to go for a pizza alone with her husband on Saturday night.

In the third session, the client reported that the task was accomplished and that they had had a very good evening. The following tasks were suggested, partly by the worker and partly by the client, for the next week. In selecting them, likes and dislikes of the couple were considered. All of these tasks were to take place between 8 and 10

P.M., after their daughter was asleep. On Monday night they were to take a bubble bath together. On Tuesday, they were to give each other back rubs. On Thursday, she would bake his favorite cookies and they would have milk and cookies by candlelight. Although the tasks may seem somewhat childish, they had the desired effect. Mr. and Mrs. K thoroughly enjoyed themselves and each task set the stage for a pleasurable sexual encounter if they desired it. Mrs. K said their sex life had not been so good since their first year of marriage, 17 years ago. It was decided by the client to repeat these tasks.

The following week an additional task was agreed on, one that would include the daughter. From 7 to 8 P.M. on Wednesday the three of them would make popcorn and have a family party. Another successful week followed. There were variations made by the client on the repeated tasks: showering together instead of a bubble bath, and pizza delivered instead of going out for one. Serendipitously it turned out that she and her husband were having not only good times but also talks about good and troublesome aspects of their marriage. Her husband began to look forward to being home and participated willingly (and at his own initiation) in chores, etc. Previously Mrs. K would go out alone with their daughter on weekends, but now Mr. K began to take them out on activities.

By the fifth session, Mrs. K felt it was no longer necessary to come in. She told of the ways she and her husband had discussed to further improve their marriage. They were all constructive. New and different activities were planned for future weeks, such as dancing, movies, but most importantly, that hour each night alone together enjoying themselves. Mrs. K reported the following as a comment her husband made to her: "It is too much," he said, "when it takes a social worker to tell us how to make our marriage better than it has ever been."

An Innovation in the Use of the Task-Centered Model

An innovation called "continuation contracts" was tried in the clinic during 1975 (Sentner, 1975). It involved the use of several task-centered sequences with the same client. It can be used primarily with chronic schizophrenics, as Mr. L, who may present an array of intransigent problems. However, it may as readily seem applicable to persons experiencing less severe disorders as long as they request assistance with problems too numerous for one sequence. So-called multiproblem families or, more properly, families or individuals suffering from extreme hardships, may fit this category.

Continuation contracts are not open-ended treatment, but are a series of task-centered treatment sequences, each one being contracted separately, i.e., target problem, goal, tasks, duration. One young man, diagnosed as paranoid schizophrenic, received two such sequences with successful results. In the first sequence the target problem was his extreme fear of leaving his parents' house alone. Within seven sessions he was coming to treatment and going other places alone. In this case, auditory hallucinations, which prevented his leaving his house alone, were treated as obstacles to task achievement. During the sequences he developed some measure of cognitive control over the frequency and magnitude of the voices he heard. In the second sequence the target problem was the client's short attention span. By the end of the sequence, he was able to spend an hour with a chosen activity. Previously his limit was 5 to 10 minutes.

The task-centered approach appears to be a means of providing a relatively quick alleviation of client stress; but it still allows for more extended treatment if a client so wishes. No claim is being made that the task-centered model can be used effectively with all clients, or that it can resolve underlying pathology. The major claim is that it seems to be efficacious with most problems that clients in this psychiatric setting want to work on. Additionally, it has provided a means to serve more clients within a shorter period of time.

Conclusions

Our experience suggests that the task-centered model can be adapted successfully for use in an outpatient psychiatry setting or in a community mental health agency. In using the model in such settings it is crucial that practitioners develop skill in perceiving and concentrating on target problems rather than on psychiatric disease syndromes. Thus the solution to the client's problems in living become central by plan. Expectations about influencing the presumed mental illness are avoided. As experienced clinicians know, it is common to concentrate treatment on "limited goals" despite frustrations about the intractability of the "disease." The task-centered model's perspective legitimates concentration on problems in living experienced by persons generally (perhaps too often) labelled mentally disturbed. By legitimating such treatment objectives, efficient and systematic interventions can be planned and implemented without wasting time on global, and usually futile, efforts to affect underlying pathology. As psychiatric and community mental health facilities extend services to larger numbers of people, they must turn increasingly to brief treatment models, like the task-centered one, which provide readily learned and applied technologies for the rapid alleviation of problems of living.

References

Reid, William J. 1975. "A test of a task-centered approach." *Social Work* 20:3–9.

Reid, William J., and Epstein, Laura. 1972. *Task-centered casework.* New York: Columbia University Press.

—— 1974. "Task-centered methods for multi-problem families: A proposal for research and development." Chicago: School of Social Service Administration, University of Chicago.

Sentner, Peter. 1975. "Time limited treatment of schizophrenics." Chicago: unpublished paper.

Chapter 16

~.~

Carvel Taylor, A.C.S.W.

Counseling in
a Service Industry

The Counseling Center at CNA Insurance in Chicago was established in October 1973 under the auspices of the company's employee medical department. One social worker is employed full-time. From time to time, there is one additional social worker, part-time. The company has six thousand employees who work in one high-rise office building. The majority are women clerical workers. The smaller number of managers and executives are men, although a few women are found at that level. The work force is young, the median age under thirty. Nineteen percent are black, and there are a few Latinos and recent Near and Far East immigrants. Most of the work force lives at considerable distance from their downtown Chicago workplace.

Services and Clients of the Center

Since the Counseling Center started, 505 employees have requested its assistance. The Counseling Center offers three services: referral to resources in the community; task-centered counseling; and consultation to supervisors and management on employee-related issues. Resource referral is the largest service. Sixty-five percent of all applicants requested and used referrals for financial planning, day care, home placement for aged relations, medical care, and legal aid. Legal problems concern matters of divorce, arrests, consumer fraud, immigration problems. Management consultation services are highly individualized. Task-centered counseling services were provided to eighty-five employees. An equal number of employees were referred to a community resource because the Center itself lacked resources: e.g., cases where behavior was of psychotic proportions and medical-psychiatric interventions were desired by the client; cases where the family of the employee wished to obtain family group treatment; cases where the employees' spouse wanted marital treatment for the couple; or cases where the employee made a request for a specific form of treatment (Transactional Analysis, Gestalt Therapy, Feminist Therapy, and so forth). Effective resource referral provides a base for the acceptance and value of the entire program. The Center has developed a network of resources which respond quickly, do not impede appointments with formidable intake procedures, and maintain hours compatible with the schedule of working people who are commuters.

Employees are able to meet with the Center's social work staff on company time, over lunch or on breaks. Except for emergencies, an appointment must be made. Waiting time is rarely more than two days. If a resource only is requested, direction to that resource is provided. Staff inform employees of the task-centered counseling available. When counseling is requested, the staff explains the different sorts of therapy available in the community and in the Center, the relative costs, and the applicability of the Major Medical Insurance provided by the company. The employees themselves decide where they believe they fit best.

The employees who requested service so far have been similar to the overall make-up of the company in terms of ethnic identity, sex, and job status. Those who chose to use the task-centered treatment component have been similar to the total group who requested service. However, divorced persons, those under thirty, and those living in one particular suburban area have been seen in higher proportion in the task-centered cases.

Application of the Task-Centered Approach

Half of the employees who accepted task-centered counseling wanted assistance in two problem categories: interpersonal conflicts and dissatisfaction with social relations. The rest of the problems were distributed among social transition, inadequate resources, reactive emotional distress, and role performance. Most complained of tense and disagreeable situations with people close to them: parents, spouse, friends, or supervisor. Others saw their own habits and internal conflicts as contributing to the problem. Many cast the problems in terms of their inability to perform within an expected role. Difficulties in adjusting to new expectations were common. For example, a newly divorced man with custody of his children needed assistance taking on some duties formerly performed by his wife. There have been instances of employees with clerical backgrounds being unable to perform when promoted to a management job. A number of employees could not deal with systems or demands outside their own family: they had overextended themselves financially, had unusually heavy financial responsibilities, or they were unable to communicate effectively with schools, courts, or business systems. Some suffered from unresolved emotional distress: grief, anxiety, anger, depression, which did not allow them to lead a normal life.

After employees decided to come to the Center for task-centered counseling a time-limit was set. The mean number of sessions for the eighty-five persons was 5; but the range varied from 2 to 21. The employee was asked to state the problem as simply as possible. For example, many would say, "My parents (mother, boyfriend, boss) are driving me crazy." or "I feel depressed." Others would be less vague. They would say: "I believe my son's teacher is not teaching my child how to read," or "The loan company is having my paycheck garnisheed."

Whenever the complaint was vague or unquantifiable, the employee was asked to give examples of situations when distress was felt. These "critical incidents" were then examined and analyzed. The employee described the incident precisely, noting who was there and what sort of people they were, where the incident took place, the time, the client's mood, and *exactly* what was said. The "critical incidents" represented conditions perceived by the employees as acute distress. Their identification and clarification enabled them to pin down target problems.

Case Illustrations

A young employee, Ann, 22, white, of working-class and Polish background, complained about her mother and her woman cousin, who lived with them. She felt depressed and inadequate whenever she was with either of them, but was unable to define the problem further. The contract was for six sessions. In order to specify the problem, Ann was asked to keep a diary of all contacts with these two people for a week. From the diary, two incidents appeared to exemplify the problem. One incident took place in the kitchen after the client came home from work. Her mother and cousin began trying to talk her into entering a beauty contest. Ann was excited about the possibility. She began feeling depressed when the other women started planning her hairstyle and dress without consulting her. She was unable to protest or to express her anger. The depression continued into the next day. That evening her mother set a time limit for Ann's returning home from a date. Ann was still angry from the episode the day before. She was unable to tell her mother how she resented this latest demand. Ann's target problem was: inability to stop her mother and cousin from imposing on her, classified as "dissatisfaction with social relations." It was judged that Ann's inability to tell her mother and her cousin how much she resented being manipulated and treated like a teenager was triggering her depressions. Her overall goal was to establish a more equal relationship with her mother and cousin. When it developed that her father also treated her like a child, problems with him were included. Tasks chosen were: "to come to an agreement with parents defining Ann's role as another adult in the home"; "to pay her share of the household costs"; "to be the one who decided what time to be in at night"; "to identify those times when she feels manipulated by her cousin and mother"; "to tell them how she felt as soon as possible after the incident." Ann decided to choose a time and place to discuss these issues with her mother and father. The counselor advised that these discussions not occur in the bedroom or the kitchen since the "put-downs" always occurred there. These tasks were outlined in the second interview. That evening, Ann asked her parents to come into the living room. She said she enjoyed living at home and had decided to contribute financially to the upkeep. Her parents resisted this suggestion at first. She convinced them by insisting that all adults paid their own way. During this discussion with her parents, Ann found out that they worried about her if she came in later than 1:00 A.M. She agreed to call them whenever she was out later than 1:00 A.M.

The following week Ann's cousin began "telling" her how to wear her hair. Ann was able to be firm, explaining she liked to design her own hairstyle. Ann reported that her hands were shaking when she confronted her cousin. After the third session, Ann said that she realized that there were other people with whom she had similar problems: her boyfriend and her boss. Ann decided to expand the sense of the tasks to others. She told her boyfriend she did not like the bar they frequented. She explained to her boss that he was giving her work to do in an inefficient way. At the end of the six sessions, Ann reported that she felt less depressed. She still got "extremely nervous" when she "told someone what she thought," but was "able to do it anyway."

The "critical incident" idea is useful to target a problem when some other person is identified by the client as the cause of the difficulty. Ed, 56, a repairman who had been with the company for 30 years, complained of his wife's nagging. He said he had decided to leave her because of it. The couple had been married 35 years. One daughter was married; a son, 12, was in school. Ed could not be specific about when the nagging occurred. Four sessions were agreed upon and Ed began keeping a diary. The first week Ed's wife "nagged" when Ed worked late and then went to a local bar with his friends; she "nagged" when he "slurped" his coffee. These incidents quickly blew up into serious arguments, other complaints being added. Ed decided he did not want a separation or divorce. The overall goal became to minimize the episodes of "nagging." When Ed's list of "critical incidents" were examined he saw, reluctantly, that he was precipitating the arguments. He consistently failed to inform his wife of his changing work hours and his intentions to be "out with the boys." He turned a deaf ear to his wife's complaints. She, in turn, escalated her demands until he recognized "nagging." Since he was unable to deal with his wife's anger, he felt relieved to have a "fight" develop. Then he could walk out, although nothing was resolved. Ed took this explanation, which evolved from his description of the events, as disagreeable but reasonable. Then he admitted he was afraid of his wife.

The tasks were: "to tell his wife ahead of time every time he had to work late"; "to call her once that night"; "to plan 'Dad's night out' ahead of time"; "to encourage her to do the same"; and "to plan more time out together." If a "nagging" episode came up Ed was "to hear her out." He would firmly retain his right to make decisions about his job and recreation plans. The diary was continued for two more sessions. After that time, Ed did not need it. He was able to remember episodes clearly. At the end of four sessions he reported that his wife seemed more relaxed and that they were arguing less.

The cases of Ann and Ed are illustrations of the task-centered counseling approach used in the Center. The range of problems is wider than suggested by only these two cases. Many, if not most, of the employees have never had counseling before and state they would not consider using community counseling facilities. They appear to bottle up their problems. They suffer anxiety and depression as they stoically persevere, often taking action adverse to their well-being through not knowing what else to do.

Evaluation

Accounting for outcomes is a necessary and regular practice of the Center. Information on the outcome of referral service is routinely obtained by inquiries to the referral agency. Forty-three employees who received three or more sessions of task-centered counseling between March 1, 1974, and January 1, 1975, and who were still employed in the company, were sent an evaluation questionnaire. Thirty-six (84 percent) returned the questionnaire. The majority (91 percent) of those responding indicated that their situation was improved. Most of them (87 percent) indicated that they received the help they wanted. Most (97 percent) would return to the Center if there were a need; and all (100 percent) believed the counseling was useful. Fifty-four percent stated that the Center helped job performance. Since only six persons primarily sought help for job related problems, it appeared that helping employees with personal and family problems influenced job performance.

In a real sense, evaluation of the service takes place in a public way. Employees tell others about help received. Their supervisors and managers observe change. All this has contributed to an assessment throughout the whole work community that there is positive value in the service. The evidence of satisfaction with the service is the continual increase in the number of applicants and the support the management gives to the Center.

Conclusions

During the year and a half that the service has been in operation, the task-centered model appears to be appropriate to an industrial setting. The concentration on target problems and time limits fits the characteristics of a work place. It is my opinion that the most important action is determining as early as possible, ideally in the first conversation, precisely and graphically what the client perceives as the problem(s). If the problem can be simply stated, that definition is accepted as the basis for task formulation. If the problem appears to be vague or not able to be stated—unhappiness, depression, lack of communication—the experience of the Center shows that the "critical incident" route to target problem definition is helpful.

The evaluative data we have obtained are in accord with the results reported elsewhere in this volume, particularly by Ewalt (chapter 2) and Brown (chapter 15). When task-centered methods are applied to specific, agreed-upon problems, a very high proportion of the problem situations so treated will show at least some degree of alleviation.

Chapter 17

~~~~~~

Andrew Weissman, A.C.S.W.

In the Steel Industry

The Counseling Center at the United States Steel–South Works, Chicago Illinois, opened in April 1974. It is administered by Human Affairs, Inc., a private social work consulting firm, under contract with the steel works. Staff consists of two social workers with Master's degrees, one with a Bachelor's degree, and a secretary. The Center's office is located off company premises, but geographically close to the plant. The Center will assist any employee and his family. Three services, which may overlap, are provided: (1) task-centered casework, (2) linkage, and (3) emergency service, including a twenty-four-hour "hot line" (Taylor and Weissman, 1975).

Clients are attracted by advertising in the company media. Our slogan is "Get Help Without Hassle." As Center Director, I conduct meetings at the plant with employees to explain the service, and consult with management and union officials to develop programs. It is widely understood by the work force that both management and the union support the objectives of the program. The Center makes no refusals. It is our hope that every employee who comes will receive assistance with the problem which he presents. Because of its no-refusal policy and emphasis on solving problems in the terms stated by the employees, the Center has found the task-centered approach well suited to its purposes.

Clients Served and Their Problems

During the Center's first twelve months of operation, it served 996 plant employees and 438 family members. The majority (85 percent) of the employees were men. The largest number were black (48 percent). The remainder were white (38 percent) and Latino (14 percent). Most of the employees served were blue-collar, hourly-rated workers. Only 18 percent were management and white-collar personnel. The majority (65 percent) were married and had been employed in the plant for more than five years (51 percent). Fifty-three percent of the employees asked for assistance with behavior or social adjustment difficulties, such as marital conflict, child behavior problems, lack of education and job training, lack of child care arrangements, and alcoholism. The balance of the employees (47 percent) needed legal and financial assistance to deal with divorce, arrests, garnishments, debts, consumer fraud, poor credit ratings, unemployment compensation claims, and the like. In 30 percent of the cases, the employee's social problems were judged to be seriously detracting from his work performance.

Counseling is provided on the basis of a verbal contract. Duration is set at between two and nine sessions. In cases with shorter duration we try to help a client analyze and act on a problem for which he has resources. The interventions usually occur at the initial phase of the task-centered model: the problem is defined concretely; exploration is confined to the immediate question; alternatives are clarified; and direction and advice are provided to help set quickly upon a problem-solving course of action. More extensive counseling, up to nine sessions, is provided when the target problem is not immediately obvious or when the client needs to experiment with different tasks in order to find a solution to his problem.

For example: Matthew, 23, a construction worker and son of a plant employee, had used heroin for two years. For the past six months,

Matthew had been attending a methadone clinic but had quit. He saw his major problem as inability to have any friends outside the drug culture. Matthew described painful loneliness, being alienated from former friends whom he respected, tense awkwardness in social relations. All this left him with no alternative to drug-induced "happiness." The target problem, the condition which was to be changed in treatment, was Matthew's loneliness, his lack of friends. In the first session a list was made of people from his high school days with whom he would like to reestablish contact. Matthew's tasks were to telephone at least three of these people, and to attend a social activity with at least one of them, all before the next session. Matthew proposed to add that he cut down on heroin intake to once for the following week. He thought that his former friends had rejected him because of his drug-dominated life. He believed he could not reestablish these relationships without also trying to control his drug use. He thought he could make progress on this change by himself, without returning to the methadone program, because at the moment he was not "strung out" on heroin. In the second interview, Matthew reported participating in a basketball game with some of his old friends whom he had phoned. He had gone with them to a party after the game. He complained of not being able to overcome shyness with girls unless he was drinking or smoking pot.

During the next six sessions, Matthew's tasks were to go out socially with his rediscovered friends, to make a date with a woman acquaintance at least once each week. He was to go on that date without using drugs or alcohol. Dates were first made only with women with whom Matthew retained some marginal relationship, whom he knew from high school. This was easier for him than to try himself out with women he was meeting for the first time. During each session, Matthew rehearsed his dating behavior. By the fourth week of the middle phase of treatment (the sixth session of the sequence) Matthew was able to approach a woman he had met at a party whom he had never known before.

During the seventh week of treatment, Matthew had a car accident and his car was in the shop for repairs. He was not insured and had to take a loan from the credit union to repair his car and the one he hit. He exhausted his savings. Low in funds and relying on public transportation, Matthew continued to attend social activities with his friends and to date. He was extremely surprised to find that old friends welcomed him back and enjoyed his company. He was surprised that women liked him. These experiences heavily reinforced his commitment to cut out heroin. Because of the expenses of the car accident, Matthew lacked funds to purchase drugs. He was not willing to risk arrest by stealing money for drugs, which he had sometimes done in the past.

In the eighth session, at termination, Matthew had succeeded in making a few valued friends, both men and women. He was happier with his parents and was being more reliable at his job. He was using marijuana occasionally.

Linkage

The term "linkage" is preferable to the usual term "referral" (Pincus and Minahan, pp. 18–26). Obtaining expeditious connection to a relevant and accessible community service is the Center's most visible and valued activity. The Center's linkage techniques have been reported elsewhere (Weissman). Briefly, they consist of the following: (1) being continuously informed of all the resources available; (2) maintaining sufficient personal contact to open access for the Center's clients; (3) selecting the resources with best fit; (4) following up with clients and resources to evaluate the effect of the linkage on the client's expressed problem; and (5) intervening with negotiations and perhaps a new resource if the original connection has failed. Knowing the resources and negotiating access are program development functions. Selecting, following up, and renegotiating are adaptations of the task-centered model.

Linkage service is used to help clients with the many problems for which the Center itself has no resources. There is no dearth of relevant services in the community for clients who are employed by a powerful company, have good insurance and fringe benefits, or have savings and property. Clients who want counseling are linked to treatment agencies or private practitioners if they have need of medication, or if the Center treatment load is full and they wish to avoid waiting.

In providing linkage service the initial steps of the task-centered model are followed in this fashion: target problem defined, contract made, exploration and assessment of the problem, evaluation of appropriate resources, negotiation with the resource by the Center staff and the client, assumption by the client of tasks to obtain the resources, followup with client and the resource to obtain information about results. If the linkage has failed, the Center takes initiative to consult the resource and the client to clarify misunderstandings or to make a substitute linkage. Followup is provided until the connection is effected or the need is no longer perceived. If the linkage breakdown is due to the client's uncertainty or to the impact upon him of other problems, there will be an additional step: undertaking a set of tasks involving changes in the client's attitudes and skills to free him to make use of the resource.

An example of a linkage service is the case of Mr. and Mrs. Lorenz. He and his wife came to the Center overwhelmed by the following: they had recently moved from a modest house to a larger one in a more expensive neighborhood; they had extensive debts far exceeding their ability to pay, were behind in payments, were daily besieged by threatening telephone calls and letters from creditors, were being threatened with wage garnishment, were afraid Mr. Lorenz would be fired if the company received wage garnishments; their unmarried teen-age daughter was pregnant; their young son was in trouble in his new school; Mr. and Mrs. Lorenz were beside themselves and quarrelled incessantly. They were offered a contract for service and immediate direction was given to deciding upon target problems and priorities. The Lorenzes were informed that the union contract prohibited the company from using wage garnishment as a reason for firing. With that issue out of the way, Mr. and Mrs. Lorenz decided they could manage on their own and did not need the Center.

Two weeks later, the first garnishment took effect and they were broke. This time the couple chose to work on their financial stress and to handle the problems of their own relationship, their daughter's pregnancy, and their son's school difficulties on their own. They were directed to explore the exact amount of their indebtedness and how it was distributed. Mr. Lorenz's task was to get a list of all firms who had wage assignments on file for his purchases, and all firms who were preparing to submit garnishments to the company. Mrs. Lorenz was to gather together all bills and contracts signed by either of them. Mr. and Mrs. Lorenz, together, were to itemize all their normal monthly expenses. In the second and final interview the Lorenzes brought all these accounts, now intelligible, and were overwhelmed by the amount. They saw themselves as "deadbeats." After being given the name of a suitable lawyer, the tasks were: to make an appointment, to get legal advice on what type of bankruptcy procedure to follow, and to put aside funds for filing the necessary papers in court.

One month later, the Center made a telephone followup. The Lorenzes had accepted legal advice. All wage assignments had been voided by the bankruptcy court. A court-supervised plan of regular payments were in effect. The Lorenzes had made their first installment payment as directed by the court. Creditors had been barred from harrassing the family with telephone calls and letters.

Emergency Services

The Center's emergency service responds to urgent calls for help which arise from sudden events of an overwhelming nature. Often there is a need to protect the employee or his family and coworkers. This service is available after office hours through an answering service which contacts the staff after receiving a call. A call back is guaranteed immediately. After-hours calls often have to be answered by making a home visit, no matter what the hour. The feature of the task-centered model used is concentration upon the immediate issues. The staff assumes a great deal of responsibility to bring such a situation under control. It is rare that employees or their families seek additional help once control has been established. Staff had been called out, for example, when the problem was a sudden and dangerous fight which had broken out between an employee and his neighbors, or when a mentally ill employee had suddenly behaved in a frightening manner.

Evaluation and Future Directions

Client views of the service were obtained from 269 usable replies to a questionnaire mailed to 350 employees who received service. Eighty-six percent of the respondents thought they received a service they wanted. Eighty-four percent stated that the problem that they came with initially had improved. Continuous monitoring of the linkage service revealed that in 75 percent of the cases employees obtained satisfactory use of that service. Most of the unsatisfactory results are explained by clients' having changed their minds about wanting the referral. This type of explanation, however, raises further questions about linkage methods and is being studied further.

At the Center, we are particularly interested in developing a typology of linkage techniques. Despite the emphasis in social work on selecting resources to fit clients' needs, an effective technology remains to be developed (Middleman and Goldberg; Kirk and Greenley). The capability of the task-centered model would be improved by a linkage technology. Analysis of data collected in the course of the Center's practice suggests there are probably patterns of use in linkage techniques. Research is being conducted at present to specify these patterns as well as test the utility and outcomes of the linkage technology.

References

Kirk, Stuart A., and Greenley, James R. 1974. "Denying or delivering services?" *Social Work* 19:443.

Middleman, Ruth, and Goldberg, Gale. 1974. *Social service delivery: A structural approach to social work practice.* New York: Columbia University Press; p. 66.

Pincus, Allen, and Minahan, Anne. 1973. *Social Work Practice: Model and Method.* Itasca, Ill.: F. E. Peacock.

Taylor, Carvel V., and Weissman, Andrew. 1975. *Handbook for the organization of an employee assistance program.* Philadelphia: Human Resources Network.

Weissman, Andrew. 1976. "Industrial social services: Linkage technology." *Social Casework* 57(1).

Chapter 18

~.~

E. Matilda Goldberg and James Robinson

An Area Office of an English Social Service Department

Within a relatively short time major changes have taken place in the British local authority social services in which over 90 percent of social workers are employed. These services have been transformed from three specialist departments with fairly well defined functions in the fields of welfare for the disabled and elderly, the care of deprived children, and social services for the mentally ill and handicapped, to an increasingly more open and integrated social service agency which serves all comers. Recent legislation concerned with the welfare of children and the care of the chronically sick and disabled has added new statutory duties to the steadily increasing volume of referrals to these integrated social service departments. Requests for help range from simple information and advice to the most intractable problems our society is capable of producing. The activities of this social services department include extensive domiciliary services such as home-helps (homemaker services), meal services, and various forms of residential and day care. Income maintenance is not included. It is administered by the central government although the social services department has small cash resources at its disposal. The social services personnel, headed by a Director of Social Services, are accountable to the Social Services Committee, comprised of elected councillors, so that decisions about the allocation and deployment of resources are in the last resort political ones.

Social work with individuals and families constitutes a small but vital part of the social services department. Social workers form only about 10 percent of its personnel. Further, much of the social work effort goes into the assessment of client needs and the provision of services. Only a small part of the social workers' activities can be described as casework. Social work methods have not yet been fully adjusted to the changing nature of the local authority social services, nor has the training of social workers been sufficiently adapted to meet the changing demands on them. There are many indications that if social work is to survive as a viable discipline its aims and input in different client situations will have to be more clearly specified and the skills required will need to be examined afresh. For instance, we shall have to look critically at the open-ended surveillance duties placed on social workers under various statutes concerned with the welfare of children and the care of the disabled, often resulting in large, relatively static caseloads and aimless "visiting."

The introduction into the social service departments of "intake teams" has aroused great interest in expert assessment and short-term work and hence in the task-centered approach (Loevenstein, 1975; Bywaters, 1975; and Hutten, 1974, 1975). The slowly increasing number of social service consumer studies in Britain (Mayer and Timms, 1970; McKay et al., 1973; and Rees, 1974) have repeatedly shown misperceptions of needs and aims between clients and social workers. These findings strongly support the notion, inherent in the task-centered model, that clients might be better able to tackle their problems if aims and means of intervention were more clearly defined and understood by client and social worker. Evaluative and descriptive studies of casework intervention carried out in Britain in the late sixties also point to the relative success of goal-oriented, short-term casework (Goldberg et al., 1970; Goldberg and Neill, 1972).

Thus the model of task-centered casework has evolved at a critical moment in British casework when its contribution to the whole spectrum of the social services provision is very much in question and stands in danger of being squeezed out altogether unless it can make a vital and visible impact.

The Setting

Soon after the publication of *Task-Centered Casework*, by Reid and Epstein (1972), we decided to explore and test the model in a local authority social services department.

The ideas underlying the task-centered approach were introduced at a staff seminar for the social services personnel in the county of Buckinghamshire some fifty miles northwest of London. Great interest was aroused and the project was set up in one of the department's five area offices situated in Aylesbury, which serves a population of 116,000 and covers some 220,000 acres, a mixture of urban and rural areas. Four professionally trained social workers with at least one year's experience volunteered to take part, as well as the assistant area officer and James Robinson, the department's research officer. The project, which was financially supported by the Department of Health and Social Security, was recognized as part of the county's development program. The work generated by the project—regular meetings, some time for thought, special recording—was additional to the ordinary activities of these workers, who carried a normal mixed caseload of between forty to fifty clients, including the elderly and physically disabled, child care cases, and problems of mental disability.[1] The project could only develop slowly and on occasion was accorded low priority, since the social workers had to respond to crises, staff shortages, and other pressures of an expanding general social services agency.

Aims

The aims of the project were to assess the usefulness and appropriateness of the task-centered model for different types of cases, by com-

[1] Many of the ideas presented have arisen in the project discussions. The case material has been contributed by Lyn Wishlade, David Walker, Jill Pick, and Cliff Thomas, who in a very real sense are the authors of this chapter.

paring those situations in which the method appeared to work and those in which it did not seem applicable; and to evaluate outcome in terms of client and social worker opinions.

Procedure and Methods

From the autumn of 1972 onward the participating staff met fortnightly with Tilda Goldberg to study the model and try it out on some selected cases. During this phase special record forms, modelled on Reid's instruments for classifying problems and tasks and for measuring progress on task achievement, were tried out and adapted to the British context (Appendix). An independent follow-up interview carried out by a social work assessor was also piloted.

The main study began in March 1974 with the target of completing fifty task-centered cases within approximately a year. The project ended in December 1975 without achieving this target for reasons which will become evident in the subsequent discussion. Since we wanted to test the suitability of the method in a variety of problem situations referred to a social services department, it was decided to accept cases into the study more or less at random as they were allocated by the team leaders to the social workers in the course of their duties. Each worker undertook to carry at least two task-centered cases at any one time, on which they filled in the special record forms and wrote fairly full narrative notes. At the final interview the client's permission was sought for a follow-up visit by the independent assessor, who visited soon after closure. She only knew the client's home address and household composition and had no contact with the participating social workers.

Some minor adaptations were introduced into the record forms, notably a checklist of outside agencies with whom the social workers are in touch on behalf of their clients, and a method of measuring the relative proportions of different intervention strategies used in any one case interview. There was only one major conceptual alteration we felt compelled to make after encountering repeated confusion over the concept of "task" which Reid and Epstein describe as referring "both to means and ends" (page 98). The confusion ceased when we began to distinguish between the "task," defined as the specific objective of intervention within the area of the target problem, and "work," defined as the means by which the task is to be achieved. We use these terms continually on the record forms and in our discussion. Thus in the case of the "sewing lady" to be described later the task was the improvement of her financial position, and the client's and the social worker's "work" varied from week to week. For example, the client's work in the second week was to ask her son for an increase in her allowance for board and lodgings. In the third week the client was to read job advertisements in the local paper and visit the employment exchange. The social worker's work was to consult the general practitioner and to approach a voluntary society for a cash grant.

Task-Centered and Non-Task-Centered Cases

During the eighteen months of the main study, 68 cases were included in the project.[2] As said before, these cases were not selected for their potential suitability for the method. Whenever a case did not prove workable according to the task-centered model, it became part of the social worker's ordinary caseload, and another case was taken on. We decided early on that we would only call a case fully task-centered when the following three basic requirements of the method were being met:

1. A target problem or problems had been agreed upon between social worker and client.
2. A task or tasks had been established and were being worked on.
3. A reasonable time limit for service was made explicit and adhered to.

Cases were considered to be partially task-centered when one or two, but not all three features were adhered to. We regarded those cases as not task-centered where the method was not being applied, or was abandoned for a variety of reasons which will be discussed below. No pressure was exerted on the workers to apply the method when they felt it to be inappropriate.

[2] One of these cases, Mrs. D (in Table 18.1) was referred twice to the project. Because the paper was written shortly before the project ended, the actual number of cases served in the project was somewhat larger than the number cited and data on a few of the cases are incomplete.

The project cases were classified as follows: fully task-centered, 22; partially task-centered, 5; non-task-centered, 41. This distribution should not come as a surprise in view of the very broad service, surveillance, and statutory functions of the British social services department described in the introduction. Indeed it is noteworthy that nearly a third of the cases were apparently amenable to a task-centered casework approach.

The first question that arises is whether the task-centered cases differed in any important respects from the non-task-centered cases, for example, in relation to clients' age, sex, household composition, the sources of and reasons for their referral, and so on. Caution is indicated as numbers are very small, but certain small differences raise interesting questions. Proportionately, more clients in the fully task-centered group were referred by medical sources or on their own initiative (77 percent) than clients who were dealt with in other ways (52 percent). Financial difficulties formed the background of the fully task-centered cases relatively more frequently (32 percent) than in the non-task-centered group (12 percent). The age range shows differences between the fully task-centered and non-task-centered groups. While less than one-third of the fully task-centered group were under the age of 40, over half of the non-task-centered group were in this age range. Related to this age difference is the fact that in nearly half of the non-task-centered cases the main client is referred to as the family while only one case is so described in the fully task-centered group. In other words, the social worker usually worked with one designated client in the fully task-centered group. This may suggest that the model lends itself better to work with individuals with its emphasis on specific objectives and clearly defined ways of achieving them. It may also be that we have not yet found a way of working in a task-centered way with couples or with the multifaceted situations affecting whole family groups.

Reasons for the nonapplication of the model in the 46 cases in which it was either not used or only partially used were examined. The cases were distributed as follows: no problem revealed, 6; specific service or information only requested, 8; problem present (according to worker) but not acknowledged by client or no agreement on problem, 9; no task agreement, 7; client incapable of collaboration, 3; time limits not kept, 6; administrative or other reasons (e.g., other agencies involved, client moved), 7.

If we look more closely into the reasons for the nonapplication of the task-centered model, they form two clusters. One group of reasons is mainly related to the agency's functions and the other reasons are mainly associated with the client's problem situation. The very broad welfare, surveillance, and preventive functions of the social services department led some clients to be referred because they were *potentially* at risk; for instance, the parents of an epileptic boy, who were coping well at the time but glad to know where to turn should the need for help arise in the future. Similarly, a few partially sighted persons were referred who did not require or wish for social work help but who agreed to registration as handicapped persons, which entitled them to certain aids and services. Other clients had practically found their own solutions before the social worker arrived, or they only required a specific piece of information or advice to work out their own solutions. As described in the introduction, the social services department under various Acts of Parliament has the duty to provide all manner of domiciliary services for the chronically sick and disabled, and day or residential care for various client groups, such as the elderly, the mentally disordered, deprived children, and so on. Thus in a proportion of cases the social workers' functions were mainly those of assessment and arrangement for specific services involving a great deal of liaison with other agencies, rather than casework.

The social services department has surveillance and protective functions, for example, in relation to the mentally handicapped, to children at risk, to those mentally ill clients who need compulsory admission to a psychiatric hospital, to young delinquents under supervision orders, and so on. In these situations a target problem may be clearly perceived by the referrer or the surrounding community but not necessarily acknowledged by the "client" or his family. For example, the headmaster of a special school for mentally handicapped children felt that a 16-year-old girl, on leaving school, should be encouraged to attend an industrial training unit daily. However, her uninterested parents would not cooperate with these plans, so the social worker was asked to try and persuade the parents to let their daughter attend the industrial training unit. By very persistent efforts the social worker eventually found the mother, and in an unannounced visit, managed to persuade her to view the unit with the girl and to allow her to attend for a trial month; but at first this could only be achieved behind the father's back! The girl improved greatly by her attendance—her enuresis practically cleared up and she took much more pride in her appearance—so that the mother eventually accepted a permanent place for her: she also undertook the difficult task of telling her husband. We felt that these manipulative and highly successful techniques employed for the sake of the handicapped girl's long-term well-being did not fulfil the requirements of the task-centered model.

In the second group of cases in which the task-centered model did not appear to "fit," the reasons mainly resided in the clients' complex problems and attitudes, and occasionally perhaps also in the social worker's uncertainty. In some of these situations a target problem was either not acknowledged by the client or not agreed upon between client and worker, and in yet other cases no feasible task could be evolved.

For example, a client may insist that his major problem (e.g., housing, in one of our cases) is one which the referring agent and the social worker only consider a minor one. In one example the referring agency, the school, and the social worker saw the behavior problems of a mentally handicapped daughter as the main cause for concern. Although the social worker tried to acknowledge and work with the parents on the problem as they saw it, namely housing, events soon overtook them, and the handicapped girl who kept disappearing from home had to be received into care. There were several families beset by a multiplicity of problems in which the most important problem seemed to be ever-shifting, and the social worker did not find it possible to home in on a target problem, let alone to delineate and work on a realistic task.

There were also cases in which the client and social worker were agreed on the target problem, but they either could not find a real task to work on, or there was disagreement about the appropriateness of the task suggested by the client. For example, in one family the husband had got into considerable financial tangles, and there were also many signs of conflict and maladjustment in the family. Although the target problem of inadequate resources was established, it proved impossible to find a specific task in the course of five interviews. In her concluding notes the social worker commented:

> Despite several efforts to elicit a task, not one has come up which the client was willing to work on in any planned or concerted way. If this were not a task-centered case there would still have been the problem of focusing or directing the social work intervention. On my last visit Mr. H commented that he was more in need of a merchant banker than a social worker.

In another case a family facing severe housing stress thought they could achieve more by hanging on until public housing became available, rather than working with the social worker on the solution of obtaining temporary accommodation meanwhile.

The cases which we considered to be only partially task-centered were mainly situations of chronic mental illness or frailty in old age. A problem area was agreed upon and a task worked out but largely owing to the chronic nature of the difficulties the time limits became rather indefinite and the tasks less and less specific.

The Task-Centered Cases

The 22 task-centered cases were referred for a great variety of problems (see Table 18.1). Some families had got into serious financial difficulties through unemployment, illness, or separation from a spouse; two families needed help in coping with a severely disabled child; marital problems were the presenting difficulties in some cases; and two mothers were having trouble in handling their children's aggressive behavior. Needs arising from progressive disablement and frailty in old age formed the background of several cases. As can be seen from Table 18.1 the most frequently identified target problem was that of inadequate resources (8), followed by problems in social transition (6), dissatisfaction in social relations (5), interpersonal conflict (2) and role performance (2).

Inadequate Resources

In a third of the task-centered cases the target problem was defined as inadequate resources. As the table shows, in most of these cases there

was considerable task achievement and problem reduction. Only a minority of situations called for fairly straightforward resource provision
with the social worker acting either as the client's agent or advocate. In
most cases the aim was not merely to raise a loan to stop eviction or to
prevent the Electricity Board from cutting off the current, but to enable clients to manage their resources more realistically or to find their
way around the maze of British welfare provisions—in short, to cope
more effectively with the material aspects of their lives. In almost all
these situations nonmaterial problems (such as marital difficulties,
physical or mental disability) contributed to the financial crisis. These
contributory problems were recognized by both clients and social
workers, but they were left untouched either because the clients considered them of lesser importance or unalterable, or because clients
felt they would be more able to cope with the nonmaterial stresses
once the material need was met. For example, a young family (Q) was
referred for the installation of a telephone because the young mother
had contracted a progressive disease which necessitated immediate
contact with a doctor at crisis points. There were heavy travelling expenses to a hospital many miles away; the care of the two small children was a cause for concern as well as the general upheaval generated
by this catastrophic change in circumstances. After very careful exploration it was established that the young father was able to take care of
most of his problems with the help of relatives and friends, except the
need for the telephone. The social worker made it clear that counselling and providing supportive domiciliary services were also part of
his function. On his final visit after the young wife's discharge from the
hospital, he found that the couple had a realistic appreciation of the future and were continuing to cope well, supported by relatives. The
social worker concluded his notes by saying that the method, concentrating on the problem uppermost in the client's mind, was particularly
helpful in allowing him *not* to push the area of readjustment which
both husband and wife clearly did not see as being a problem. On the
follow-up visit the young couple said that their problem had been
resolved (the telephone application had been accepted), and they had
appreciated the social worker's concern about their ability to manage; it
had given them "a new view on what the social service people were
like" and they felt that if anything occurred that they could not deal
with they would not mind asking the social worker for advice.

Table 18.1

Characteristics and Outcomes of 22 Task-Centered Cases

CLIENT IDENTIFICATION	AGE	REASON FOR REFERRAL	PRIMARY TARGET PROBLEM(S)	PRIMARY TASK(S)	LENGTH OF SERVICE (IN WEEKS)	NUMBER OF INTERVIEWS	RATING OF TASK ACHIEVEMENT (BY SOCIAL WORKER)	RATING OF PROBLEM REDUCTION (CLIENT FOLLOW-UP BY INDEPENDENT ASSESSOR)
Mrs. A	67	Referred by family doctor. Assistance with rehousing to combat depression	Dissatisfaction in social relations	To work out ways to overcome loneliness	9	9	Partial	No Follow-up
Fam. B	20's	Help with finances of separated mother	Inadequate resources	To get financial problems into manageable proportions	15	10	Partial	A lot better
Mrs. C	87	Change from private home to welfare accommodation	Dissatisfaction in social relations	Application for welfare accommodation	17	6	Complete	Inconclusive
Mrs. D * Episode 1	45	Husband's desertion	Problems of social transition	To work out plan for future	16	12	Partial	Worse
Episode 2	46	Inability to cope	Dissatisfaction in social relations	To find ways of meeting people	—	—	—	—
Mrs. E *	33	Marital problems	Problems of social transition	To help find accommodation	—	—	—	—
Mrs. F	56	Finding alternative living arrangements	Problems of social transition	To explore various possibilities of accommodation	4	3	Partial	No Follow-up

Name	Age	Problem	Category	Goal			Goal attainment	Outcome
Mrs. G	74	Financial and material assistance	Inadequate resources	To investigate possibility of financial and practical assistance	22	4	Substantial	Refused
Mrs. H	27	Acute financial difficulties	Inadequate resources	Provision of financial help	8	7	Substantial	A lot better
Mrs. I	57	Anxiety over money problems; hypertension	Inadequate resources	To improve financial situation	8	6	Complete	Problem no longer present
Mrs. J.	65	Help with debts	Inadequate resources	To improve financial situation	5	2	Complete	A lot better
Mrs. K	29	Help with housing application; conflict with father	Interpersonal conflict	To make housing application to get away from intolerable conflict	6	4	Substantial	A little better
Mrs. L	60's	Day care to relieve relatives	Problems of social transition	To visit welfare home	1	2	Substantial	About the same
Mrs. M	58	Need for transport to hospital; dog phobia	Dissatisfaction in social relations	To find means to meet and mix with people	24	5	Complete	A lot better
Mrs. N	32	Support to family for handicapped child	Inadequate resources	To obtain voluntary help and support to ease strain without further financial commitments	12	9	Complete	Problem no longer present
Mr. O	51	To be registered as partially sighted	Problems of social transition	To find niche in community	46	14	Substantial	A lot better

Table 18.1 (*Continued*)

Characteristics and Outcomes of 22 Task-Centered Cases

CLIENT IDENTIFICATION	AGE	REASON FOR REFERRAL	PRIMARY TARGET PROBLEM(S)	PRIMARY TASK(S)	LENGTH OF SERVICE (IN WEEKS)	NUMBER OF INTERVIEWS	RATING OF TASK ACHIEVEMENT (BY SOCIAL WORKER)	RATING OF PROBLEM REDUCTION (CLIENT FOLLOW-UP BY INDEPENDENT ASSESSOR)
P (child)	6	Behavior difficulties in school and foster home	Difficulties in role performance	To decide which school would help P and if it would affect his behavior	9	5	Complete	No follow-up
Fam. Q	20's	Telephone for chronically sick and disabled persons	Inadequate resources	To apply for telephone (through social worker)	9	4	Complete	Problem no longer present
Mrs. R	42	Threat of expulsion to common law wife	Interpersonal conflict	To devise strategies to reestablish relations	9	5	Not achieved	Same
Mr. S	50	Financial difficulties after severe disablement	1) Problems of social transition	1) To find ways of dealing with financial situation	8	8	Substantial	About the same
			2) Dissatisfaction in social relations	2) To come to terms with feelings of rejection and to find out about social activities	(8)	6	Not achieved	About the same
Mrs. T	41	Widowed mother unable to cope with children	Difficulties in role performance	To find ways of coping better with children	6	5	Substantial	A lot better
Mrs. U	42	Financial difficulties of deserted mother	Inadequate resources	To improve financial situation by claiming benefits	5	3	Substantial	A lot better

* Case still open when report was prepared.

Perhaps the most instructive and successful example of task-centered casework in the area of inadequate resources was Mrs. I. She was a middle-aged woman referred by her medical practitioner. She suffered from hypertension and unspecified back pains for which no physical cause could be traced. Mrs. I, aware that her doctor felt that these symptoms could be exacerbated by anxieties, admitted to having financial worries. Divorced, with only the youngest of her three children still at home, she seemed to be a pleasing, independent person who was losing her ability to cope with her financial problems. She expected numerous bills which she saw no hope of meeting. An extensive exploratory interview firmly established inadequate resources as the target problem and subsequent interviews focused on this. The allowance she received from her husband was low, but because he was a chronic invalid she felt unable to press for more. The divorce settlement had given her the house and the millstone of a mortgage. Her son paid her only a small sum for bed and breakfast, and she supplemented her income by many hours of dressmaking for which she charged very little. She was now unable to meet a monthly payment of her annual insurance policy. The task the social worker and the client formulated for Mrs. I was "to find ways of improving her general financial position while the social worker would try to meet some specific debts."

In the first interview following the task formulation the social worker and client looked at the possibility of Mrs. I's asking her son for an increase in his payment to her and they rehearsed how she might word such a request. They also discussed the possibility of Mrs. I's getting a part-time job and settled on some "work" for Mrs. I during the following week: to read advertisements in the local paper and to visit the employment exchange. Finally, the social worker was to consult the medical practitioner about the advisability of Mrs. I's seeking alternative employment and to approach a voluntary society about a grant. The "work" thus mapped out, the client and social worker agreed on an eight-week period to achieve the task.

By the second interview Mrs. I had approached her son, who had readily given her an immediate increase and a promise for more in the future. Mrs. I had read the local papers, been surprised at the rates of pay, and wondered whether she could be undercharging for her dressmaking work. She eagerly took up the social worker's suggestion of obtaining prices for a variety of jobs from local firms and asking magazines for advice. She was also to make a note of the number of hours she was working. The social worker had done her job and written to the voluntary society for a grant.

By the third interview Mrs. I seemed more cheerful, said that she was feeling better and coming to grips with her finances. She produced several lists of prices being charged in the vicinity for comparable work, all higher than her charges. She had made a note of her working hours and had not realized how many she put in for such a poor return. She had gone to see the Department of Health and Social Security on her own initiative and had learned that she might be exempt from having to pay a self-employed insurance stamp. The social worker was able to tell Mrs. I that the check from the voluntary society was on its way. By the next interview the check had arrived, and client and social worker decided how best to meet the bills. A visit to her doctor had encouraging results; he was pleased with Mrs. I's health and did not want to see her for two months.

At the fifth interview progress was reviewed again. Bills had been paid and Mrs. I had received further replies about price ranges. Again these charges were higher and she had gathered confidence to put up her prices. She had thus increased her income by £2 per week and experienced no shortage of work. She had also decided to limit her number of working hours and the amount of work she took in. She thought she might write to other magazines for price lists and pursue the insurance issue with the Department of Health and Social Security. The social worker encouraged her to go ahead with all these plans. Gradually all the suggestions and initiatives were coming from Mrs. I, and she began to see more clearly what she herself could do about her situation.

At the final interview Mrs. I was intending to take up the cudgels further with the Department of Health and Social Security and to reconsider the possibility of a part-time job. They reviewed her initial problems and what had been achieved over the last two months. Mrs. I said that she had found it helpful to talk with someone outside the family: it had enabled her to be more objective and regain control over her finances by deliberate planning and methodical tackling of her difficulties.

In the independent follow-up interview the client was quite clear about the target problem and the plan that was agreed upon between her and the social worker. The client felt that she had been helped to make the decision to change her scale of charges, but she clearly thought that the decisions had been hers, encouraged by the "approval" of the social worker. It was *she* who had gone round to the shops and written to the magazines. She felt that the social worker had contributed greatly in the matter of the grant, that she had been a valuable source of contact with outside agencies, and that she had helped by listening and by being really interested; the client was able to clarify her problems and deal with them one at a time with the social worker's help. She also helped by agreeing with the client on a course of action suggested by the client. Mrs. I thought that the length of contact was just right. Asked whether she felt that the social worker really understood her problems, she said that this had been the most important thing—the social worker really seemed interested and would listen.

It is clear from this account that while the social worker raised some money at a crisis point, the basic task was to enable Mrs. I to discover more effective ways of managing her affairs which helped her to increase her earning capacities. In common with a number of other clients, she emphasized that the decisions and achievements had been hers and expressed her pleasure in regaining autonomy. She was also able to verbalize another strength of the task-centered method: she had been able to specify her problems and to tackle then one at a time. In this way she could break down a multiplicity of overwhelming problems into manageable bits.

Problems of Social Transition

The six cases in which the target problem was identified as social transition (three marital break-ups and three cases of coming to terms with disability) raised a number of problems about the method. As will be seen from the table, the outcomes were much more problematical than those in the area of inadequate resources. The issue that stands out most clearly is the time limit.

Even the most successful case (Mr. O) took one year and may well need further occasional involvement by a skilled social worker. Mr. O, who had lost his job because of increasing blindness, had been referred for registration as a partially sighted person. The social work was divided into two phases: the first consisted of helping the client to work through some of his depression and grief over losing his job and his sight, helping him to make connections with various other services, and stimulating him to use them. The social worker also encouraged him to accept a residential training course which entailed separation from his elderly mother and complicated domestic arrangements for her. The time limit for this piece of work (some four months involving five interviews) was determined by the date of a vacancy at the training center. This phase was considered to be only partially task-centered since the client could not bring himself to acknowledge his problem of readjusting to a new life as a blind person. He was only able to do so in retrospect, when he and the social worker looked back on their achievements prior to his entering the training center.

In our group discussion we questioned whether it is always appropriate to insist on explicit clarification of the problem area when a client who is prepared to work on a task directed towards his problem finds it too painful to name it. When Mr. O returned from the training center he remarked, "Before we seemed to be aiming towards something, and now what?" He went on to say that his problem now was to "find a niche in the community." This was the thing to concentrate on. He suggested that previously the time limit was determined by the vacancy in the center but that now they would have to create a time limit to work towards; three months was agreed upon. During this period the client began to attend the occupational therapy center and to attain more mobility. The social worker encouraged him to take as much initiative as possible in shaping his new life. She kept in touch and gingered up a whole network of agencies involved in the rehabilitation of the blind. The case ended with a conference between the client, mobility officer, occupational therapist, and the Disabled Employment Officer for the Blind. They reviewed both achievements so far and prospects and further plans for the client's increased mobility. In his

final appraisal with the social worker, the client said, "Coming to occupational therapy has given me a shape to my week; I don't wake up
and wonder what I'm going to do today; I've found a niche, not perhaps the one I thought of." He felt that quite a bit had been achieved
and that he had contributed to it by attending the occupational training
unit and by taking the initiative in asking for more instruction in handi-
craft. He was still hoping to find work eventually. The social worker
considered the task-centered method was helpful in this case but felt
that this man may need further social work support and that there was
a need for a social worker to ginger up other agencies on his behalf.

The client mirrored these feelings by telling the assessor that he
hoped that there would be someone to see on a fairly regular basis. His
appraisal of the task-centered approach was: "At the beginning it was a
help to have someone to help sort things out—when you are out on a
limb on your own. I like the way she accepted suggestions and my own
ideas. She made the social services work for me." He felt that he made
use of all help offered and used the social worker to find out other
sources of assistance. To the question of whether he felt that the social
worker understood his problem, he remarked that no one who is not
blind or partially sighted can really understand, "but she did well." He
divided his problem into three categories: short-term, to arrange his attendance at the occupational therapy center; long-term, to find light
employment; and the continuing need to adjust to life with deterio-
rating sight. We can, therefore, see in the client's own words that although imaginative task-centered casework has made a considerable
impact on helping a newly blind person to find a new niche in the community, there are continuing long-term needs for support, possibly by
a skilled social worker.

In three other cases in which social transition was identified as the
target problem, the outcomes were more doubtful and pressure towards long-term social worker involvement on the part of the clients
was very great. These clients were seriously disturbed individuals who
felt quite unable to cope with their change of circumstances and who
wanted to cling to the social workers as listeners and sources of support. Two of the clients gave vent to their feelings of being "let down"
in bitter comments to the assessor, but both admitted that the social
worker had helped them to survive crucial weeks and to sort out op-

tions. They also said that the social worker had pointed out consequences of proposed actions not seen by the client. Both clients knew
of long-term social work; as one of them said, "Why put a time limit?
Patients often go on for years with their social workers. I have been
thrown out. If crying helps to relieve tension then I need to continue to
see a social worker."

The experience in this very small sample seems to indicate that if
very unstable personalities face fundamental changes in their lives, a
limited piece of sharply focussed social work is difficult to maintain,
since such clients want to cling to a life line, ventilating their uncertainties and their problems as they go along, unable to stick to a specific
focus, at any rate during the period of upheaval. A longer-term perspective appears to be necessary, but, as the assessor remarks about
one of these cases: "Long-term treatment would be ineffective too, I
guess. No one could be the friend/wife/lover he has never had." It will
be instructive to observe how the task-centered strategy succeeds in
one of our still open cases in which work on problems of social transition is being carried out with the "healthy" marital partner, who is
proposing to leave her physically disabled husband became he incurs
constant debts and so far remains unwilling to work on his problems of
role performance.

Dissatisfaction in Social Relations

Five cases were in the problem area of dissatisfaction in social relations. In the context of a social services department these situations are
often related to loneliness and isolation in elderly people, or to impov-
erished relationships occasioned by physical or psychological handicaps. It looks a potentially fruitful field for task-centered casework,
provided that community resources such as day care, clubs, and volunteer help are available to supplement the skilled social worker's "mo-
tivating push."

A good example is Mrs. M, who had started outpatient treatment for
her excessive dog phobia, but was unable to keep her appointments
with the psychologist because of transport problems. Hence she was
referred to the social services department. Mrs. M was a timid and

sensitive person, embarrassed about her fear of dogs. She believed that others thought her stupid and that she needed to pull herself together. Her husband seemed to have little understanding of her fears, although they were of long standing. Mrs. M felt herself to be socially and intellectually inferior to her husband and would become distressed about and dwell on any disagreements they had, but she was not able to get away from these problems, as she could never leave the house on her own.

The transport problems were soon resolved by finding a volunteer, but in the second interview Mrs. M expressed her feelings of loneliness, as the phobia was isolating her socially. She had no social network of family and childhood friends: the family had only recently moved to Buckinghamshire from London, and she was unable to go out to make friends. The social worker suggested that Mrs. M might be interested in making contacts by joining a club, either as a member or in a helping capacity if transport could be found. Mrs. M showed considerable enthusiasm for this.

The problem was thus defined as "dissatisfaction in social relations," and a task was formulated: "finding some means by which Mrs. M could meet people, preferably with transport provided." With Mrs. M's agreement the social worker contacted the psychologist to indicate how they proposed to work and to discuss if this dovetailed with her treatment plans for Mrs. M. The upshot was that the social worker and the psychologist worked in tandem: Mrs. M and the psychologist on the phobia, and Mrs. M and the social worker on the alleviation of the loneliness it created. The social worker and the client hardly ever mentioned again the unsympathetic relationship with her husband or her guilt about a mentally handicapped son whom she had not visited for many years: these were long-standing problems about which both client and social worker agreed they could do little.

Three more interviews followed, which took place within an agreed upon two-month period. During this time the client decided, from a list produced by the social worker, on the club she would like to join in a helping role. Mrs. M started to help at a luncheon club once a week. Although she played a retiring role, she found the team of helpers friendly and was beginning to know one or two of the club members well.

The final interview started with a somewhat dejected Mrs. M relating that she and her husband had had a misunderstanding the previous night and as usual she had become rather introspective. Client and social worker discussed again her feelings of inferiority and the temptation to dwell on these and stressed the need to go out and take up other activities and interests to counteract these feelings. They then reviewed what had been achieved: Mrs. M was arranging her own transport and had made one or two friends at the club. She had been invited out to tea by one of the team of helpers. She was enjoying the club so much that she was thinking of offering help to other clubs. Mrs. M concluded by saying that she thought she would always be afraid of Alsatians!

At the follow-up visit this client said that her problem was a lot better and that the contact with the social worker had enabled her to get out of the house at least once a week. The social worker had shown her how she doubted her own abilities and capacity for success: for example in knitting or getting on with the old folks at the club. She believed her problem of the dogs to be insoluble.

This case illustrates strikingly the advantages of the task-centered method in settling for modest, achievable objectives whilst recognizing seemingly unalterable life-long difficulties. Although Mrs. M will presumably never lose her dog phobia or her feelings of guilt over her mentally handicapped son, task-centered casework enabled her to try out some new ways of achieving social pleasures despite her permanent handicaps. The temptation was resisted to explore her experiences surrounding her visits to the handicapped son, during one of which she was attacked by a dog. Also resisted was the inclination to probe the precarious marital equilibrium established over some thirty years.

Another case, which unfortunately could not be followed up because the client was admitted to hospital, illustrates a different facet of task-centered casework—how clients seem able to move ahead once obstacles to task achievement are successfully grappled with. Mrs. A, a widow of 67, was referred by her medical practitioner for rehousing in a Warden-supervised flat as a solution for her depression and loneliness. The problem search revealed dissatisfaction in social relations as her most pressing problem and a task was formulated of "finding ways to relieve her loneliness." A time limit of eight weeks was agreed on.

Throughout seven interviews the social worker produced a number of suggestions for more social contact, most of which the client rejected. She made a few attempts herself to find more suitable housing, but mainly she talked about her isolation and loneliness. In the eighth interview she revealed much intense guilt about her late husband's suicide, which she had kept a dark secret; she also talked about the circumstances of her mother's death. In the next interview, she seemed much brighter and announced her own solution to her problem, namely to sell her house and buy a flat nearer her sister and other relatives and friends in a town a few miles away.

Role Performance

Role performance was formulated as the target problem in only two of the task-centered cases. However, one might argue that in a number of the episodes in which inadequate resources was the main target problem, much work was accomplished in the area of role performance, as clients learned to cope better with their financial and practical problems of daily living. They often acknowledged this in the independent follow-up interview. Problems of role performance also figured largely among multiproblem families for whom the task-centered method did not seem to work on the whole.

One case stands out clearly as one in which problems of role performance were tackled very successfully. After four years of widowhood, Mrs. T felt increasingly unable to cope with her four boys. Other problems, such as ill health and concern about its seriousness and, implicitly, an unresolved grief, were also revealed during the problem search, but finally she agreed that her main problem was her inability to cope with the boys' continued fighting, arguing, and general abusiveness. She felt that she was failing as a mother, was concerned about what the neighbours thought and very much wanted help to improve her capabilities and tolerance. Discussion indicated that the early morning presented a particularly trying time. Mrs. T would lie in bed and listen to the fights going on downstairs, getting more and more agitated. A plan was worked out that she would always get up with the boys and just be with them, try to ignore the arguments and concentrate on herself. For the rest of the day Mrs. T would behave according to how she felt. There were several topics which the social worker purposefully did not take on, for example, the death of Mr. T and the children's reactions to it, or the interactional conflict aspects of the present situation. Rather he tried to use these as material for helping Mrs. T to work out her reactions and to behave differently.

She managed to perform her "work" as agreed and was pleased with the result. The morning situation improved, and more importantly, Mrs. T felt better simply by having got up! During the next two or three interviews the social worker also talked about what children are like at various stages of development and how they behave so that she could put her own into context. By the fourth interview she started to discuss not only the incidents that had arisen but how she had handled them, clearly seeking approval, which was easy to give. She was relieved to find that the children responded to her change in behavior. By the fifth interview Mrs. T's confidence was noticeably increased so that the social worker suggested they should terminate their meetings earlier than the eight interviews they had planned. They discussed what she had learned and how she would cope in the future.

At the follow-up interview this mother was able to describe the task in the following words: "to help me face out the boys first thing in the morning instead of lying upstairs listening to the fights rigid with tension, and then to deal with their behavior problems as they arose with discussion." She also told the assessor that after five weeks the social worker thought she was ready to stand on her own again and that she herself felt that they were going over the same ground and that it was right to stop. She considered that things were very much better and she felt that most of the achievement came from herself with the social worker's support and approval. It helped to talk to a stranger who listened and who was willing to say yes or no. She wasn't ashamed to tell him things which her family would see as her failure in bringing up the children. She felt that she had learned a method of solving problems: "not to scream at the kids, to show trust in them, and to ignore their attempts to shock her." The assessor remarked in her comments that one would have expected resentment at the social worker's withdrawal, but this did not seem to be the case: "she was strengthened by his intervention, was not becoming dependent, lost no sense of her own worth, and gained some." Perhaps the most remarkable feature in this case is that although the husband was ever present in photographs and in references to him the social worker did not try to probe and deal with possible unresolved grief, but helped this widow and mother to cope in the present as she had requested. Is it too fanciful to suggest that in this way he acknowledged and strengthened her as a separate, effective human being in her own right?

Interpersonal Conflict

Normally one would expect problems of parent/child or marital relationships to occur frequently in a general social service agency and hence interpersonal conflict to be a common target problem. As the table shows this was not so in this small series of cases. Since the social services department is often a last resort when things have gone badly wrong, many of the marital relationships have already broken down by the time the clients come to the agency. Thus a number of the marital situations were dealt with as problems of social transition or even inadequate resources when the deserted spouses, especially young mothers, could not cope. Again, many of the parent/child problems occurring in the natural family or in foster homes are either part of long-term surveillance cases or embedded in the multiplicity of problems and catastrophes that befall the so-called problem families. The only marital case in which interpersonal conflict was eventually pinned down as the target problem proved extremely difficult to work according to the task-centered method, possibly because only one partner in the conflict was prepared to see the social worker. It was a desperate situation in which a common law wife of 20 years standing was being told to leave so that the husband could install another girl. Throughout the five interviews she veered between devising strategies to win him back and giving up. While seeing the social worker she was also in touch with a solicitor, her general practitioner, and a psychiatrist, all giving conflicting advice. It was impossible to know what the husband felt and there was no opportunity of developing a joint task. The contact was terminated without any resolution of the problem, and in the follow-up interview Mrs. R did not feel that anything had been achieved by her contact with the social worker. Thinking about this case one wonders whether the social worker should have tried harder to involve the husband. Alternatively, one might have led towards the target problem of social transition with the aim of helping Mrs. R to come to a decision about leaving or not leaving her husband.

Contributions of the Model

Even within a general social services agency which dispenses many services and has to undertake a good deal of long-term statutory and voluntary surveillance, the task-centered approach has much to offer. It stimulates clarity of thinking, more explicitness about aims and ways of achieving them, and more forward planning of individual cases. It invites greater participation by the client, who is encouraged to accomplish as much as possible by his own efforts; the evidence of the follow-up interviews shows how proud the clients are of their achievements. The method discourages aimless "visiting," unnecessary follow-ups, and a kind of vague responsiveness to any problems that might emerge.

The project social workers felt strongly that the model enhances respect for the client, stresses the client's equality as a participating contractor, and helps to demystify social work by clarifying the social worker's role. Since they have set out with their clients to achieve a relatively modest objective, the social workers have felt much less guilty than usual about the things they have not been able to change. As we have seen, many problem areas have been deliberately left unexplored, however tempting the psychopathology of the "underlying problems" may have been. Closure of cases has been by explicit agreement rather than by an unexplained reduction of contacts. We have also a hunch that since the social workers have not intruded into areas the clients are not willing to work on, their enhanced autonomy may lead them to recontact the social workers when they feel ready to tackle more painful problems.

The method has highlighted the effort involved in achieving a genuine agreement on the most important target problems in a setting where many clients are referred for difficulties which are paramount in the referrer's mind, but not necessarily acknowledged by the client.

The model reveals much more clearly than any other whether the social worker is there as an agent of control or protection or as a needed therapist. In other words, the method, which maximizes the self-determination of the client, shows that the aims of the client and those of the social worker as a concerned member of society are by no means always identical and reminds us that this conflict has often been evaded in the past.

The method has also brought home to us in a challenging way how paternalistic some of the British service arrangements are, particularly those which require a social worker to act as an intermediary, controller, and rationer of service resources in situations in which the clients could be encouraged to make their own applications for various services and benefits. Thus, in many cases, no task could be found for the client to work on, as the social worker had to act as the client's agent. This emphasizes the dual role of the social worker in a social services department: as an agent determining eligibility to services the department supplies, and as a client enabler. The two roles tend to conflict. If community workers can mobilize poor and uneducated tenants' groups into acquiring social skills which enable them to apply for an urban aid grant in order to establish and run a play group, it should also be possible for caseworkers to increase the social skills of their clients so that they feel capable of applying directly for certain resources and services without needing the social worker to intervene as an agent or advocate.

The task-centered method has helped to differentiate more sharply between change-oriented, short-term social work to which the task-centered model can be applied, and long-term surveillance and maintenance which may need to be followed in statutory or chronic situations. The former probably requires skilled caseworkers, while the latter may be carried out by auxilliaries, community groups, and neighbourhood networks of various kinds.

Some Unresolved Questions

There have also been a number of question marks about the model. In some cases, particularly those of complex interpersonal relationships, the requirements of the method have been experienced as restrictive to the therapeutic relationship: the maintaining of a sharp focus has seemed almost like a business transaction on occasions. As one client put it, "I did not like the cut and dried approach." It has also been questioned whether the equality between client and social worker, which this method enhances so much, is at times more apparent than real, since the social worker has far greater access to resources and can manipulate them better than the client. Our experience so far suggests that this method may be more successful in a relatively uncomplicated situation where a client is anxious for change rather than with clients who are bombarded by many vicissitudes. On the other hand, we feel that we have not yet experiemented in a sufficiently bold way by partializing problems and pursuing modest tasks fairly single-mindedly.

We have already indicated that the explicitness of the method may be inappropriate where clients cannot face certain basic threats, although they may be willing and able to work on tasks whose eventual purpose is implicitly understood but not explicitly articulated.

It seems that more empirical evidence is needed to determine appropriate time limits for task-centered casework in different problem areas.

Finally, we have found that the method calls for a good deal of reeducation both of social workers and of the community at large. In particular, referring agents need to be informed about the role of social workers. Social workers have on the whole been trained to be subtle and implicit, rather than articulate and explicit: responsive and indeterminate, rather than goal-oriented. Referring agents, such as general medical practitioners, school personnel, and other agencies in the community have to be weaned away from the idea that, once referred to a social worker, a client will be looked after and "visited" forever and that the social worker is a kind of general aunt who takes care of all the client's problems and needs.

References

Bywaters, Paul. 1975. "Ending casework relationships." *Social Work Today* 6(10 and 11).

Goldberg, E. M.; Mortimer, Ann; and Williams, B. T. 1970. *Helping the aged: A field experiment in social work*. London: Allen and Unwin.

Goldberg, E. M., and Neill, J. E. 1972. *Social work in general practice*. London: Allen and Unwin.

Hutten, Joan M. 1974. "Short-term contracts." *Social Work Today* 4(22).

—— 1975. "Short-term contracts, III." *Social Work Today* 6(17).

Loevenstein, Carol. 1974. "An intake team in action in a social services department." *The British Journal of Social Work* 4(2).

Mayer, John E., and Timms, Noel. 1970. *The client speaks.* London: Routledge and Kegan Paul.

McKay, A.; Goldberg, E. M.; and Fruin, D. J. 1973. "Consumers and a social services department." *Social Work Today* 4(16).

Rees, S. 1974. "No more than contact: An outcome of social work." *British Journal of Social Work* 4(3).

Reid, William J., and Epstein, Laura. 1972. *Task-centered casework.* New York: Columbia University Press.

Chapter 19

~~~~~~

Naomi Golan, Ph.D.

Work with
Young Adults in Israel

In their search for better ways to help troubled clients, social work practitioners in Israel have increasingly turned their attention to the various forms of short-term treatment that have proliferated in recent years (Barten, 1971; Mann, 1973). Of particular interest has been the task-centered treatment model developed by Reid and Epstein (1972). Experience with our variation of that model has shown that it is a particularly useful method of treatment for youth and young adults facing specific problems that have arisen during the course of their normal life situations.

A Special Program

Use of the model with this client group and others was examined in a series of two seminar-practicums conducted by the University of Haifa

School of Social Work from 1973 to 1975. The program will be described briefly to show the context in which the model was tested and to present one way of training experienced practitioners from different settings in its use.

The program was addressed to the kind of questions practitioners ask about the task-centered model: For what kinds of problems is it most appropriate? For what types of clients? In what kinds of settings? What training is needed? Participants were some 38 professional social workers practicing in the northern part of Israel, who had been brought together by their common interest in improving their practice competence and by their frustrations in trying to adapt conventional treatment procedures to work with multiethnic, multilingual, and multiproblem clients.

Participation was limited to graduate social workers with clinical experience. The workers in the groups had a median of 11 years of experience; all but one participant had at least 2 years. The agencies from which they came included public welfare offices, regular and special school settings, medical services for the acutely and chronically ill, rehabilitation services for civilians and soldiers, family and student counseling centers, child guidance and mental health clinics, mental hospitals, and private practice—a broad and representative sample of social work practice in the area. While a number of the participants were currently functioning as directors of services, senior supervisors, and university field instructors, all identified themselves primarily as practitioners and enthusiastically accepted as a condition for participation that they complete and report on a minimum of two practice cases in which they would utilize the task-centered model under ongoing supervision.

The program itself was divided into two parts. During the first ten weeks, participants took part in a two-hour weekly seminar in which we laid the theoretical framework for the task-centered approach as we used it. Relevant concepts from ego psychology, role theory, systems analysis, crisis intervention, and behavioral modification were explored and developed.[1] A number of short-term approaches, ranging from simple case studies to complex programs, were investigated and com-

[1] Many of these theories can be found in concentrated form in Turner (1974).

pared. Research evaluations of various kinds of crisis-oriented and planned short-term programs were analyzed, with some time spent in discussion of appropriate strategies and techniques.

The background and rationale of the task-centered model were examined in terms of types of social problems experienced by clients in Israel, the abilities of different client populations to participate in such a demanding treatment program, and the willingness of both agencies and workers to offer this type of service. Finally, our own model, adapted from the work of Reid and Epstein (1972) was developed as the basis for further operation.

During the second part of the program, the seminar was broken up into small work subgroups of six to ten members each. These groups met on a regular weekly basis for 16 to 20 weeks. Initially, each participant reported on the agency in which he planned to operate and on the nature and dimensions of the cases he was considering for treatment. The group discussed each situation, made suggestions, raised reservations, and suggested alternatives.

Once the green light was given, workers started to treat their new clients and report back periodically on their progress: what the initial treatment plan was, how the tasks were shaping up, what changes in focus and structure took place, how to handle the inevitable straying from the original plan for action. Priorities were usually given to urgent questions and requests for immediate advice and consultation.

These work sessions became the highlight of the program. Each group rapidly developed its own process and personality. Participants became deeply invested in each others' cases and developed a proprietary interest in their progress. Members became very supportive of misgivings, outspoken in pointing out deviations, and generous in offering suggestions from their growing familiarity and experience in the use of the task-centered model.

As director of the program, my role was generally low-keyed at this stage; as long as the group momentum carried on its own, I remained in the background. Occasionally I would deflect a too-detailed examination of dynamics or an overheated discussion of administrative interference to return the discussion to the use of the model. At times I would raise questions of relevance or validity of focus or procedures, point out how the theoretical issues raised in the first part of the program were reflected in practice, and suggest new directions or techniques based on my own experience.

Since a research component had been built into the program, each practitioner, on completing a task-centered case, reported first to the group and then met with me separately to go over in detail the five research schedules which he filled out during the progress of the case. These instruments, based on the series of task-centered research projects currently being carried out under the guidance of the University of Chicago, had been modified to meet the needs of the Israeli program. (See Appendix.)

Initially the schedules were considered very difficult to complete, since workers felt more comfortable reporting in their usual free-floating, rambling style. However, when the program was evaluated at the close of each year, participants agreed that filling out the instruments helped them to sharpen their practice thinking and become more focused in reporting exactly what they had been doing.

Modifications in the Model

Our work in the seminars has led us to make certain modifications in the model. The primary one has been to interject a second major concept between the *target problem* and the *task,* that of the *target goal.*[2] This is in keeping with Briar and Miller's (1971) position that:

> In mapping a treatment strategy, it is not enough simply to arrive at a diagnostic assessment—that is, to decide what the problems are—it must also be determined what the outcome of the treatment should be. *If change is not to be aimless and haphazard, the case-worker needs some conception of the specific goals that he and the client are attempting to achieve. And these goals should be defined in specific, behavioral terms.* (p. 276) [Italics added.]

While this notion is stated in Reid and Epstein's (1972) discussion of the client's goals and actions and in their definition of the task as "what the client agrees to attempt to do to alleviate a problem" (p. 96), we have found it simpler to use the following triad:

[2] Editor's note: In response to the work of Golan and others, we have given a more prominent place to the goals of service in recent formulations of the model.

A. The *target problem:* the "felt difficulty," in specific behaviors or circumstances, for which the client asks help and on which he expresses his willingness to work.

B. The *target goal:* the projected situation in which the client would feel he no longer needs help, the stage at which he might continue on his own.

(Operationally, the worker is asked, "Under what conditions would you and the client agree that the problem would be solved or reduced to manageable proportions?" Or, even more specifically, "How would you define the conditions under which you would feel you could close the case or reduce or terminate your activity?")

C. The *task* becomes, then, the means of going from Point A to Point B. The *general* tasks become paths of action and the *operational* tasks and subtasks become the specific stepping stones along the path.

This differentiation has been useful in clarifying the relationship between means and ends in treatment planning. It also gives client and worker an endpoint on which to focus in the hectic pace of dealing with a series of tasks within a specific time limit. While theoretically the target goal can be renegotiated at the end of the time limit set for the case, it has been found that, once worker and client have the goal clearly in mind, it becomes the natural termination point in almost every case. Using a different vocabulary, Goldberg and Robinson (chapter 18) arrived at a similar clarification between means and ends.

Implementation of Program

The task-centered model was applied to various types of clients. Of the 34 cases completed in the 1973–74 group, 16 dealt with individual adults; of these, 10 were in the 19–30 year range. Another 3 of the 6 couples seen also were in this age group. Similarly, in the 1974–75 sample of 33 cases, 19 were individual adults, of whom 12 were in the young adult age range. Again, 3 out of 6 couples seen were also young adults.

It should be pointed out that the selection of these clients was not

random. Since workers were interested in learning how to use the
model, choosing clients with a hopeful prognosis seemed to be indicated. Thus, the only condition for selection was to start with two cases
from new applicants for service on which the task-centered model
could be applied. In some instances, workers reported deliberately
choosing clients in the young adult range because they thought that
such clients generally make good use of treatment. Some agencies
themselves catered to this age range: for example, the Family Department of the Ministry of Defense, which dealt with war widows; the
student counseling services of the two universities in the area; or the
mental health services of the army. Sometimes the seminar groups advised against particular choices because they appeared contraindicated.

Target problems chosen reflected the areas in which the task-centered model was tried out. As seen in Table 19.1, interpersonal conflicts, reactive emotional distress, social transition difficulties, and
problems in role performance accounted for 80 percent of the cases
treated the first year and 81 percent of those treated the second year of
the program.

Table 19.1

Nature of Primary Target Problem Chosen for Treatment by Year

| | 1973–74 | | 1974–75 | |
PROBLEM CATEGORY	NO.	PERCENT	NO.	PERCENT
Interpersonal conflict	9	26	8	24
Social transition	7	21	4	12
Reactive emotional distress	6	18	10	30
Role performance	5	15	5	15
Relations with formal institutions	3	9	3	9
Dissatisfaction in social relations	3	9	1	3
Inadequate resources	1	3	2	6
N =	34		33	

The type of situation for which the task-centered model seemed
most appropriate is illustrated by the following case, in which the client
was experiencing reactive emotional distress to a family crisis:

Rachel, a slender young woman of 20, was referred to the medical
social worker at the Outpatient Clinic of the Workers' Sick Fund by
the chief physician of the Admitting Service of Rothschild Hospital,

after she had been treated there for the third time within two weeks for hyperventilation, faintness, vomiting, and stomach pains for which no organic basis could be found. She was very frightened and agitated and said she had been very tense for the past month, had been unable to go to work at her office job, had refused to see or go out with her bewildered boyfriend, and had spent her time at home, either bickering with her mother or crying in her room.

After some probing, the worker learned that these changes in her customary patterns of behavior started a month ago when her father left home to live with his current girl friend. Rachel had long been an "involved participant" in her parents' marital problems and her father had not only informed her of his plan to leave, but promised to send for her and her two young brothers "when things are ready." Since then she had been waiting tensely to hear from him and was now faced with the dilemma: should she take the initiative to call him herself?

After allowing Rachel to ventilate her feelings of loss and anger at her father's desertion, the worker suggested that they concentrate on two target areas: to help Rachel differentiate between her parents' situation and her own, and to help her return to her own normal functioning. In the first area, Rachel took on a series of tasks, starting with her defining how she felt about her father's desertion, then how her parents felt about each other, then what they wanted from themselves, and finally, what they wanted from her.[3] When her father returned home the following week, the tasks helped her observe objectively how her parents alternately stimulated and provoked each other.

At the same time, Rachel assumed the task of returning immediately to work, then beginning to meet her girl friends, and finally, starting to go out again with her boyfriend, who was anxiously waiting for her to resume their relationship. By the end of the third week, Rachel joyously reported that her physical symptoms were almost entirely gone, that she felt "wonderful" at work, and that she had gone dancing with her boyfriend the night before at a discotheque. She also felt less involved with her father since her return and could see that he was really a "flitter"; conversely, she said she was getting along better, for the

---

[3] Editor's note: These tasks provide good illustrations of Ewalt's concept of "mental tasks" (chapter 2).

first time, with her mother and could even sympathize with her at what she had to take.

With the close of treatment after three concentrated weeks, she announced that she had decided to stop mixing into her parents' lives and live her own instead. Her final words to the worker were, "Don't laugh, but I feel I have really grown up in these last few weeks!"

While it was anticipated that the task-centered model would be used for critical situations with persons who normally functioned at an adequate level, we were gratified to learn that it was also an excellent way to partialize a multiproblem case. Workers found that by concentrating on a relatively limited segment of a chronic chaotic situation, *particularly if it involved some new development,* marked change could be affected. Typical is the following case:

Eli, 19, a "marginal" school dropout from a Moroccan family living in a slum area of Haifa, had spent a number of years in an institution for predelinquent boys and, since then, had drifted around the lower port area of the city, working intermittently as a porter. Home presented a very complex, disordered picture: Eli's mother had remarried; quarters were very crowded with four of her seven children from her first marriage plus four from her second still at home. Eli did not get along with his stepfather, an inveterate card player, who regarded his stepchildren as a nuisance and a burden.

Eli came in to the Youth Followup Service with a desperate request: he could no longer stand living at home and wanted to strike out for himself. Yet he was afraid of antagonizing his mother and of burning his bridges; moreover, he had no idea of how to go about becoming independent.

The worker, who recalled Eli and two of his brothers from earlier contacts, recognized this as a legitimate request, during a period of role transition, with the potential for ego growth for the youth. Together they agreed to concentrate on helping him "leave home in a positive manner" and "set up an independent living arrangement."

Events flowed from one task to the next. Hesitatingly, Eli tried to approach his formidable mother for permission to leave home; finally he accomplished this indirectly, through his oldest brother, a policeman. The mother, predictably, came in to attack the worker furiously but, because of their previous relations, soon cooled down and agreed that it was appropriate for Eli to leave the house where father and his friends played cards and drank all night. She even promised to provide him with household utensils and linens.

Once this key permission was obtained, Eli, with the worker's support, began to carry out the program of starting a household. After several ineffectual attempts on his part to rent an inappropriate apartment, the worker steered him to a room with an older, retired widower who was delighted to share his overlarge flat, now that his children were married. Eli took great pride in furnishing his room and setting up cooking arrangements. The worker also helped him obtain the necessary documents for independent living—an identity card and sick fund booklet—and showed him how to open a savings account. By the end of the fourth week, Eli was working regularly in the factory where he had worked intermittently and triumphantly brought in to her a rudimentary bookkeeping system he had devised to keep track of his increased earnings.

Although several setbacks occurred in his progress towards independence, by the time the case was closed after nine weeks, Eli was working steadily and had developed a new air of responsibility and purposiveness. He told the worker he was "looking around" for a regular girlfriend now and thinking of taking a course in auto repair work to improve his job prospects.

Time Limits, Tasks

Armed with the theoretical background and fortified by the support of their work groups, workers began to implement the model with surprisingly few difficulties. Almost all reported being able to arrive at one or two mutually agreed upon target problems and to establish time limits either in terms of a set number of interviews ("Let's start with a series of 12 interviews and then evaluate our progress"), or a definite period of time ("Why don't we try this for the next two months and see if we reach our goal?).

In virtually all cases, they were able to remain within the time limits set. The figures were found to be almost identical for the two groups: in the first year, the number of interviews ranged from 3 to 16, with 9 as the median, while in the second year, the number ranged from 4 to 16, again with 9 as the median. The time span in the first year spread from 3 to 18 weeks, and in the second from 4 to 20 weeks, with the medians 9 and 10 weeks respectively.

The specification and delineation of tasks proved to be the most difficult and challenging part of the implementation of the task-centered model. Again and again we concentrated on spelling out typical tasks and on differentiating between different types of tasks carried out by the client. Throughout the program some workers found it difficult to operationalize their tasks and could only come up with one or two comprehensive ones to span the duration of the case. Others, particularly those with a background in behavior modification, tended to break down each task into discrete activities which could be recorded and charted in minute detail.

We found that the total number of recorded tasks varied in the two groups. During the first year, the number ranged from 2 cases with 3 tasks apiece to 4 cases with 9 tasks each. In the second year, when more attention was paid to spelling out the tasks, the range was broader: from 1 case with just a single task to another with 23 separate tasks listed. However, the median number of tasks per case in the first year (5) was only slightly less than the median number for the second (6).

In discussing reasons for difficulties in task formulation it became apparent that the structure and purpose in some social agencies, such as hospital social services, National Insurance, and work evaluation centers in rehabilitation services, lent themselves naturally to the focus on specific behavioral tasks and the setting up of limited goals. In other less structured settings, practitioners gloomily doubted whether the task could be set up at all: clients were too disturbed, problems too pervasive, agency structure too rigid, etc. Nevertheless, despite these misgivings, considerable gains were accrued when workers were pressed to adhere to a task orientation.

The following case, from a child guidance clinic which prides itself on its leisurely paced, long-term, intensive treatment of adolescents, reflects the change in approach:

Ronit, a dark, exotic-looking 15-year-old girl, was referred by the teacher-counselor of the youth group in the kibbutz where she had been living for the past six months. Constant arguments and recriminations between her Egyptian-born father and Yemenite mother made life at home intolerable and had brought the request for placement. Now, her father had been killed in an auto accident and Ronit was reported to be crying in her room and having nightmares. Even before this, she had been doing poorly in class, was acting aggressively towards the other members of the group, and was considered an "outsider" by them.

Ordinarily the worker would have concentrated on helping Ronit work through her unresolved oedipal feelings about her father and her anger at her mother. To her surprise, the worker found that Ronit was primarily concerned, not with her home situation, but with her poor social relations with her fellow group members and whether the kibbutz would continue to keep her, in view of her unsatisfactory classroom performance.

Ronit and the worker agreed to concentrate on these two problem areas for a three-month period. Ronit started, on the one hand, to organize dance performances for social evenings in the group—her particular forte. She also made a real effort, with the worker's support, to try to control the aggressiveness which instigated much of her conflict with the other members. At one point, she asked for and received some elementary sex information which cleared up some of her uncertainties in this area and helped her decide what was appropriate behavior with the boys in the group towards whom she was alternately seductive and hostile.

Concurrently, Ronit began to concentrate on the school subjects in which she showed particular ability. Within a month, she began to show marked improvement in her grades and classroom performance. By the end of the three months, when the case was closed, she reported having made several close girl friends within the group and even had found a "special" boyfriend. The kibbutz school authorities, gratified at her school progress, had agreed to keep her in the group.

Although the worker still felt misgivings in that she had dealt "too superficially" with the situation and would have preferred to treat Ronit's basic emotional conflicts in a more open-ended fashion, she reported several months later that, surprisingly, Ronit was continuing to do well in the group, was fairly well accepted, and apparently had overcome her grief over her father's death.

The importance of concentrating on specific, limited areas and working out a series of action-oriented tasks became particularly evident when workers were faced with tragic situations with which they might ordinarily tend to over-identify with their clients. The following case summary illustrates this point:

Following the death of their older son, Uri, 26, in the Yom Kippur War, the Vered family had literally fallen apart. The parents, both in their early 50's, were sunk in a depression over the loss of their first-born, refused to admit visitors to the house, and were functioning at a minimal level. Their younger son, Amir, 20, who had served in the same unit with his brother, had suffered a nasty head wound, which he refused to have treated. Instead of reporting for medical care, he remained stretched out on his bed at home most of the time, castigating himself as to why death had happened to his idol, Uri, and not to him. His parents would occasionally rouse themselves from their grief to alternately scold Amir for not getting proper medical care and to compare him unfavorably with his brother.

The social worker from the Ministry of Defense's Family Department, who was also a friend of the family, decided to focus treatment in two areas: to help Amir obtain the necessary medical treatment and to help the family members improve communication between themselves.

In the first area, she worked with Amir in a carefully structured manner, to help him plan and carry out, step by step, the obtaining of medical care: first he was examined by his field unit doctor, then underwent the necessary neurological tests, and finally was examined by a psychiatrist to determine his fitness to return to duty. At first Amir remained passive and even hostile and the worker had to take the initiative in carrying out many of the preliminary tasks such as inquiring as to procedures and setting up appointments. Gradually Amir became involved and active, assuming the initiative in arranging his own appointments and deciding on next steps. Using techniques of anticipatory guidance and role rehearsal, she helped Amir see what lay ahead and what needed to be done in the immediate future.

Meanwhile, combined interviews were held with the two parents and Amir. For the first time they began to talk openly about the loss of Uri and what it meant to each of them and to recall past good times they had experienced together as a family. Mother and father began to see Amir as a person in his own right and not just as a poor substitute for his brother. They could agree that they still had one son who needed them and whom they needed as well. (This was the first time Amir felt that there was still some hope for him as their son.) Step by step, using reality testing and reflective introspection, the worker helped them begin their grief work.

By the end of 12 weeks, Amir had returned to his army unit and was able to continue his medical care on his own. The Vereds had roused themselves sufficiently to begin to go out to do necessary shopping and to welcome a few friends at home; they also had lessened their deification of Uri and had begun to recall him in a more realistic light. They were still grieving but had moved on in the bereavement process.

The worker, profoundly affected herself by the family's pain, reported that the task-centered structure not only gave her a "handle" by which to deal with the situation, but helped her to deal with her own feelings and to keep her helping role in mind.

Worker's Evaluation of Model

With the close of each practicum, workers were asked to evaluate the usefulness and utility of the task-centered model in the light of their experiences in the program. As seen in Table 19.2, both groups felt that the large majority of clients had improved their ability to cope both with their target problems and their problems in general.

The difference in ratings between the two sets of cases perhaps reflects the fact that Israeli workers in general were rapidly becoming more familiar with task-centered and other short-term methods. Also, by the second year, I had become more experienced in how to teach the utilization of the model.

Finally, workers were asked to speculate retroactively on modifications they would have made if they could treat the same problem situation over again. In 80 percent of the first year's group of cases and in 90

Table 19.2
Workers' Assessment of Client Functioning at Close of Case

| LEVEL OF IMPROVEMENT | CLIENTS' ABILITY TO COPE WITH TARGET PROBLEMS | | | | CLIENTS' ABILITY TO COPE WITH OVERALL PROBLEMS | | | |
| | 1973–74 | | 1974–75 | | 1973–74 | | 1974–75 | |
	NO.	PERCENT	NO.	PERCENT	NO.	PERCENT	NO.	PERCENT
Extensive, considerable	22	65	26	79	16	47	19	58
Some, slight	9	26	6	18	15	44	11	33
No change	2	6	—	—	3	9	1	3
Unable to assess	1	3	1	3	—	—	2	6
Total	34	100	33	100	34	100	33	100

percent of the second, the participants felt they would have kept to the same primary target problem and the same client configuration. In 65 percent of the first group and in 72 percent of the second, they would have maintained the same timing arrangements. And finally, in 74 percent of the first group of cases and 88 percent of the second set of cases, the workers declared that they would have retained the task-centered model. The explanation given above for the differences between the two groups in respect to outcome may apply to these differences as well.

Conclusions

Three major conclusions have been drawn from this experience. First, adults—particularly at the younger age levels—can be helped significantly with their problems of reactive emotional distress due to external events (often experienced as crises), their difficulties during periods of developmental and social transition, their interpersonal conflicts with inmates (usually marital partners, parents, or children), and their struggles in carrying out their vital life roles.[4] When worker and client jointly selected one or two specific problems on which to concentrate, set up definite goals as "success points" towards which to direct their efforts, and structured treatment in terms of a series of client tasks aimed at bringing about behavioral changes, not only was the client's

[4] Our conclusions received subsequent support in others' studies: see Rosenberg (1975).

ability to cope with these specific problems generally enhanced, but his overall level of social functioning usually improved.

Second, regardless of the practitioner's theoretical orientation, his style of treatment, and the setting in which he operated, the key to successful use of the task-centered model appeared to be his *initial* conviction that significant change could take place within a planned, limited time and his ability to impart this conviction to his client. The mutual commitment on the part of worker and client seemed to provide the underlying impetus for successful implementation of the model.

Finally, the seminar-practicum format described in the paper seemed to be an effective way to help practitioners learn the model. At the close of the program, the great majority of the participants reported that they were integrating the basic principles of the model into their work and that it had already significantly changed the nature of their practice.

References

Barten, Harvey H. 1971. *Brief therapies.* New York: Behavioral Publications.

Briar, Scott, and Miller, Henry. 1971. *Problems and issues in social casework.* New York: Columbia University Press.

Mann, James. 1973. *Time-limited psychotherapy.* Cambridge, Mss.: Harvard University Press.

Reid, William J., and Epstein, Laura. 1972. *Task-centered casework.* New York: Columbia University Press.

Rosenberg, Bianca N. 1975. "Planned short-term treatment in developmental crises." *Social Work* 56(4):195–204.

Turner, Francis J., ed. 1974. *Social work treatment: Interlocking theoretical approaches.* New York: Free Press.

Appendix

~.~

The appendix contains a selection of instruments used in the studies discussed in several of the chapters in the volume. In addition to providing a sense of the data collected in the studies, the instruments may prove useful to readers who wish to do their own studies of task-centered treatment or to develop recording forms for this model of practice.

The Problem Assessment Schedule, Task Review Schedule, and Task Achievement Scale served as the basis for practitioner recording of data reported in papers by Reid (chapter 4), Epstein (chapter 9), and Brown (chapter 15). The Client Questionnaire was used to obtain the client data presented by Reid, and the Closing Interview Schedule was used to secure the follow-up data given in the Epstein and Brown chapters.

Instruments used in the studies reported by Ewalt (chapter 2), Hofstad (chapter 14), Goldberg and Robinson (chapter 18), and Golan (chapter 19) covered similar content areas but used somewhat different items and format.

Problem Assessment Schedule

NAME OF CLIENT(S) _____

NAME OF PRACTITIONER _____

1. Write below statements of the target problems (to a limit of three) the client most wished to alleviate through treatment, starting with the problem of greatest importance to the client. After each statement indicate approximate length of time client had problem before starting treatment—e.g., 2 weeks; 3 months; a year; 10 years, etc.

   1.

   2.

   3.

2. At what point in treatment was agreement to work on these problems first reached.

When Agreement Was First Reached	Problem		
Interviews 1–2	1	2	3
Interviews 3–4	1	2	3
Interviews 5–6	1	2	3
Interview 7 or later	1	2	3

3. For each problem, indicate the amount and direction of change that occurred by the last treatment interview.

Categories of Change	Problem		
Aggravated	1	2	3
No Change	1	2	3
Slightly Alleviated	1	2	3
Considerably Alleviated	1	2	3
Problem No Longer Present	1	2	3

4. Give brief statements of evidence used for the problem rating given above. Statements for each rating should consist of from one to three sentences setting forth the evidence on which the rating is primarily based. Statements should emphasize evidence for specific changes in client's behavior or situation.

———————————

Statements of Evidence for Ratings

Problem 1
 (a)

 (b)

 (c)

Problem 2
 (a)

 (b)

 (c)

Problem 3
 (a)

 (b)

 (c)

5. Did client want additional help for any of these problems at termination of task-centered treatment? Indicate which below by number.

1. _____   3. _____
2. _____   None _____

6. What problems besides those listed in item 1 did client want help for, either during or at the conclusion of treatment? (Write problem statements below. If none, write "none." Add additional numbers and statements as necessary.) Place a check (✓) before each of the statements below that were target problems—that is, where there was explicit agreement between practitioner and the client to work on the problem. Rate approximate change in each problem by placing after each statement one of the following symbols: + is alleviation; 0 is no change; and − is aggravation.

7. For which of the problems listed in item 6 did client still want help at the end of the treatment?
 None_____   If any, indicate by number from item above_____ .

Task Review Schedule

PRACTITIONER'S NAME: _____   CASE #: ____

Task #: ____

Task Statement (begin with client's name):

Prob. # to which related: ____ When task formulated: Sess. #: ____

Date: _____

Who suggested idea for task? Client____ Practitioner____ Other____

Client's Initial Commitment to Task: $\frac{1 \quad\quad 2 \quad\quad 3 \quad\quad 4 \quad\quad 5}{\text{Low} \qquad\qquad\qquad \text{High}}$

When task reviewed:

  Session #:   ___ ___ ___ ___ ___ ___ ___ ___ ___

Progress rating (1–4 or NO)

  for each review: ___ ___ ___ ___ ___ ___ ___ ___ ___

Task #: ____

Task Statement (begin with client's name):

Prob. # to which related: ____ When task formulated: Sess. #: ____

Date: _____

Who suggested idea for task? Client____ Practitioner____ Other____

Client's Initial Commitment to Task: $\frac{1 \quad\quad 2 \quad\quad 3 \quad\quad 4 \quad\quad 5}{\text{Low} \qquad\qquad\qquad \text{High}}$

When task reviewed:

  Session #:   ___ ___ ___ ___ ___ ___ ___ ___ ___

Progress rating (1–4 or NO)

  for each review: ___ ___ ___ ___ ___ ___ ___ ___ ___

Task #: ____

Task Statement (begin with client's name):

Prob. # to which related: ____ When task formulated: Sess. #: ____

Date: _____

Who suggested idea for task? Client____ Practitioner____ Other____

Client's Initial Commitment to Task: $\frac{1 \quad\quad 2 \quad\quad 3 \quad\quad 4 \quad\quad 5}{\text{Low} \qquad\qquad\qquad \text{High}}$

When task reviewed:

  Session #:   ___ ___ ___ ___ ___ ___ ___ ___ ___

Progress rating (1–4 or NO)

  for each review   ___ ___ ___ ___ ___ ___ ___ ___ ___

Task Achievement Scale

(4) Completely achieved.

This rating applies to tasks that are fully accomplished, e.g., a job has been found, a homemaker secured, financial assistance obtained. It may also be used for tasks that are fully accomplished "for all practical purposes"; if a couple's task was to reduce quarreling a rating of (4) could be given if they reached a point where hostile interchanges occurred infrequently, no longer presented a problem, and they saw no need for further work on the task.

(3) Substantially achieved.

The task is largely accomplished though further action may need to be taken before full accomplishment is realized. Thus, if the task is to improve work performance, significant improvement would merit a rating of (3) even though further improvement would be possible and desirable.

(2) Partially achieved.

Demonstrable progress has been made on the task but considerable work remains to be done. For example, if the task is to obtain a job, a rating of (2) could be given if the client has been actively looking for work and found a job he could take (and might) but was reluctant to. Or this rating would be appropriate for a couple who had made some headway on a shared task of finding things of mutual interest to do together even though they and the caseworker may be dissatisfied with their progress. Specific evidence of task accomplishment is required however. A rating of (2) should not be given just on the basis of positive motivation, good intentions, or expenditure of effort.

(1) Minimally achieved (or not achieved).

This rating is used for tasks on which no progress has been made or on which progress has been insignificant or uncertain. If a client's task were to locate and enter a suitable vocational training program, a rating of (1) would be given if the client were unable to locate a program, even though much effort had gone into searching for one.

(NO) No opportunity to work on task.

For example, client cannot carry out task in classroom because school is closed by teachers' strike.

Closing Interview Schedule

I. *Client's Conception of Problems and Tasks*
1. What were the most important problems that you and your caseworker worked on? (Number the first three problems in order of their apparent importance to client.)

1a. (For each problem numbered above determine the amount and direction of change that client thought had occurred by the last treatment interview. Do this by reading back each problem to client and asking him to select appropriate category.)

Categories
of Change   Problem

Categories of Change	Problem		
Aggravated (worse)	1	2	3
No Change	1	2	3
Slightly Alleviated (a little better)	1	2	3
Considerably Alleviated (a lot better)	1	2	3
Problem No Longer Present	1	2	3

2. Do you feel that the caseworker grasped the true nature of your problems as you tried to describe them?

____ Yes   ____ No   ____ Uncertain

(If "No" or "Uncertain," probe for reasons for client's feelings.)

3. Did you and your caseworker come to an agreement about what you might try to do to solve these problems?

____ Yes   ____ No   ____ Uncertain

4. (If client responded "Yes" to question 3): What did you and your caseworker agree you should try to do?

(Probe for clarifying detail. Before going to next question, ask if there was anything else.)

5. (If client responds with "No" or "Uncertain" to question 3, probe for client's conception of the caseworker's expectations, e.g.: As far as you could tell, what did the caseworker expect you to do to try to solve these problems?)

II. *The Client's Assessment of Progress*

   1. How well were you able to (repeat first task as given by client in response to question 4 or 5). (Probe for details of—and evidence for—task accomplishment.) (Repeat for each task mentioned in 4 or 5.)

   2. How is your over-all situation now compared with how it was when you first came to Social Service? Is it better, worse or about the same? (Probe for clarifying details, e.g.: Better or worse in which way?)

   3. Do you have any personal or family problems now that you think you need help for? (If yes, probe for nature of problems, client's plans, if any, for getting help.)

III. *The Client's Assessment of Service*

   I am going to read you a number of statements describing possible reactions you may have had to casework service. After I read each statement please tell me whether you would agree or disagree with the statement as it applies to your experience. Please give us your frank opinion.

   1. Casework service lasted about the right length of time.

            AGREE   DISAGREE

   2. My caseworker and I decided to concentrate on one problem at a time.

            AGREE   DISAGREE

   3. My caseworker gave me too much advice about what to do.

            AGREE   DISAGREE

   4. I received the kind of help I wanted from Social Service.

            AGREE   DISAGREE

   5. There were a lot of things on my mind which we did not have time to discuss.

            AGREE   DISAGREE

   6. I liked the idea of deciding at the beginning how long service was going to last.

            AGREE   DISAGREE

   7. I am satisfied with that I was able to accomplish as a result of casework service.

            AGREE   DISAGREE

8. My caseworker should have given me more advice about what to do.

     AGREE   DISAGREE

9. Casework service was a little too brief; I could have used a few more sessions.

     AGREE   DISAGREE

10. The caseworker concentrated too much on me; he (she) should have tried to do more to change the attitude of others or to get me services that I needed.

     AGREE   DISAGREE

11. The caseworker came through with the kind of help he (she) said he was going to give me when we started.

     AGREE   DISAGREE

12. Casework service was far too brief; it should have continued for a much longer period of time.

     AGREE   DISAGREE

13. I felt I understood what my caseworker was trying to do.

     AGREE   DISAGREE

14. In my last discussion with my caseworker, I got some good ideas about what I might do about problems I still have.

     AGREE   DISAGREE

15. Too much time was spent trying to help me understand what I was doing wrong.

     AGREE   DISAGREE

16. I would have had more confidence in my caseworker if he (she) had been older.

     AGREE   DISAGREE

17. I was confused a lot of the time about what the caseworker was trying to do.

     AGREE   DISAGREE

18. If I again have personal or family problems, I would turn to Social Service.

     AGREE   DISAGREE

19. The caseworker seemed to have a lot of confidence that I would be able to work out my problems.

     AGREE   DISAGREE

20. Casework service lasted too long.

     AGREE   DISAGREE

21. Social service really did not give me the kind of help I wanted.

     AGREE   DISAGREE

22. I think my experience with Social Service will help me to handle future problems as they arise.

     AGREE   DISAGREE

23. On the whole, how would you rate the helpfulness of service?

  ———— 1. I would have been better off without Social Service contact.

  ———— 2. I was neither helped nor harmed.

  ———— 3. I was slightly benefited.

  ———— 4. I was considerably benefited.

  ———— 5. I could not have gotten along without the service.

Client Questionnaire

We hope you will be able to take a few minutes of your time to complete this questionnaire before leaving the office. The information you provide will become part of a nationwide study conducted by the University of Chicago. The study is designed to help this and other agencies to improve the effectiveness of their casework and counseling programs.

After you have completed the questionnaire, please place it in the envelope provided, seal it and leave it with the agency's receptionist who will mail it for you (you may mail it yourself if you wish). Please give us your frank opinion. Absolutely no reference to your name will be made in our use of your responses to the questionnaires, nor will your responses be revealed to your caseworker or counselor.

Thank you for your cooperation.

Name _____

Address_____

Phone No. _____

CHECK ONE RESPONSE FOR EACH QUESTION. IF YOU CHECK "OTHER," WRITE IN YOUR RESPONSE IN THE SPACE PROVIDED.

1. Do you have any personal or family problems now that you think you need further help for?
   ____ yes
   ____ no
   ____ uncertain
   ____ other _____
   _____

2. Consider the one problem that you most wanted the caseworker or counselor to help you with. How is this problem *now* compared with how it was when you started treatment here?
   ____ it is no longer present
   ____ it is a lot better
   ____ it is a little better
   ____ it is about the same
   ____ it is worse
   ____ other _____
   _____

3. On the whole, how are you getting along now compared with when you first began treatment here? (check one)
    _____ much better
    _____ a little better
    _____ about the same
    _____ worse
    _____ other _____
    _____

4. The service:
    _____ was far too brief; it should have continued for a much longer period of time
    _____ was a little too brief; I could have used a few more sessions.
    _____ lasted about the right length of time
    _____ went on too long
    _____ other _____
    _____

5. The advice I was given in counseling was:
    _____ particularly helpful
    _____ of some help
    _____ not helpful
    _____ little or no advice given
    _____ other _____
    _____

6. The encouragement I received for progress I made was:
    _____ particularly helpful
    _____ of some help
    _____ not helpful
    _____ little or no encouragement given
    _____ other _____
    _____

7. The caseworker's (counselor's) attempts to help me understand myself or others were:
    _____ particularly helpful
    _____ of some help
    _____ not helpful
    _____ few such efforts were made
    _____ other _____
    _____

8. The caseworker's (counselor's) attempt to concentrate on specific goals or tasks for me to work on was:
    _____ particularly helpful
    _____ of some help
    _____ not helpful; I would have liked more freedom to talk about what was on my mind
    _____ the caseworker (counselor) did not do this
    _____ other _____
    _____

9. Our agreement at the beginning on how long service was to last:
   ____ was "a plus" as far as I was concerned
   ____ was acceptable
   ____ didn't strike me as a good idea
   ____ we didn't do this
   ____ other _____
   _____

10. If I again have personal or family problems that I need help with I would want to have:
    ____ the kind of service I have just completed
    ____ a different kind of service
    ____ other _____
    _____

11. The service:
    ____ helped with most of the problems that were bothering me
    ____ helped me with some of the problems that were really bothering me but we did not get to all of them
    ____ didn't help me much at all
    ____ other _____
    _____

Author Index

Subject Index

Action, client: emphasis on, 12-14
Adaptations of the task-centered model, 20-22, 23, 30-35, 87-88, 104-8, 121-22, 147-56, 157-67, 170-74, 185-01, 225-26, 245-46, 273-74

Behavior modification, 5, 8, 12, 13, 14, 147-56
Brief treatment, see Planned brevity, Termination of treatment

Casework, task-centered, see Treatment model
Caseworkers: location of target problems, 3; role, 4; activities in relation to task, 4-6; see also Communication, basic types of
Child guidance (practice field), 27-49; adaptation of the model for, 30-35; research findings, 37-39, 43-44, 45-48; staff in-service training, 39-40
Client questionnaire, 293-95
Closing interview schedule, 290-92
Communication: as caseworker techniques, 4-5; in marital counseling, 23; in marital problems, research on, 100-12
Communication, basic types of: awareness-enhancement, 4, 73-74; direction, 4, 73-74; encouragement, 4, 73-74; exploration, 4; structuring, 4, 73-74
Conference on Applications of Task-Centered Treatment, vii
Contracts, 3, 9-10, 21, 25, 29, 36, 40, 42, 44, 114-15, 117-18, 156, 209
Crisis theory, 7, 271

Duration of service, see Termination of treatment, Planned brevity

Empirical orientation, 14-16, 28-29
Employee counseling (practice field), 204, 228-34; application of task-centered approach, 230-31; target problems, 230, 236; outcomes, 233-34, 240-41; linkage (referral), 238-40; emergency services, 240

Families (practice field), 19-26, 58-77; adaptations of the model for, 20-22, 23, 74-76; outcomes, 22, 67-74; staff in-service training, 23, 24, 76-77
Federal Social Security Act (Title XX), 24
Field of practice, see Practice field
Focus, treatment, specificity in, 8

Group work with adolescents, 157-67; target problem selection, 159-61, 169; group composition, 161; group formation, 162-63, 169-70; task specification, 164; task implementation, 164-66

Industrial counseling, see Employee counseling

Juvenile courts (practice field), 126-29, 183-94, 195-201; target population, 184-85; adaptations of the model, 185-91, 196-97; outcomes, 192-94, 198, 200-1; target problems, 197-98; tasks, 198

Long-term treatment, see Termination of treatment